THE POTHOLE AT THE END THE RAINBOW

By Stephen Francis & Rico

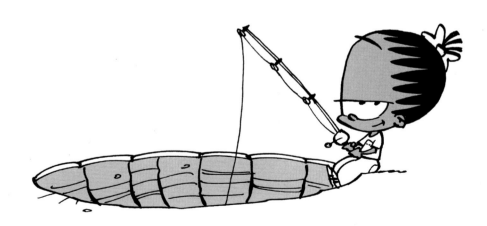

JACANA

Published in 2011 in South Africa by
Jacana Media
10 Orange Street, Auckland Park, 2092
PO Box 291784, Melville, 2109
www.jacana.co.za

ISBN 978-1-4314-0252-6
Job number 001585
Printed and bound by Ultra Litho (Pty) Ltd, Johannesburg

OTHER MADAM & EVE BOOKS

Madam & Eve Collection	(Rapid Phase, 1993, reprint 1999)
Free At Last	(Penguin Books, 1994)
All Aboard for the Gravy Train	(Penguin Books, 1995)
Somewhere over the Rainbow Nation	(Penguin Books, 1996)
Madam & Eve's Greatest Hits	(Penguin Books, 1997)
Madams are from Mars, Maids are from Venus	(Penguin Books, 1997)
It's a Jungle Out There	(David Philip, 1998)
International Maid of Mystery	(David Philip, 1999)
Has anyone seen my Vibrating Cellphone?	(interactive.Africa, 2000)
The Madams are Restless	(Rapid Phase, 2000)
Crouching Madam, Hidden Maid	(Rapid Phase, 2001)
Madam & Eve, 10 Wonderful Years	(Rapid Phase, 2002)
The Maidtrix	(Rapid Phase, 2003)
Gin & Tonic for the Soul	(Rapid Phase, 2004)
Desperate Housemaids	(Rapid Phase, 2005)
Madams of the Caribbean	(Rapid Phase, 2006)
Bring me my (new) Washing Machine	(Rapid Phase, 2007)
Madam & Eve Unplugged	(Rapid Phase, 2008)
Strike While The Iron Is Hot	(Jacana, 2009)
Twilight of the Vuvuzelas	(Jacana, 2010)
Jamen sort kaffe er pa mode nu, Madam!	(Gyldendal, Denmark, 1995)
Jeg gyver Mandela Skylden for det her!	(Gyldendal, Denmark, 1995)
Alt under kontrol I Sydafrika!	(Bogfabrikken, Denmark, 1997)
Men alla dricker kaffet svart nufortiden, Madam!	(Bokfabrikken, Sweden, 1998)
Madame & Eve, Enfin Libres!	(Vents D'Ouest, France, 1997)
Votez Madame & Eve	(Vents D'Ouest, France, 1997)
La coupe est pleine	(Vents D'Ouest, France, 1998)
Rennue-Ménage à deux	(Vents D'Ouest, France, 1999)
En voient de toutes les couleurs	(Vents D'Ouest, France, 2000)
Madame vient de Mars, Eve de Venus, Madam & Eve	(Vents D'Ouest, France, 2000) (LIKE, Finland, 2005)

MADAM & EVE APPEARS REGULARLY IN:
Mail & Guardian, The Star, Saturday Star, Sunday Times, Herald, Mercury, Witness, Daily Dispatch, Cape Times, Pretoria News, Diamond Fields Advertiser, Die Volksblad, EC Today, Kokstad Advertiser, The Namibian, iMaverick, Daily Maverick Online.

TO CONTACT MADAM & EVE:
PO Box 413667, Craighall 2024, Johannesburg, South Africa
madamandeve@rapidphase.co.za
www.madamandeve.co.za

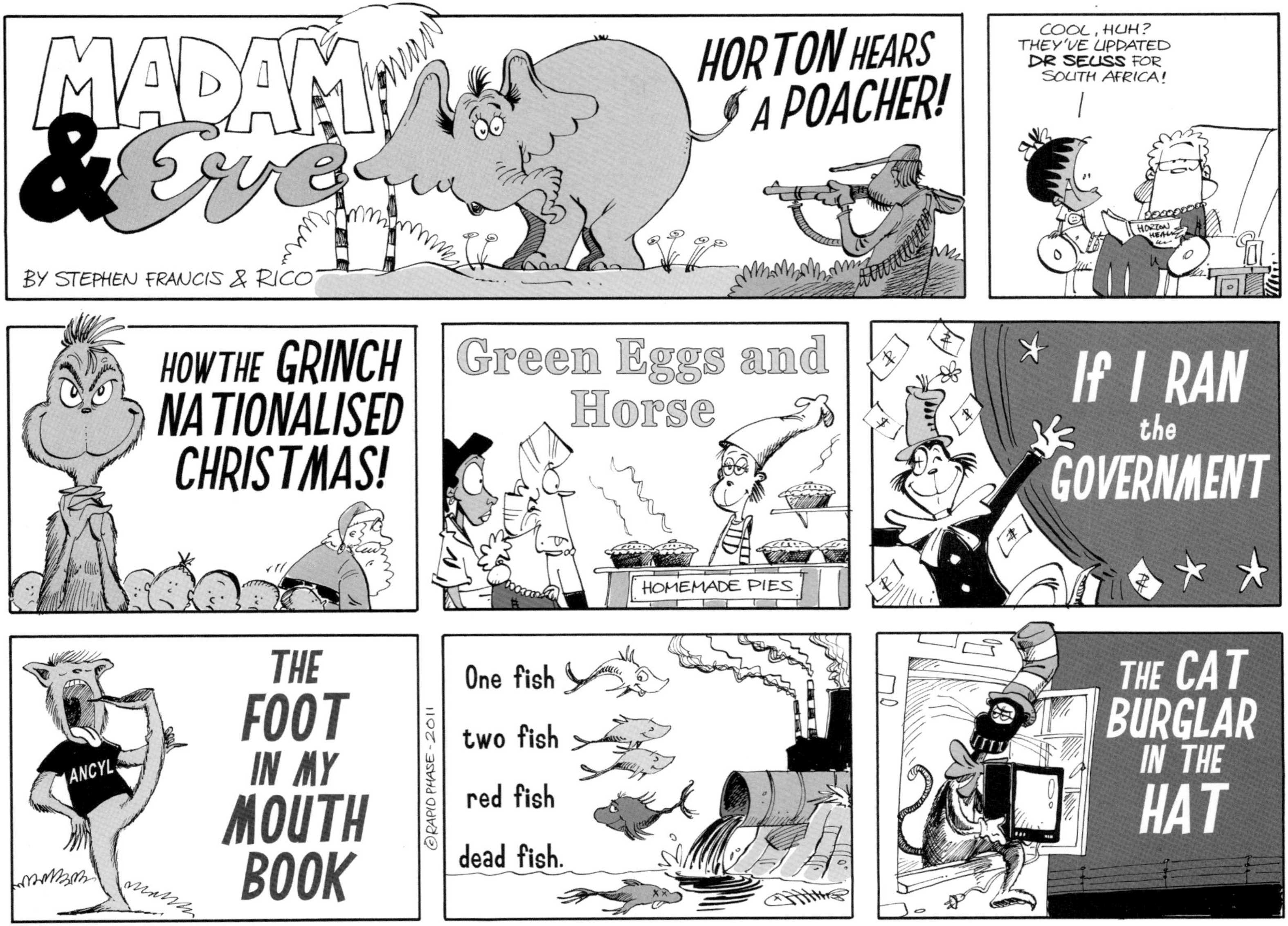
MADAM & Eve
BY STEPHEN FRANCIS & RICO
HORTON HEARS A POACHER!
COOL, HUH? THEY'VE UPDATED DR SEUSS FOR SOUTH AFRICA!
HOW THE GRINCH NATIONALISED CHRISTMAS!
Green Eggs and Horse
HOMEMADE PIES
If I RAN the GOVERNMENT
THE FOOT IN MY MOUTH BOOK
ANCYL
©RAPID PHASE - 2011
One fish
two fish
red fish
dead fish.
THE CAT BURGLAR IN THE HAT

BETTER PAY!! BETTER PAY!! CRASH! BASH!! POW!! OW!!
HAI! HAI!! HAI! BETTER PAY!! CRASH! POW!!
HEY!! THAT'S MY TEACHER! THAT'S SO UNFAIR!!
BECAUSE SHE DESERVES BETTER WAGES? AND SHE'S STRIKING?
©RAPID PHASE · 2010
BECAUSE LAST WEEK SHE SENT ME TO THE PRINCIPAL'S OFFICE FOR FIGHTING!

REACHING THE MIDDLE OF THE STREET, THE POLICE ARRIVED. BUT OUR STRIKE CONTINUES!
I CAN'T BELIEVE IT... THAT'S MY ENGLISH TEACHER!!
AND YOU'RE EMBARRASSED FOR HER?
©RAPID PHASE · 2010
I'LL SAY! SHE JUST USED A DANGLING PARTICIPLE!

YEP! THIS IS GOING TO BE A LONG STRIKE! REALLY LONG.
I MAY NOT GO BACK TO SCHOOL FOR WEEKS! MONTHS, EVEN! STUCK HERE IN YOUR LOUNGE!
©RAPID PHASE · 2010
YESIREEE! A LONNNNG STRIKE. WE'RE IN FOR THE LONG HAUL ON THIS ONE!
FINE! NEXT TIME I'LL SUGAR COAT IT!!

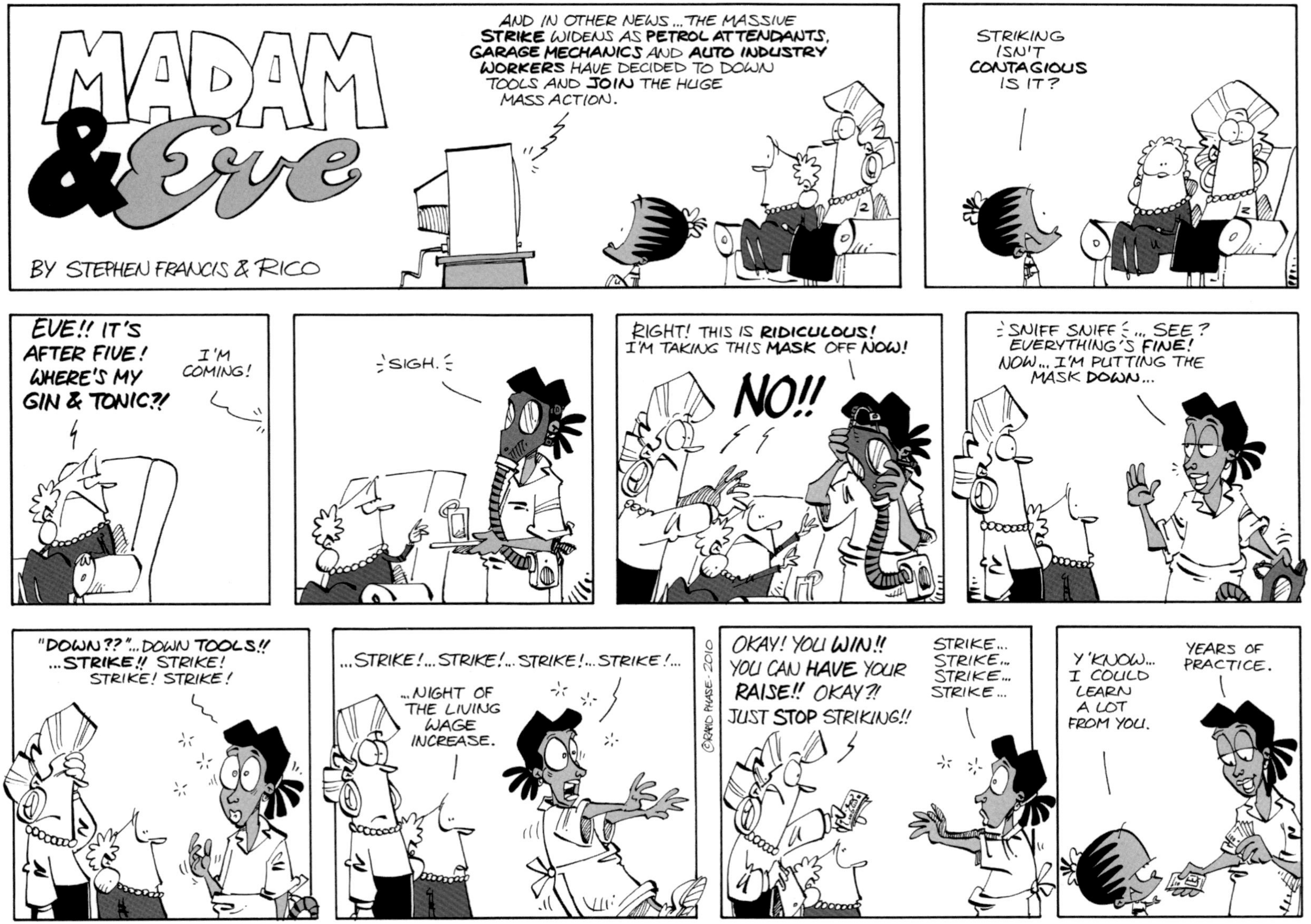
MADAM & Eve
BY STEPHEN FRANCIS & RICO
AND IN OTHER NEWS... THE MASSIVE STRIKE WIDENS AS PETROL ATTENDANTS, GARAGE MECHANICS AND AUTO INDUSTRY WORKERS HAVE DECIDED TO DOWN TOOLS AND JOIN THE HUGE MASS ACTION.
STRIKING ISN'T CONTAGIOUS IS IT?
EVE!! IT'S AFTER FIVE! WHERE'S MY GIN & TONIC?!
I'M COMING!
SIGH.
RIGHT! THIS IS RIDICULOUS! I'M TAKING THIS MASK OFF NOW!
NO!!
SNIFF SNIFF ... SEE? EVERYTHING'S FINE! NOW... I'M PUTTING THE MASK DOWN...
"DOWN??"... DOWN TOOLS!! ...STRIKE!! STRIKE! STRIKE! STRIKE!
...STRIKE!...STRIKE!...STRIKE!...STRIKE!...
...NIGHT OF THE LIVING WAGE INCREASE.
©RAPID PHASE · 2010
OKAY! YOU WIN!! YOU CAN HAVE YOUR RAISE!! OKAY?! JUST STOP STRIKING!!
STRIKE... STRIKE... STRIKE... STRIKE...
Y'KNOW... I COULD LEARN A LOT FROM YOU.
YEARS OF PRACTICE.

AND IN OTHER NEWS--THE GOVERNMENT WORKERS **STRIKE** CONTINUES...
STRIKE! STRIKE! STRIKE! STRIKE!
STRIKE! STRIKE! STRIKE! STRIKE!
...STRIKE! STRIKE! STRIKE! STRIKE!
STRIKE! STRIKE! STRIKE! STRI---
SNAP OUT OF IT!!
COOL! THE HYPNOTIC **POWER** OF MINDLESS MOB MENTALITY.
I'M CHANGING THE CHANNEL.
©RAPID PHASE · 2010

THE MODERN PUBLIC SERVANT
BYE, HONEY! I'M OFF TO **WORK**!
HAVE A GOOD DAY, DEAR. DON'T FORGET YOUR **LUNCH**!
SEE YOU TONIGHT! I LOVE YOU!
I LOVE YOU TOO! DON'T WORK TOO HARD!
I WON'T!
©RAPID PHASE · 2010
ON STRIKE

BOB'S HOUSE OF TABLES
DINING ROOM TABLE
NEGOTIATION TABLE
END TABLE
COFFEE TABLE
www.madamandeve.co.za ©RAPID PHASE · 2010

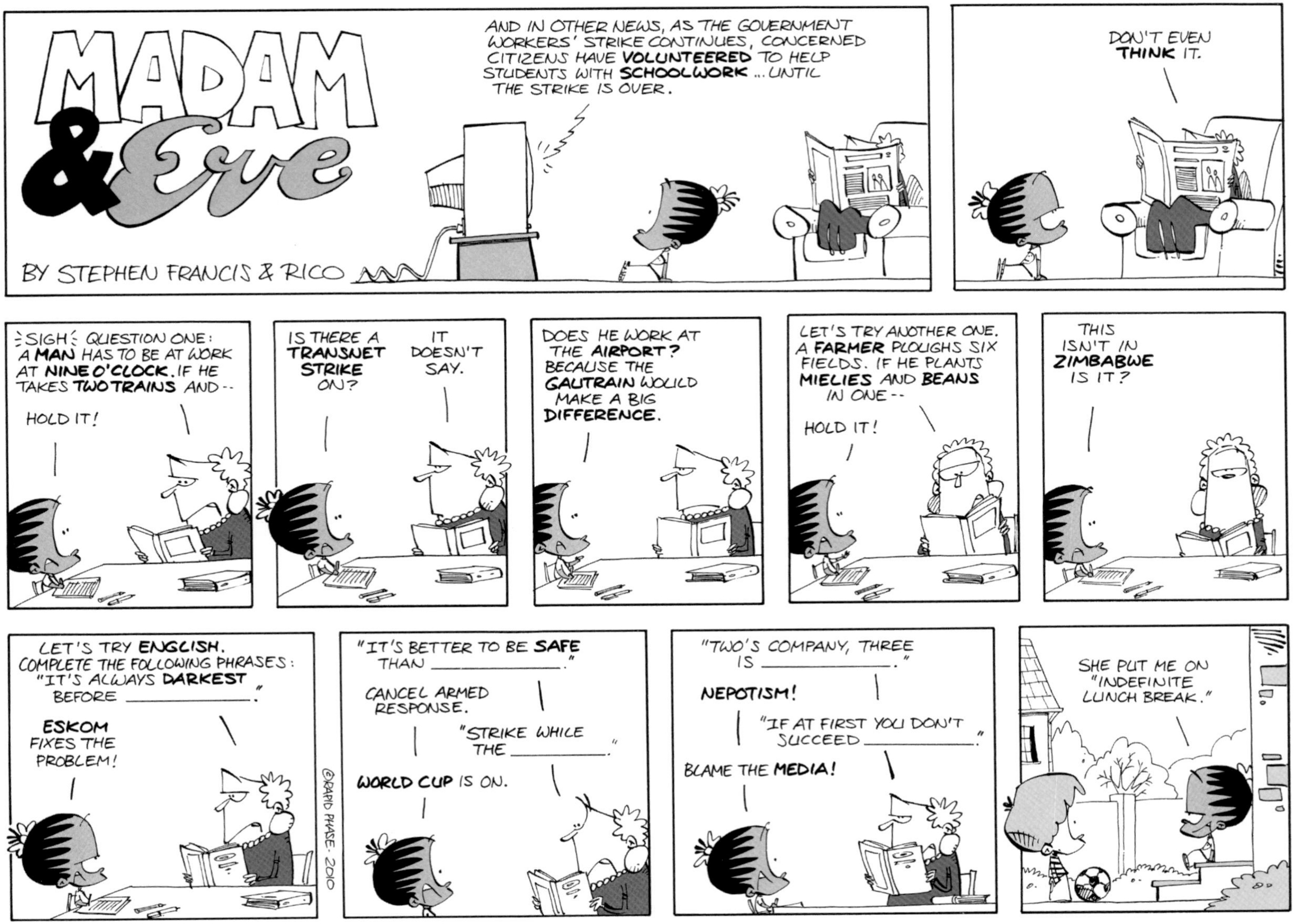
MADAM & Eve
BY STEPHEN FRANCIS & RICO
AND IN OTHER NEWS, AS THE GOVERNMENT WORKERS' STRIKE CONTINUES, CONCERNED CITIZENS HAVE VOLUNTEERED TO HELP STUDENTS WITH SCHOOLWORK ... UNTIL THE STRIKE IS OVER.
DON'T EVEN THINK IT.
:SIGH: QUESTION ONE: A MAN HAS TO BE AT WORK AT NINE O'CLOCK. IF HE TAKES TWO TRAINS AND --
HOLD IT!
IS THERE A TRANSNET STRIKE ON?
IT DOESN'T SAY.
DOES HE WORK AT THE AIRPORT? BECAUSE THE GAUTRAIN WOULD MAKE A BIG DIFFERENCE.
LET'S TRY ANOTHER ONE. A FARMER PLOUGHS SIX FIELDS. IF HE PLANTS MIELIES AND BEANS IN ONE --
HOLD IT!
THIS ISN'T IN ZIMBABWE IS IT?
LET'S TRY ENGLISH. COMPLETE THE FOLLOWING PHRASES: "IT'S ALWAYS DARKEST BEFORE ____________."
ESKOM FIXES THE PROBLEM!
©RAPID PHASE 2010
"IT'S BETTER TO BE SAFE THAN ____________."
CANCEL ARMED RESPONSE.
"STRIKE WHILE THE ________."
WORLD CUP IS ON.
"TWO'S COMPANY, THREE IS ____________."
NEPOTISM!
"IF AT FIRST YOU DON'T SUCCEED ____________."
BLAME THE MEDIA!
SHE PUT ME ON "INDEFINITE LUNCH BREAK."

...THANDI?
STRI
READ CHAPTERS 23 AND 24 OF YOUR HISTORY TEXTBOOK!
MORE PAY!!
...AND WRITE AN ESSAY ON "HOW YOU SPENT YOUR WEEKEND."
STRIKE
www.madamandeve.co.za
©RAPID PHASE · 2010
DEFINITION OF **BAD LUCK**: BUMPING INTO YOUR **TEACHER** DURING THE STRIKE AND GETTING AN EXTRA **HOMEWORK** ASSIGNMENT.

DON'T FORGET CLASS, THERE'S A HISTORY EXAM THIS FRIDAY, SO START **PREPARING**...
©RAPID PHASE · 2010
YES, THANDI?
ANY CHANCE OF ANOTHER TEACHERS' STRIKE? I'D **HATE** TO STUDY FOR **NOTHING**.
www.madamandeve.co.za
IT'S GOOD TO BE BACK.
PRINCIPAL

WELCOME BACK CLASS. I'M SURE WE'RE ALL GLAD THE **STRIKE'S** OVER.
www.madamandeve.co.za
LET'S BEGIN WITH A MATHS QUIZ.
©RAPID PHASE · 2010
HAU! HAU! HAU! HAU!
WHAT IS THE SQUARE ROOT OF 144?
HAU! HAU! HAU!
SOME HABITS ARE HARD TO BREAK.

THE LAST CONCESSION
ON STRIKE!
MORE PAY!
8,6% OR BUST!
WE DEMAND
©RAPID PHASE · 2010
www.madamandeve.co.za

MISTER PRESIDENT! YOU'VE GOT TO **DO** SOMETHING!
SIGH YES, I KNOW.
THE STRIKE'S GETTING OUT OF CONTROL! THE PEOPLE NEED **DECISIVE LEADERSHIP!**
SIGH YES, I KNOW.
... AND TRAVELLING TO CHINA AND AVOIDING THE UNIONS DOESN'T HELP EITHER!
SIGH YES, I KNOW.
SIR... YOU **REALLY** NEED TO **COME OUT** FROM UNDER YOUR DESK!
I ... UH ... DROPPED MY PENCIL.
©RAPID PHASE · 2010

ON STRIKE
MORE PAY!!
MEN STRIKING
©RAPID PHASE · 2010 www.madamandeve.co.za
MEN WORKING

BECAUSE OF THE CONFUSION OVER POWER... WE WOULD LIKE TO GO ON RECORD BY SAYING... THE TRIPARTITE ALLIANCE IS DYSFUNCTIONAL.
GASP!
©RAPID PHASE - 2010 www.madamandeve.co.za
TIC TIC TIC TIC
THE TRIPARTWEET ALLIANCE.
HOW DO YOU SPELL "DYSFUNCTIONAL?"

TRIPARTITE ALLIANCE GROUP THERAPY
RIGHT. WHO'D LIKE TO SHARE FIRST?
SHARE?! YOU MUST BE JOKING! WHY SHOULD I SHARE MY POWER WITH THEM?!
FEELINGS! I MEAN SHARE YOUR FEELINGS!
©RAPID PHASE - 2010 www.madamandeve.co.za
DUH!!
HELL-O!!
PAY ATTENTION MUCH?!
WHICH REMINDS ME... STARTING NEXT SESSION, NO MORE ENTOURAGES ALLOWED IN THERAPY.

THANDI. DID YOU DO YOUR HOME-WORK?
A FAIR QUESTION. AND WHILE I APPRECIATE YOUR RIGHT TO KNOW, I'M AFRAID THAT INFORMATION IS CLASSIFIED.
...AND ACCORDING TO THE PROTECTION OF INFORMATION ACT, THE INFORMATION MUST REMAIN CLASSIFIED, ESPECIALLY IF DECLASSIFICATION MAY RESULT IN SIGNIFICANT HARM TO NATIONAL INTEREST.
©RAPID PHASE - 2010
...TO TO MENTION, ON A PERSONAL NOTE, MY VERY OWN MATHS MARK AVERAGE.
www.madamandeve.co.za
SIGH
THANDI, CAN'T YOU JUST ANSWER WITH A SIMPLE "YES" OR "NO"?
PRINCIPAL
NOT WITHOUT MY LAWYER PRESENT.

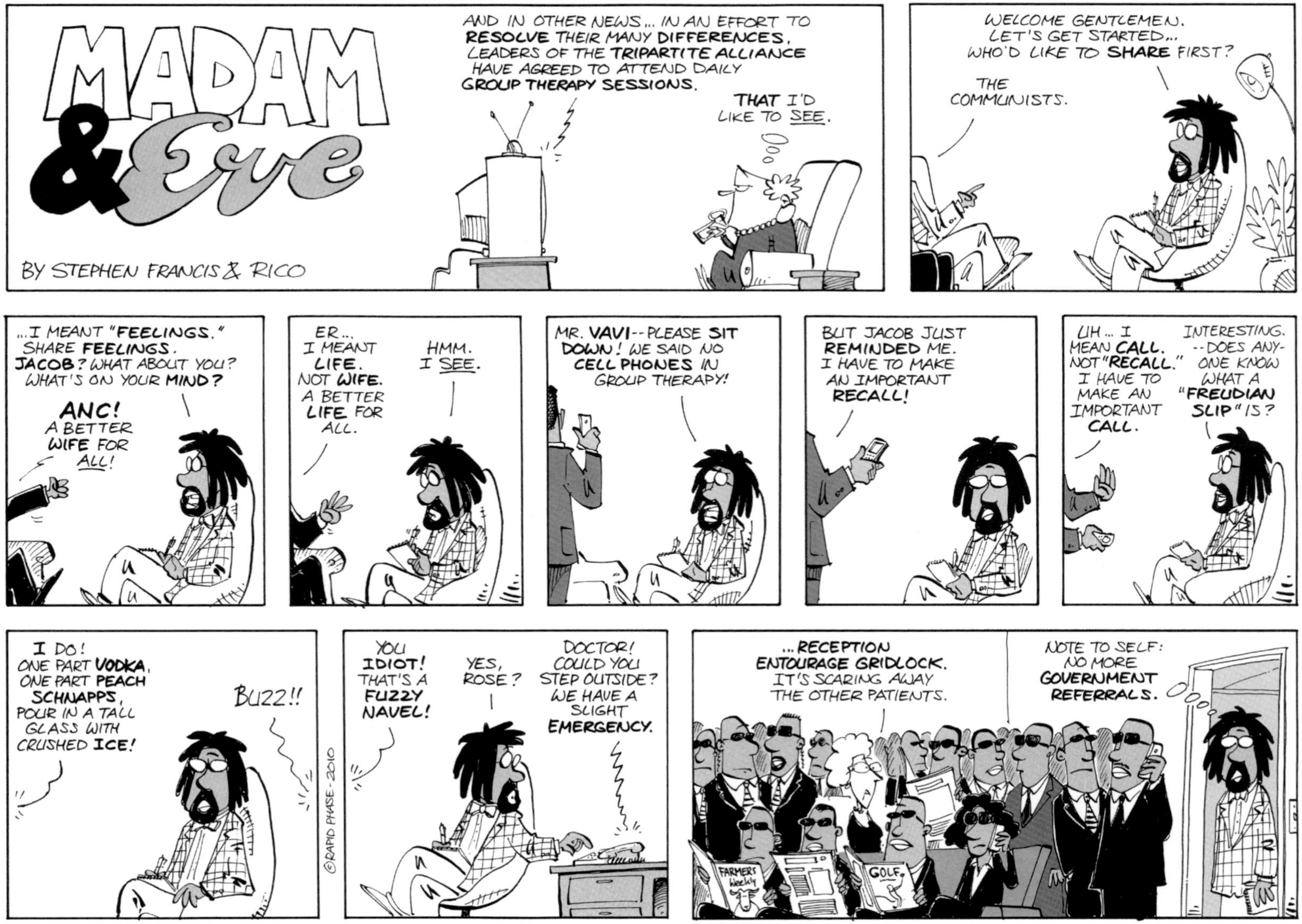
MADAM & Eve
BY STEPHEN FRANCIS & RICO
AND IN OTHER NEWS... IN AN EFFORT TO RESOLVE THEIR MANY DIFFERENCES, LEADERS OF THE TRIPARTITE ALLIANCE HAVE AGREED TO ATTEND DAILY GROUP THERAPY SESSIONS.
THAT I'D LIKE TO SEE.
WELCOME GENTLEMEN. LET'S GET STARTED... WHO'D LIKE TO SHARE FIRST?
THE COMMUNISTS.
...I MEANT "FEELINGS." SHARE FEELINGS. JACOB? WHAT ABOUT YOU? WHAT'S ON YOUR MIND?
ANC! A BETTER WIFE FOR ALL!
ER... I MEANT LIFE. NOT WIFE. A BETTER LIFE FOR ALL.
HMM. I SEE.
MR. VAVI--PLEASE SIT DOWN! WE SAID NO CELL PHONES IN GROUP THERAPY!
BUT JACOB JUST REMINDED ME. I HAVE TO MAKE AN IMPORTANT RECALL!
UH... I MEAN CALL. NOT "RECALL." I HAVE TO MAKE AN IMPORTANT CALL.
INTERESTING. --DOES ANYONE KNOW WHAT A "FREUDIAN SLIP" IS?
I DO! ONE PART VODKA, ONE PART PEACH SCHNAPPS, POUR IN A TALL GLASS WITH CRUSHED ICE!
BUZZ!!
©RAPID PHASE · 2010
YOU IDIOT! THAT'S A FUZZY NAVEL!
YES, ROSE?
DOCTOR! COULD YOU STEP OUTSIDE? WE HAVE A SLIGHT EMERGENCY.
...RECEPTION ENTOURAGE GRIDLOCK. IT'S SCARING AWAY THE OTHER PATIENTS.
NOTE TO SELF: NO MORE GOVERNMENT REFERRALS.
FARMERS Weekly
GOLF

AND...THEY'RE OFF! IT'S PROTECTION OF INFORMATION OUT IN FRONT! -- FOLLOWED BY FREEDOM OF EXPRESSION AND RIGHT TO KNOW!

COME ON, RIGHT TO KNOW!!

ROUNDING THE BEND, IT'S RIGHT TO KNOW IN THE LEAD! BUT WAIT! HERE COMES FEED AT THE TROUGH! ...FEED AT THE TROUGH LOOKS UNSTOPPABLE!!

INTO THE FINAL STRAIGHT... IT'S FEED AT THE TROUGH, FOLLOWED BY THREAT TO NATIONAL INTEREST AND CLASSIFIED DOCUMENTS... RIGHT TO KNOW HAS FALLEN WAY BEHIND!

www.madamandeve.co.za

©RAPID PHASE - 2010

AND COMING UP FAST-- MEDIA TRIBUNAL!

WHO'S WINNING?

NOT US.

HOW COME THE GOVERN-MENT ALWAYS SEEMS SO WORRIED ABOUT THE MEDIA?

THE MEDIA IS LIKE A WATCHDOG. ...CORRUPT POLITICIANS DON'T LIKE TO BE WATCHED.

SO WHAT'S WITH THIS "MEDIA TRIBUNAL?"

THE GOVERNMENT CLAIM THEY NEED THEIR OWN WATCHDOG.

www.madamandeve.co.za

...SO THE GOVERNMENT WANTS THE MEDIA TRIBUNAL TO BE A WATCHDOG WATCHING THE MEDIA WHILE THE MEDIA IS BUSY WATCHING THE GOVERNMENT?

YOU GOT IT.

©RAPID PHASE - 2010

THAT'S THE PROBLEM WITH GOVERNMENT THESE DAYS... TOO MUCH WATCHING AND NOT ENOUGH DOING.

GOOD MORNING. SO FAR... TWO WINE GLASSES, ONE DISH, ONE COFFEE CUP...

Tinkle Tinkle

...AND ONE INEXPENSIVE VASE SOMEONE LEFT ON THE EDGE OF THE TABLE.

©RAPID PHASE - 2010

www.madamandeve.co.za

WHAT WAS THAT?

...YOU'VE BEEN LISTENING TO "BREAKING NEWS" WITH EVE SISULU.

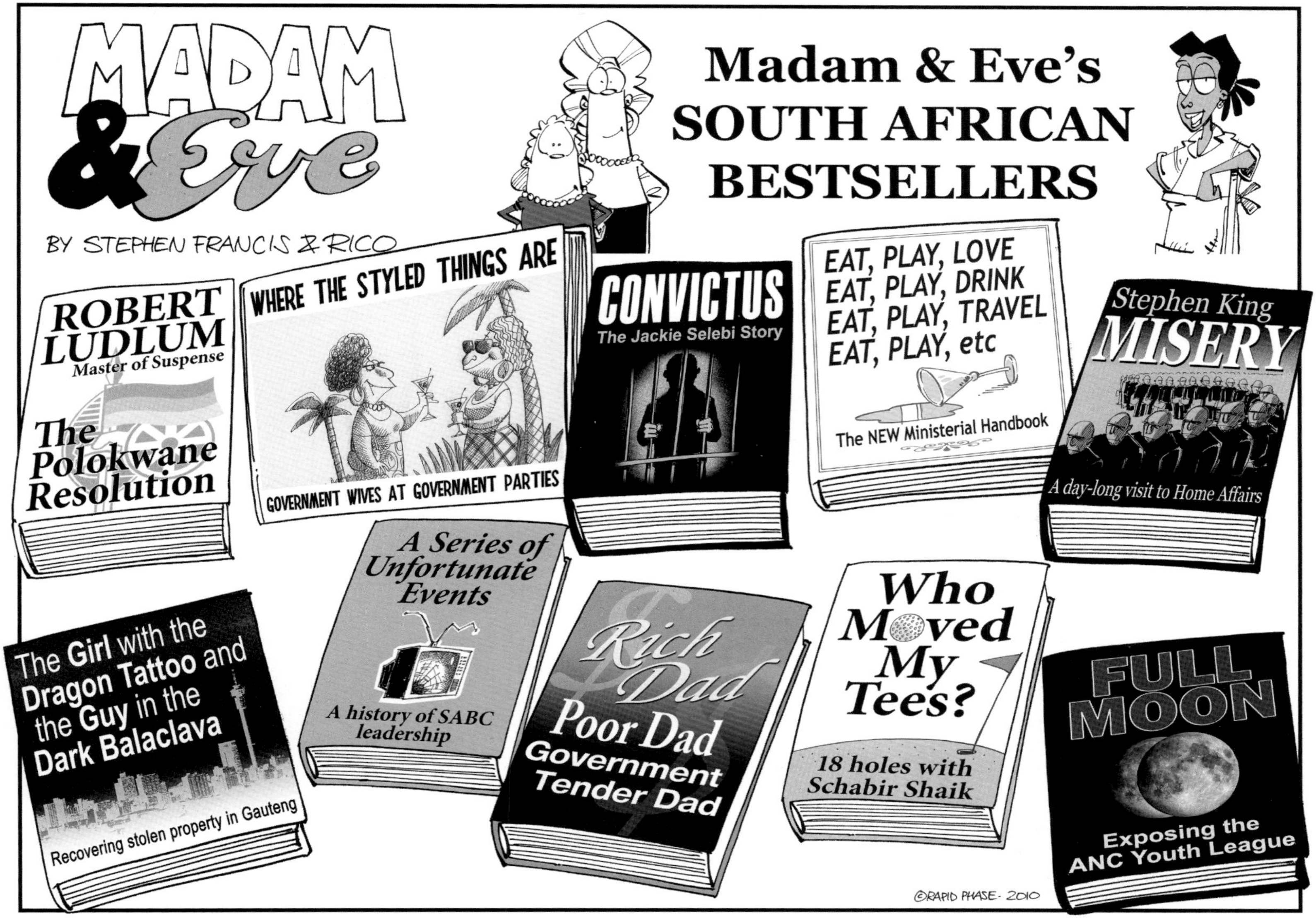
MADAM & Eve
BY STEPHEN FRANCIS & RICO
Madam & Eve's SOUTH AFRICAN BESTSELLERS
ROBERT LUDLUM Master of Suspense
The Polokwane Resolution
WHERE THE STYLED THINGS ARE
GOVERNMENT WIVES AT GOVERNMENT PARTIES
CONVICTUS
The Jackie Selebi Story
EAT, PLAY, LOVE
EAT, PLAY, DRINK
EAT, PLAY, TRAVEL
EAT, PLAY, etc
The NEW Ministerial Handbook
Stephen King
MISERY
A day-long visit to Home Affairs
The Girl with the Dragon Tattoo and the Guy in the Dark Balaclava
Recovering stolen property in Gauteng
A Series of Unfortunate Events
A history of SABC leadership
Rich Dad Poor Dad
Government Tender Dad
Who Moved My Tees?
18 holes with Schabir Shaik
FULL MOON
Exposing the ANC Youth League
©RAPID PHASE- 2010

DID YOU NOTICE THE LIGHTS CHANGE COLOUR?
CELL©
IMPRESSIVE.
© RAPID PHASE - 2010 www.madamandeve.co.za
ER,... CAN I HELP YOU?
WE'RE HELPING OUT WITH A LITTLE MARKET RESEARCH FOR YOUR NEW AD CAMPAIGN.
MARKET RESEARCH?
MY WIFE AND I ARE HOMELESS. AND YOU'VE BEEN WONDERING "IF A CELLPHONE STORE COULD BE A COOL PLACE TO HANG OUT."
WE'LL LET YOU KNOW. GIVE US A FEW WEEKS TO GET OUR GROOVE ON.
SO FAR, WE'RE LOVING THE COOL MUSIC AND FREE COFFEE.

RING! RING!
LOOK! MY VERY FIRST TEXT MESSAGE! ON MY VERY FIRST CELLPHONE!
WHAT'S IT SAY?
© RAPID PHASE - 2010
"PAY YOUR TV LICENSE."

SIR -- THE ANC NATIONAL GENERAL COUNCIL MEETING'S STARTING! THEY WANT TO KNOW IF YOU'RE FINISHED WRITING THE SPEECHES!
LISTEN TO THIS: "THE ANC IS NOT AN EMPLOYMENT AGENCY! THE ANC IS NOT A PLACE FOR THE ENRICHMENT OF FRIENDS AND RELATIVES!"
© RAPID PHASE - 2010
BOLD...YET HONEST. I LIKE IT, SIR. YOU'RE A GREAT SPEECH-WRITER.
THANKS. HAVE IT COPIED, AND RUN IT DOWN TO THE MAIN PODIUM.
NO PROBLEM, UNCLE VUSI.
ON YOUR MOTHER'S SIDE! ON YOUR MOTHER'S SIDE!

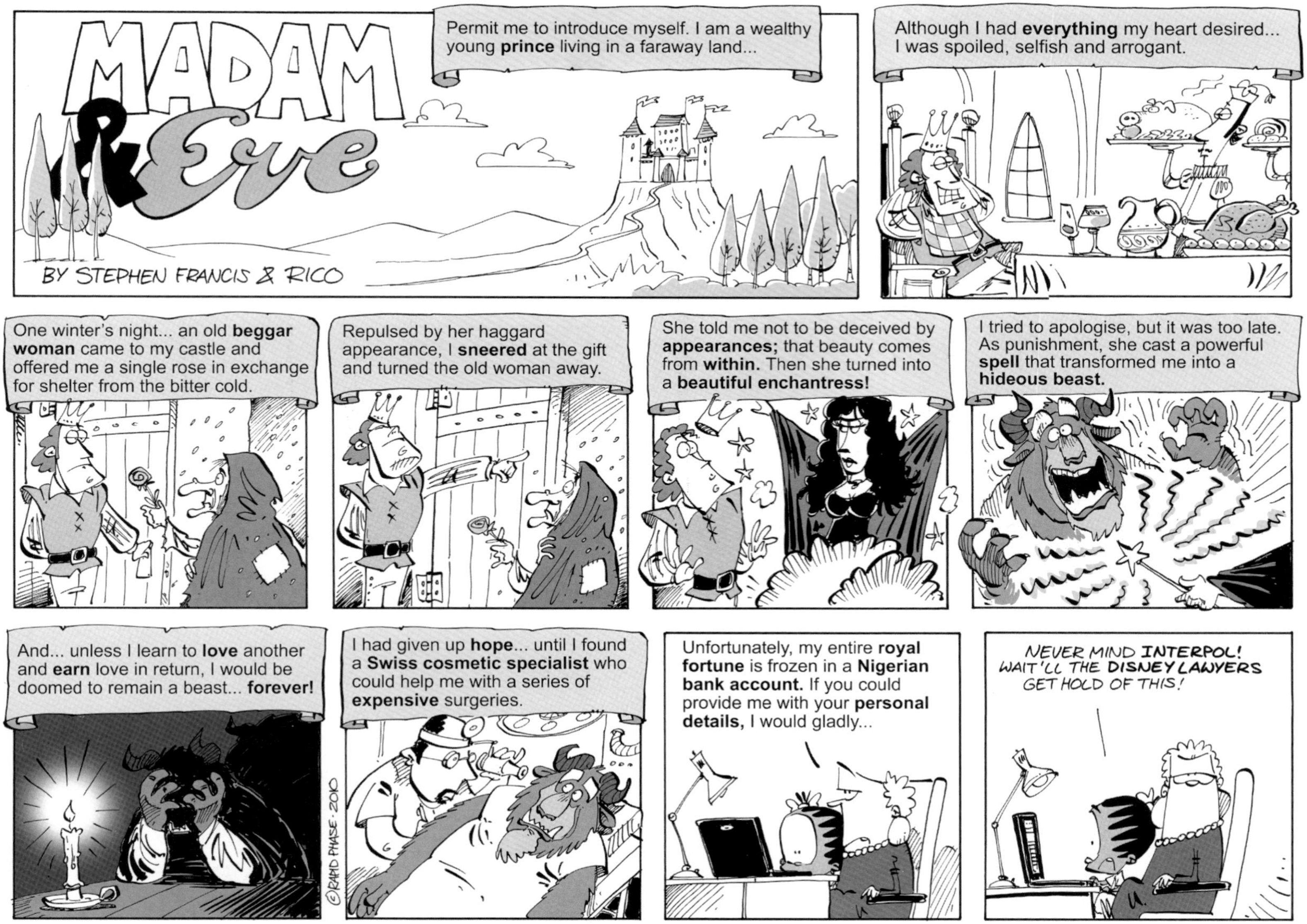
MADAM & Eve
BY STEPHEN FRANCIS & RICO
Permit me to introduce myself. I am a wealthy young prince living in a faraway land...
Although I had everything my heart desired... I was spoiled, selfish and arrogant.
One winter's night... an old beggar woman came to my castle and offered me a single rose in exchange for shelter from the bitter cold.
Repulsed by her haggard appearance, I sneered at the gift and turned the old woman away.
She told me not to be deceived by appearances; that beauty comes from within. Then she turned into a beautiful enchantress!
I tried to apologise, but it was too late. As punishment, she cast a powerful spell that transformed me into a hideous beast.
And... unless I learn to love another and earn love in return, I would be doomed to remain a beast... forever!
I had given up hope... until I found a Swiss cosmetic specialist who could help me with a series of expensive surgeries.
©RAPID PHASE · 2010
Unfortunately, my entire royal fortune is frozen in a Nigerian bank account. If you could provide me with your personal details, I would gladly...
NEVER MIND INTERPOL! WAIT'LL THE DISNEY LAWYERS GET HOLD OF THIS!

www.madamandeve.co.za
©RAPID PHASE · 2010
WIRE RHINOS
R 500.00
WIRE RHINO HORNS
R 15000.00

LOOK WHAT I BOUGHT FOR THE GARDEN. A RHINOCEROS... MADE ENTIRELY OUT OF WIRE.
RUMBLE!
©RAPID PHASE · 2010
TWANG!
ZING!
www.madamandeve.co.za
SPROING!!

I'LL HAVE THE EGGS BENEDICT. ARE THE EGGS FRESHLY POACHED?
OH YES.
©RAPID PHASE · 2010
...THEY JUST CAME IN THIS MORNING.

AND IN OTHER NEWS... MEMBERS OF AN ALLEGED LARGE RHINO POACHING SYNDICATE WERE ARRESTED TODAY.
YES!
©RAPID PHASE · 2010
SCORE ONE FOR THE RHINOS!
www.madamandeve.co.za
AND THEY SAY NEWS HEADLINES ARE ALWAYS DEPRESSING.
UNLESS YOU'RE A RHINO POACHER.

MADAM--THE VACUUM'S ACTING UP AGAIN! I'VE CALLED THE APPLIANCE WHISPERER!
"APPLIANCE WHISPERER?"
TAKE ME TO THE AFFLICTED APPLIANCE.
FOLLOW ME.
©RAPID PHASE · 2010
www.madamandeve.co.za
VRRRR!!
SHHH... SUCH A NICE BOY... SUCH A NICE VACUUM.
TOLD YOU HE'S GOOD.
VRRRRRR

WHO'S THAT GUY TALKING TO THE WASHING MACHINE?
EVE CALLED HIM IN. HE'S THE APPLIANCE WHISPERER.
Bsst. Bsst. Bsst.
WELL?
BAD NEWS. YOUR VACUUM'S DEPRESSED AND YOUR WASHING MACHINE'S LOST ALL SELF ESTEEM.
©RAPID PHASE · 2010
www.madamandeve.co.za
RIGHT. I'M OUTTA HERE.
Bzzt. Bzzt. Bzzt.
AND WHO'S BEEN PUTTING GIN & TONICS ON TOP OF THE DRYER?
UH-OH.

... AND FINALLY, THE LAST OF THE **CHILEAN MINERS** HAS BEEN RESCUED.
POOR GUYS. WHAT'S **WORSE** THAN BEING A MINER **TRAPPED** UNDERGROUND?
BEING A MINER TRAPPED UNDERGROUND IN A **NATIONALISED** MINE.
©RAPID PHASE - 2010 www.madamandeve.co.za
Hello. You've reached the **Nationalised Mining Hotline.** A better life for all. All our representatives are busy right now. If you're involved in a cave-in, press ONE...

Madam & Eve's
THE CHILEAN MINERS
-
THE UNTOLD STORY
©RAPID PHASE - 2010
CLOSE CALLS #14: THINKING ERRONEOUSLY IT MIGHT LIFT THEIR SPIRITS, RESCUERS SEND DOWN SEVERAL **VUVUZELAS**...
PLONK!
PLONK!

GASP!
FREE!! I'M FREE!!
©RAPID PHASE - 2010 www.madamandeve.co.za
THIS WAY AMIGOS! I FOUND A SHORT CUT!!
WELL, AT LEAST **POTHOLES** ARE GOOD FOR **SOMETHING.**
VIVA CHILE! VIVA!

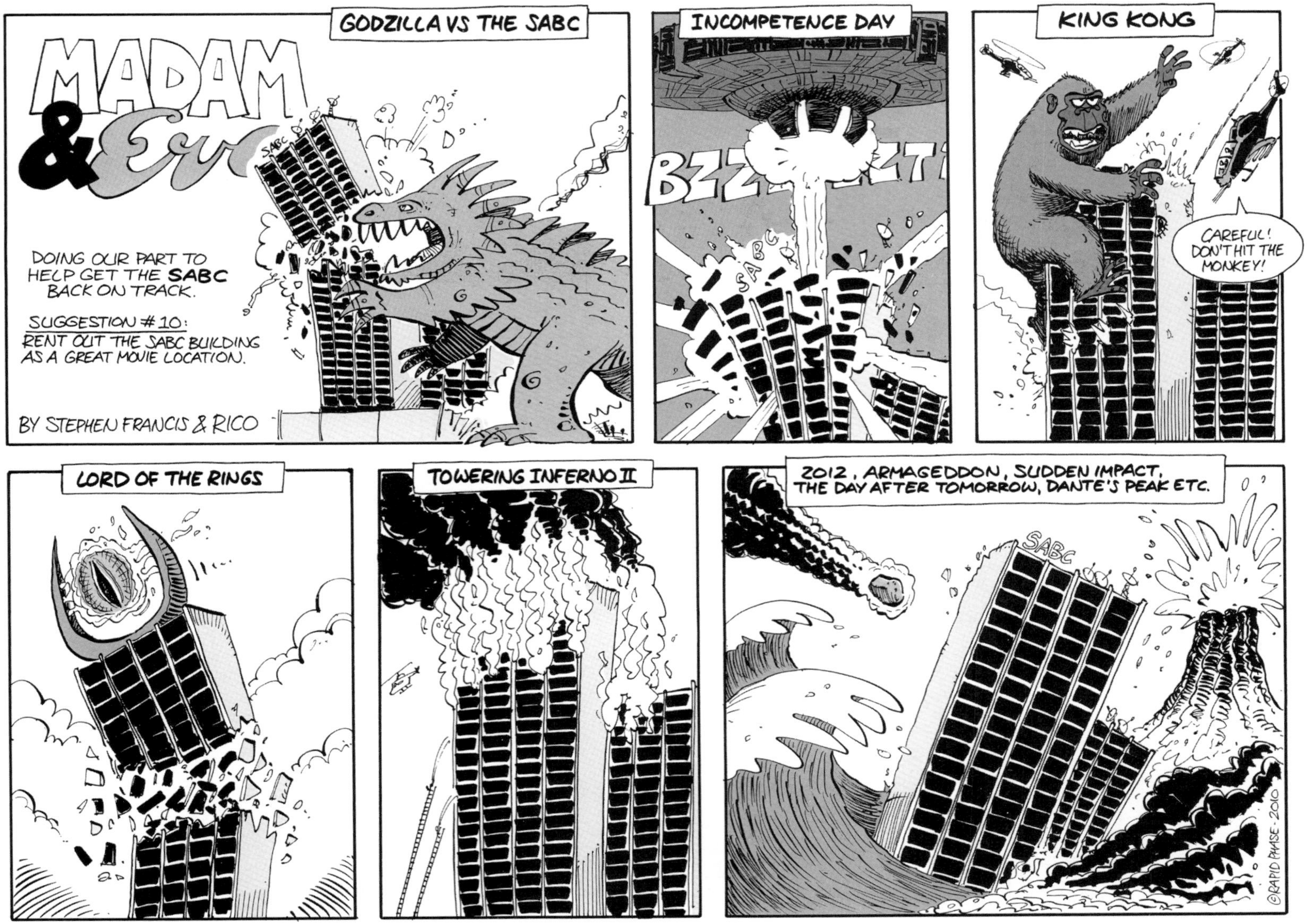
GODZILLA VS THE SABC
MADAM & Eve
SABC
DOING OUR PART TO HELP GET THE SABC BACK ON TRACK.
SUGGESTION #10: RENT OUT THE SABC BUILDING AS A GREAT MOVIE LOCATION.
BY STEPHEN FRANCIS & RICO
INCOMPETENCE DAY
SABC
KING KONG
CAREFUL! DON'T HIT THE MONKEY!
LORD OF THE RINGS
TOWERING INFERNO II
2012, ARMAGEDDON, SUDDEN IMPACT, THE DAY AFTER TOMORROW, DANTE'S PEAK ETC.
SABC
©RAPID PHASE · 2010

AND SO, AFTER THE **SABC** HAD FAILED TO BROADCAST AN IMPORTANT SPORTS EVENT...
SABC
THE PEOPLE GATHERED WITH THEIR **VUVUZELAS**...
PARRP! PARRP!
www.madamandeve.co.za
... AND THE WALLS CAME TUMBLING DOWN.
RUMBLE! CRASH!
©RAPID PHASE · 2010
SO **JERICHO** WAS A SUBURB OF AUCKLAND PARK?
YUP.
MOM!!

WHAT DO YOU THINK?
DOESN'T WORK FOR ME.
WHAT ABOUT THIS?
HMM.
... CARELESSLY STREWN WITH PAGES OPEN AS IF RECENTLY **READ** ... YET **TITLE** STILL VISIBLE TO GUESTS.
GOOD.
www.madamandeve.co.za
©RAPID PHASE · 2010
WHAT ARE YOU TWO DOING?
POSITIONING **NELSON MANDELA'S** NEW **BOOK** ON OUR NEW COFFEE TABLE.

Madam & Eve's
COMICAL HIGHLIGHTS from the MINISTERIAL **HUMOUR** HANDBOOK
©RAPID PHASE · 2010
QUICK! FOLLOW THAT CAR! HEH-HEH! **GET** IT?! **"FOLLOW THAT CAR!"** HEE-HEE! HOO-HOO! HAHAHA!!

MADAM... I THINK IT'S TIME TO HAVE THE **ELECTRIFIED FENCE** SERVICED AGAIN.
REALLY? WHAT MAKES YOU SAY THAT?
OH... JUST A FEELING.
SQUEAK SQUEAK SQUEAK SQUEAK
©RAPID PHASE · 2010 www.madamandeve.co.za

POLICE
I GUESS THE PHRASE "WATCHING THINGS LIKE A HAWK" TAKES ON A WHOLE NEW MEANING.
©RAPID PHASE · 2010 www.madamandeve.co.za

AND IN OTHER NEWS... A **POLICE** SPOKESMAN HAS ADMITTED THAT ONLY **14% OF DETECTIVES** WORKING TODAY HAVE BEEN PROPERLY **TRAINED**.
COLD!!
CHILL!!
FREEZE!!
DAMN! I **KNEW** THAT ONE!
©RAPID PHASE · 2010 www.madamandeve.co.za

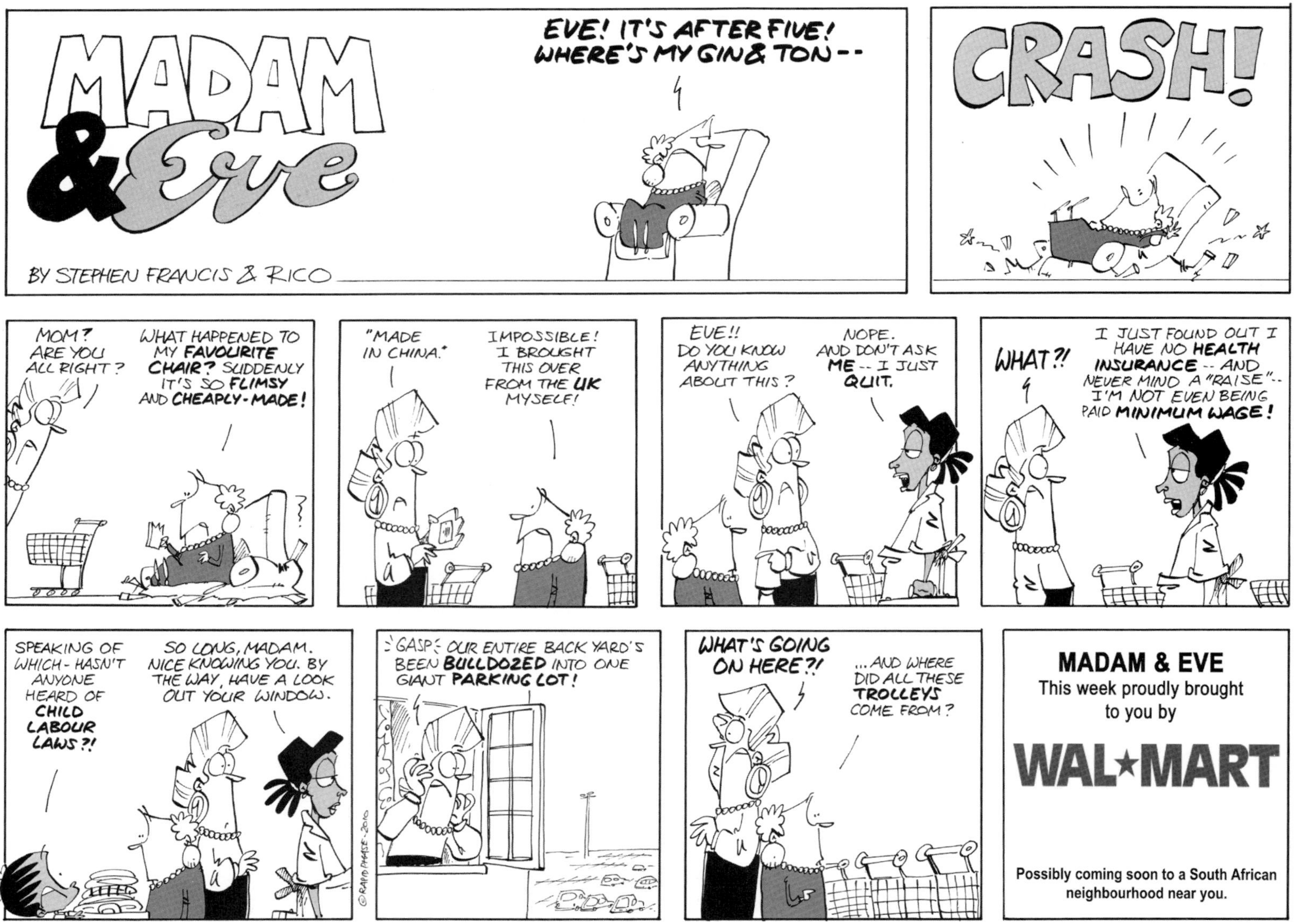
MADAM & Eve
BY STEPHEN FRANCIS & RICO
EVE! IT'S AFTER FIVE! WHERE'S MY GIN & TON--
CRASH!
MOM? ARE YOU ALL RIGHT?
WHAT HAPPENED TO MY FAVOURITE CHAIR? SUDDENLY IT'S SO FLIMSY AND CHEAPLY-MADE!
"MADE IN CHINA."
IMPOSSIBLE! I BROUGHT THIS OVER FROM THE UK MYSELF!
EVE!! DO YOU KNOW ANYTHING ABOUT THIS?
NOPE. AND DON'T ASK ME -- I JUST QUIT.
WHAT?!
I JUST FOUND OUT I HAVE NO HEALTH INSURANCE -- AND NEVER MIND A "RAISE"-- I'M NOT EVEN BEING PAID MINIMUM WAGE!
SPEAKING OF WHICH - HASN'T ANYONE HEARD OF CHILD LABOUR LAWS?!
SO LONG, MADAM. NICE KNOWING YOU. BY THE WAY, HAVE A LOOK OUT YOUR WINDOW.
© RAPID PHASE - 2010
GASP OUR ENTIRE BACK YARD'S BEEN BULLDOZED INTO ONE GIANT PARKING LOT!
WHAT'S GOING ON HERE?!
...AND WHERE DID ALL THESE TROLLEYS COME FROM?
MADAM & EVE
This week proudly brought to you by
WAL★MART
Possibly coming soon to a South African neighbourhood near you.

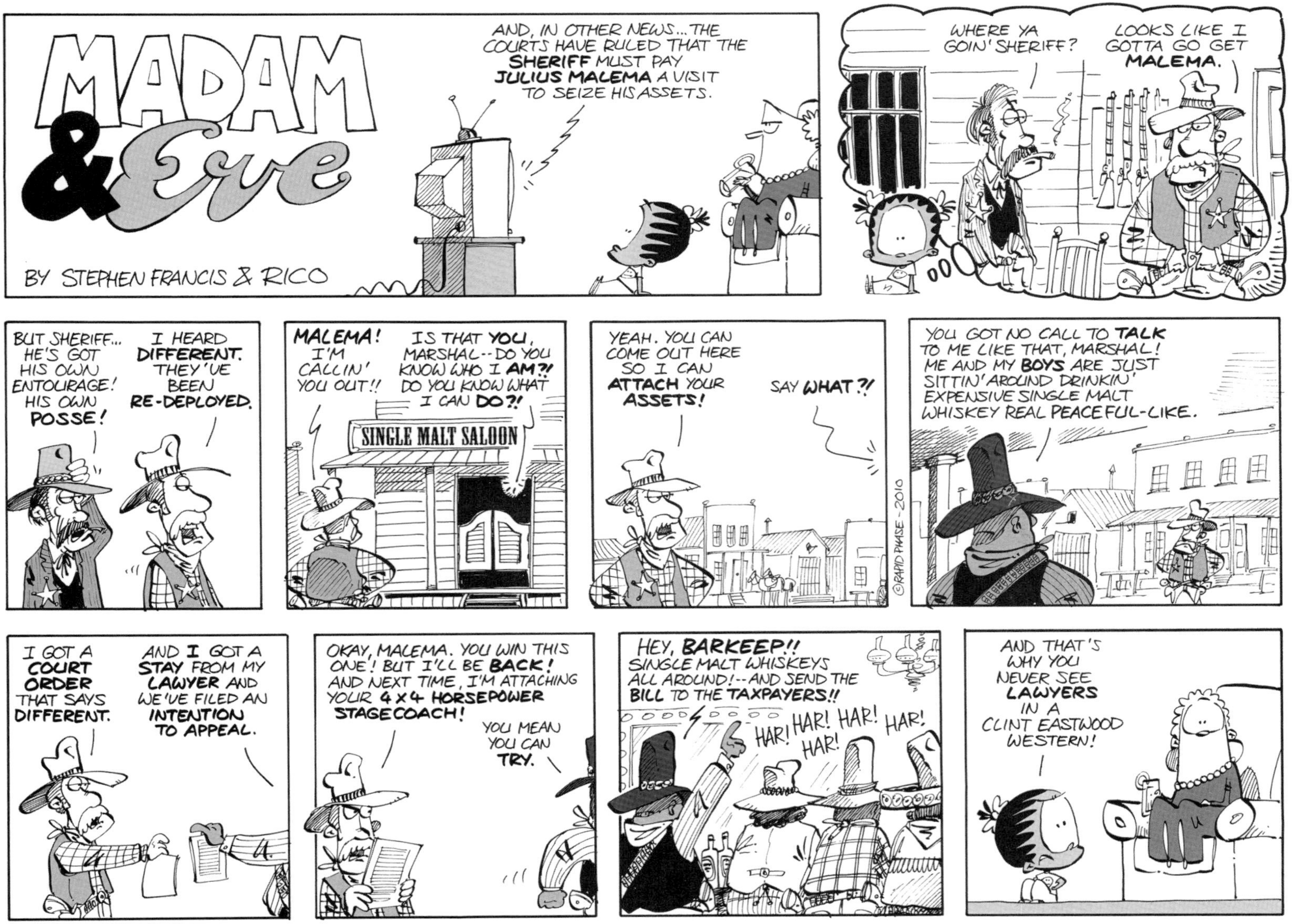
MADAM & Eve
BY STEPHEN FRANCIS & RICO
AND, IN OTHER NEWS... THE COURTS HAVE RULED THAT THE SHERIFF MUST PAY JULIUS MALEMA A VISIT TO SEIZE HIS ASSETS.
WHERE YA GOIN' SHERIFF?
LOOKS LIKE I GOTTA GO GET MALEMA.
BUT SHERIFF... HE'S GOT HIS OWN ENTOURAGE! HIS OWN POSSE!
I HEARD DIFFERENT. THEY'VE BEEN RE-DEPLOYED.
MALEMA! I'M CALLIN' YOU OUT!!
SINGLE MALT SALOON
IS THAT YOU, MARSHAL--DO YOU KNOW WHO I AM?! DO YOU KNOW WHAT I CAN DO?!
YEAH. YOU CAN COME OUT HERE SO I CAN ATTACH YOUR ASSETS!
SAY WHAT?!
©RAPID PHASE - 2010
YOU GOT NO CALL TO TALK TO ME LIKE THAT, MARSHAL! ME AND MY BOYS ARE JUST SITTIN' AROUND DRINKIN' EXPENSIVE SINGLE MALT WHISKEY REAL PEACEFUL-LIKE.
I GOT A COURT ORDER THAT SAYS DIFFERENT.
AND I GOT A STAY FROM MY LAWYER AND WE'VE FILED AN INTENTION TO APPEAL.
OKAY, MALEMA. YOU WIN THIS ONE! BUT I'LL BE BACK! AND NEXT TIME, I'M ATTACHING YOUR 4x4 HORSEPOWER STAGECOACH!
YOU MEAN YOU CAN TRY.
HEY, BARKEEP!! SINGLE MALT WHISKEYS ALL AROUND!--AND SEND THE BILL TO THE TAXPAYERS!!
HAR! HAR! HAR! HAR! HAR!
AND THAT'S WHY YOU NEVER SEE LAWYERS IN A CLINT EASTWOOD WESTERN!

NO! COME BACK! IT'S NOT FAIR!!
©RAPID PHASE · 2010
I HEAR THEY TOOK AWAY JULIUS MALEMA'S BODYGUARDS.
DO YOU KNOW WHO I AM?!!

HELLO? CAN I SPEAK TO JULIUS MALEMA PLEASE?
©RAPID PHASE · 2010
IT'S THANDI SISULU. I'M OFFERING MY SERVICES AS A FREE BODYGUARD SO I CAN FOLLOW HIM AROUND AND ONE DAY... BECOME A POWERFUL YOUTH LEADER LIKE HIM.
www.madamandeve.co.za
HUH? HE IS? OKAY... I'LL CALL BACK LATER.
HE CAN'T TALK RIGHT NOW. THE SHERIFF'S SEIZING ALL HIS ASSETS.

WHY ON EARTH WOULD YOU VOLUNTEER TO BE JULIUS MALEMA'S BODYGUARD?
TO GET MY FOOT IN THE POLITICAL DOOR.
AND WHAT DO YOU KNOW ABOUT POLITICS?
HOW HARD CAN IT BE?
DRIVE FLASHY CARS, HANG WITH MY ENTOURAGE, PARTY HEARTY, JOCKEY FOR MORE POWER... AND NATIONALISE SOMETHING EVERY NOW AND THEN.
©RAPID PHASE · 2010 www.madamandeve.co.za
WHAT?! DID I LEAVE SOMETHING OUT?!

ARMS DEAL Cluedo

WAS IT...

...COLONEL KICKBACK?

...MISTER GREENBACKS?

...PROFESSOR PAYOUT?

...MISTER MINISTER?

©RAPID PHASE - 2010

THE ADVENTURES OF SCORPY & HAWKY

www.madamandeve.co.za

©RAPID PHASE - 2010

HEY HAWKY-- I HEARD YOU GUYS DROPPED THE ARMS DEAL INVESTIGATION.

HAD TO, SCORPY. IT WAS A MATTER OF "NATIONAL SECURITY."

NATIONAL SECURITY?

YEAH! NOW THAT WE'VE DROPPED IT... GOVERNMENT OFFICIALS FEEL A LOT MORE **SECURE**!

HAW! HAW! HAW! HAW!

BILL PLEASE.

THE ADVENTURES OF SCORPY & HAWKY

www.madamandeve.co.za

©RAPID PHASE - 2010

HEY HAWKY-- I HEARD ONLY 14% OF YOUR **OFFICERS** HAVE RECEIVED **PROPER POLICE TRAINING**.

OH, SHUT THE FRONT DOOR! THAT'S A LOAD OF **RUBBISH**!

AND ANYWAY, **SMILE** WHEN SAY THAT, PAL.

WHY SHOULD I?

MY **FIREARM**!! I LOST MY DANG **FIREARM**!!

NOT AGAIN. --BILL PLEASE!

I'M READY TO MAKE AN ACCUSATION.
I SAY IT WAS... PROFESSOR PAYOUT IN THE FIVE STAR RESTAURANT WITH THE CORVETTE!
©RAPID PHASE · 2010
HAH! WRONG! IT WAS COLONEL KICKBACK IN THE BILLIARD ROOM WITH THE LIGHT UTILITY HELICOPTER!
www.madamandeve.co.za
ARMS DEAL CLUEDO.

YOUR TURN.
THREE! ONE... TWO... THREE! SAXONWOLD DRIVE! I'LL BUY IT!
www.madamandeve.co.za
AND... I'M BUILDING LOTS OF HOUSES! HERE'S ONE FOR THE PRESIDENT'S SON! YOUR TURN!
©RAPID PHASE · 2010
TWO! ONE... TWO! DAMN. ...NEW AGE NEWSPAPER.
YOU WANT IT OR NOT?
...GUPTA BROTHERS' MONOPOLY.

HEY!! MY HANDBAG!!
QUICK!! FOLLOW THAT MAN!!
TAXI
TAXI
www.madamandeve.co.za
©RAPID PHASE · 2010
TAXI
FOLLOW ME ON TWITTER

NO FOOD NO JOB FOLLOW ME ON TWITTER
©RAPID PHASE · 2010
www.madamandeve.co.za

"DRINKING SINGLE MALT WHISKEY AND JUST CHILLING."
WHO'S THAT?
I'M FOLLOWING JULIUS MALEMA ON TWITTER.
www.madamandeve.co.za
©RAPID PHASE · 2010
"WHO IS THIS? LEAVE JULIUS ALONE OR I'LL BREAK YOUR PHONE!"
HE HIRED A NEW TWITTERGUARD.

"HOW COULD SHE DO THIS TO ME?"
"HEADS ARE GOING TO ROLL FOR THIS!"
©RAPID PHASE · 2010
"AND THAT
HAS HAD HER LAST SHOPPING TRIP!"
www.madamandeve.co.za
I'M FOLLOWING ROBERT MUGABE ON TWITTER.

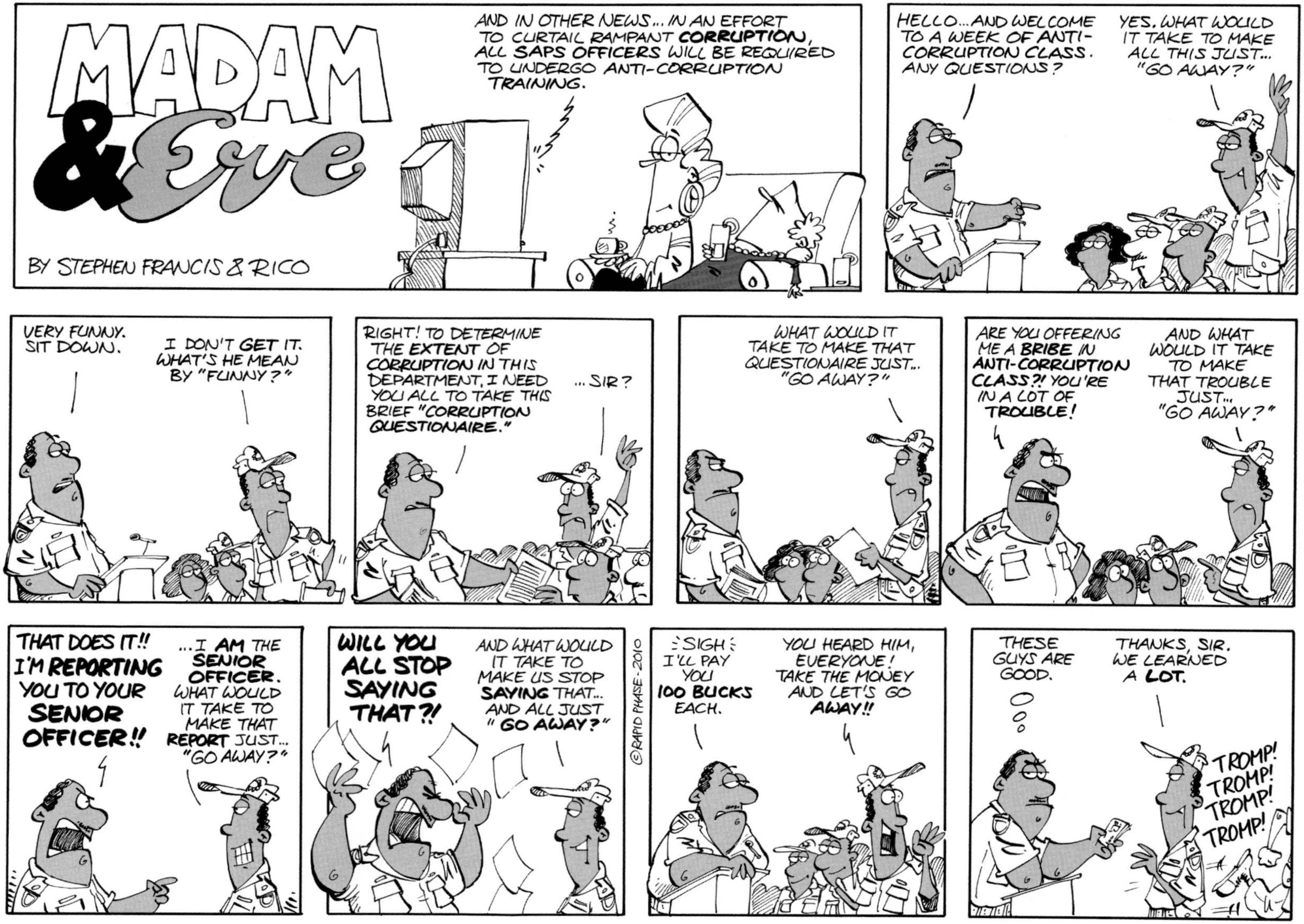
MADAM & Eve
BY STEPHEN FRANCIS & RICO
AND IN OTHER NEWS... IN AN EFFORT TO CURTAIL RAMPANT CORRUPTION, ALL SAPS OFFICERS WILL BE REQUIRED TO UNDERGO ANTI-CORRUPTION TRAINING.
HELLO... AND WELCOME TO A WEEK OF ANTI-CORRUPTION CLASS. ANY QUESTIONS?
YES. WHAT WOULD IT TAKE TO MAKE ALL THIS JUST... "GO AWAY?"
VERY FUNNY. SIT DOWN.
I DON'T GET IT. WHAT'S HE MEAN BY "FUNNY?"
RIGHT! TO DETERMINE THE EXTENT OF CORRUPTION IN THIS DEPARTMENT, I NEED YOU ALL TO TAKE THIS BRIEF "CORRUPTION QUESTIONAIRE."
...SIR?
WHAT WOULD IT TAKE TO MAKE THAT QUESTIONAIRE JUST... "GO AWAY?"
ARE YOU OFFERING ME A BRIBE IN ANTI-CORRUPTION CLASS?! YOU'RE IN A LOT OF TROUBLE!
AND WHAT WOULD IT TAKE TO MAKE THAT TROUBLE JUST... "GO AWAY?"
THAT DOES IT!! I'M REPORTING YOU TO YOUR SENIOR OFFICER!!
...I AM THE SENIOR OFFICER. WHAT WOULD IT TAKE TO MAKE THAT REPORT JUST... "GO AWAY?"
WILL YOU ALL STOP SAYING THAT?!
AND WHAT WOULD IT TAKE TO MAKE US STOP SAYING THAT... AND ALL JUST "GO AWAY?"
© RAPID PHASE - 2010
SIGH I'LL PAY YOU 100 BUCKS EACH.
YOU HEARD HIM, EVERYONE! TAKE THE MONEY AND LET'S GO AWAY!!
THESE GUYS ARE GOOD.
THANKS, SIR. WE LEARNED A LOT.
TROMP! TROMP! TROMP! TROMP!

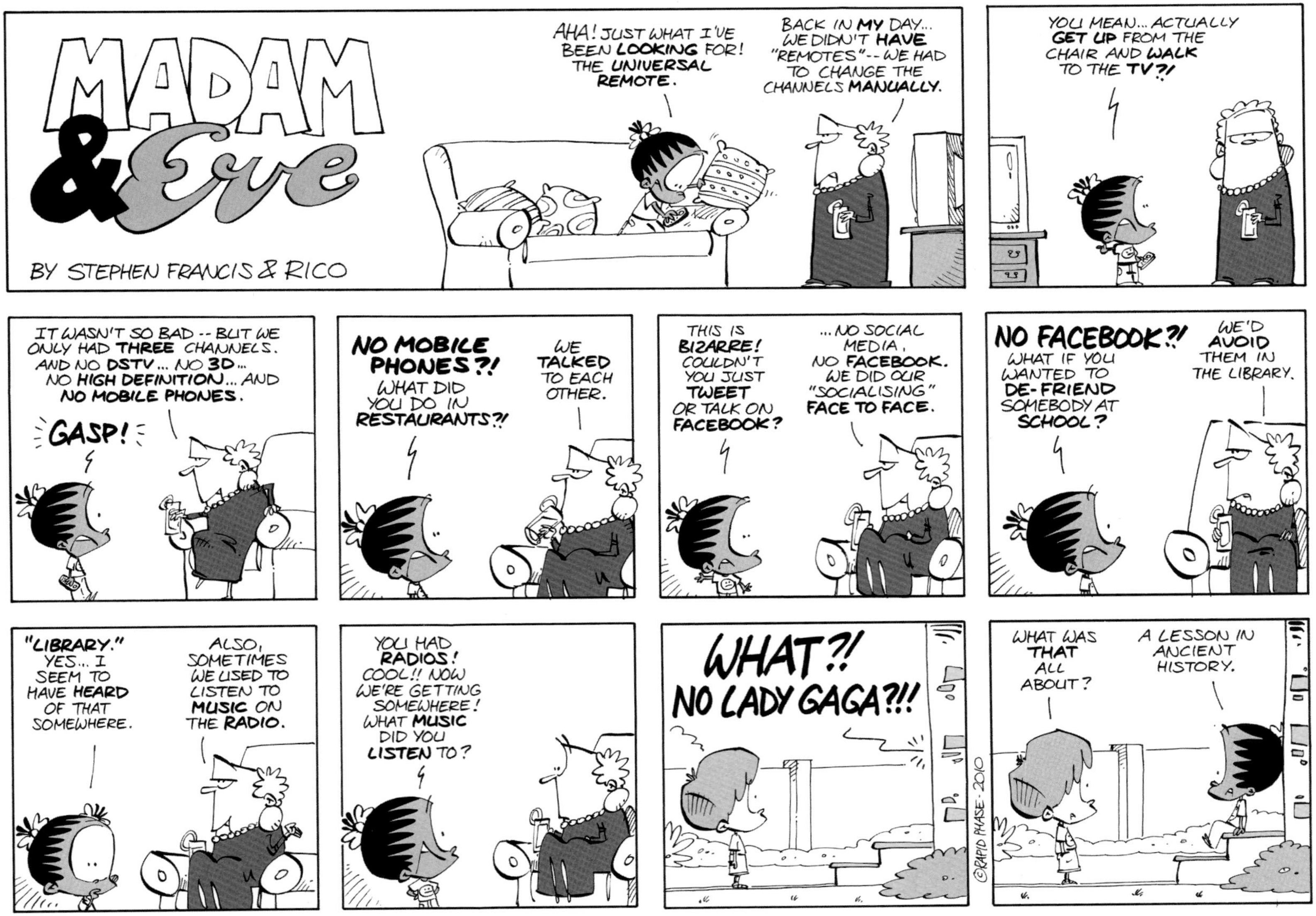
MADAM & Eve
BY STEPHEN FRANCIS & RICO
AHA! JUST WHAT I'VE BEEN LOOKING FOR! THE UNIVERSAL REMOTE.
BACK IN MY DAY... WE DIDN'T HAVE "REMOTES"-- WE HAD TO CHANGE THE CHANNELS MANUALLY.
YOU MEAN... ACTUALLY GET UP FROM THE CHAIR AND WALK TO THE TV?!
IT WASN'T SO BAD -- BUT WE ONLY HAD THREE CHANNELS. AND NO DSTV... NO 3D... NO HIGH DEFINITION... AND NO MOBILE PHONES.
GASP!
NO MOBILE PHONES?! WHAT DID YOU DO IN RESTAURANTS?!
WE TALKED TO EACH OTHER.
THIS IS BIZARRE! COULDN'T YOU JUST TWEET OR TALK ON FACEBOOK?
...NO SOCIAL MEDIA, NO FACEBOOK. WE DID OUR "SOCIALISING" FACE TO FACE.
NO FACEBOOK?! WHAT IF YOU WANTED TO DE-FRIEND SOMEBODY AT SCHOOL?
WE'D AVOID THEM IN THE LIBRARY.
"LIBRARY." YES... I SEEM TO HAVE HEARD OF THAT SOMEWHERE.
ALSO, SOMETIMES WE USED TO LISTEN TO MUSIC ON THE RADIO.
YOU HAD RADIOS! COOL!! NOW WE'RE GETTING SOMEWHERE! WHAT MUSIC DID YOU LISTEN TO?
WHAT?! NO LADY GAGA?!!
©RAPID PHASE · 2010
WHAT WAS THAT ALL ABOUT?
A LESSON IN ANCIENT HISTORY.

MOM -- THE **PRESIDENT'S OFFICE** IS ON THE PHONE.
GASP!
THEY'RE RESHUFFLING THE **CABINET** AND **YOU'VE** BEEN CHOSEN TO HEAD UP A **NEW PORTFOLIO.**
REALLY? WHAT IS IT?
"MINISTER OF 80 YEAR-OLD DISGRUNTLED WHITE WOMEN."
www.madamandeve.co.za
©RAPID PHASE · 2010
TELL HIM I ACCEPT! **I ACCEPT!!**
WAKE MOM UP. IT'S TIME FOR DINNER.

MOTHER ANDERSON'S DREAM OF MINISTERIAL GLORY CONTINUES...
NEW MINISTER ANDERSON REPORTING FOR DUTY.
GO RIGHT IN. THEY'RE WAITING FOR YOU.
www.madamandeve.co.za
EDITH ANDERSON. YOUR CEREMONIAL **BLUE LIGHT.**
©RAPID PHASE · 2010
GASP MY OWN **ENTOURAGE!**
CHOKE EXPENSIVE SINGLE-MALT **WHISKEY.** I-I DON'T KNOW WHAT TO SAY!
WELCOME TO GOVERN-MENT.

MOTHER ANDERSON'S DREAM OF MINISTERIAL GLORY CONTINUES.
WELCOME TO THE **MINISTER'S CLUB**, Ms ANDERSON.
THANK YOU.
I NOW PRESENT YOU WITH THE SECRET **MINISTERIAL HANDBOOK** GUIDELINES FOR ALL MINISTERS.
GASP IT REALLY EXISTS?!
HUH? ALL THE PAGES ARE **BLANK!**
EXACTLY! THERE **ARE** NO **GUIDELINES** FOR MINISTERS. **WE** DO WHAT-EVER **WE** WANT! BWAHAHAHA!!
www.madamandeve.co.za
©RAPID PHASE · 2010
GOOD LUCK. SEE YOU IN TWO WEEKS. I'M TAKING MY FAMILY TO **DISNEYLAND!**
WAIT! WHAT ABOUT MY MINISTERIAL CREDIT CARDS?

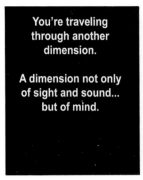

You're traveling through another dimension.
A dimension not only of sight and sound... but of mind.
It is the middle ground between light and shadow. Of science and superstition. This is the dimension of imagination. And often, incredible stupidity.
It is an area we call...
HEY! I'VE GOT AN IDEA! WE'LL SHUT DOWN TWITTER.
©RAPID PHASE - 2010
...The ANCYL Zone
Coming soon to a social media near you.

You're traveling through another dimension.
A dimension not only of sight and sound... but of mind.
And often, incredible stupidity.
It is an area we call...
©RAPID PHASE - 2010 www.madamandeve.co.za
HOW IS OUR PLAN 9 TO TURN OFF TWITTER PROGRESSING?
IT'S MORE DIFFICULT THAN WE THOUGHT, SIR.
BUT DON'T WORRY... WHEN IT COMES TO TURNING THINGS OFF... WE'RE CONSULTING THE BEST THERE IS!
Eskom
...The ANCYL Zone
Coming soon to a social media near you.

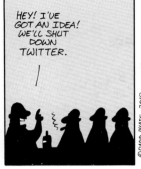

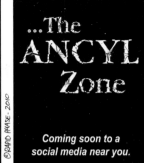

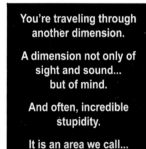

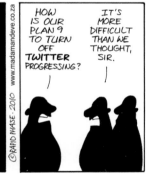

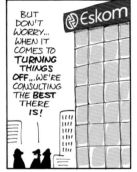

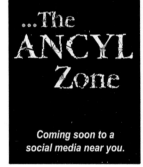

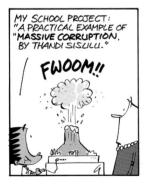

MY SCHOOL PROJECT: "A PRACTICAL EXAMPLE OF "MASSIVE CORRUPTION, BY THANDI SISULU."
FWOOM!!
"CORRUPTION?" YOU MEAN ERUPTION! THAT'S AN EXAMPLE OF VOLCANIC ERUPTION! ...NOT VOLCANIC CORRUPTION!
©RAPID PHASE - 2010
YOU MEAN... I HAVE TO DISQUALIFY MY ENTIRE PROJECT... BECAUSE OF A SIMPLE MISTAKE IN DEFINITION?
YEP.
www.madamandeve.co.za
MAYBE IF I GIVE THE TEACHER TWENTY BUCKS... SHE'LL GIVE ME AN A.

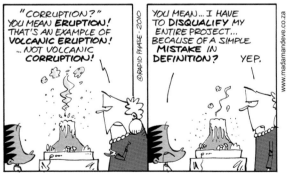

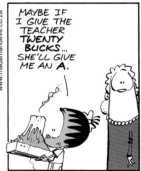

CONGRATULATIONS
YOU ARE THE 10.000th PERSON TO PASS BY This ROBOT WITHOUT GIVING ME MONEY.
©RAPID PHASE · 2010
www.madamandeve.co.za

NOPE. THIS ONE DOESN'T WORK. NO MOVEMENT AT ALL.
SIGH
...TRY THIS ONE.
©RAPID PHASE · 2010
WHAT ARE YOU DOING?
www.madamandeve.co.za
TESTING ENERGY DRINKS.

BEEN THERE... DONE THAT.
OH PLEASE! GIVE ME A BREAK!
©RAPID PHASE · 2010
SIGH
BEEN THERE... DONE THAT.
...HERSCHELLE GIBBS BIOGRAPHY.
BIG DEAL. I'VE DONE THAT TOO.

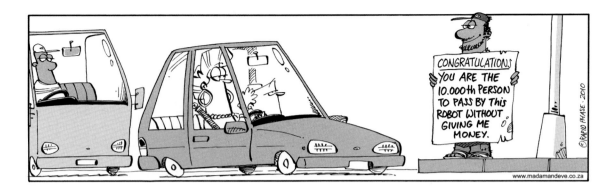

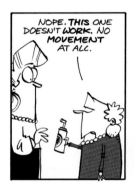

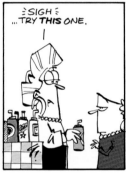

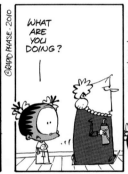

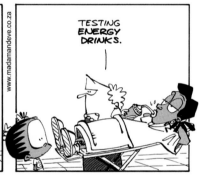

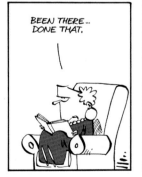

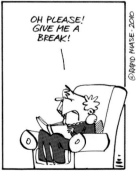

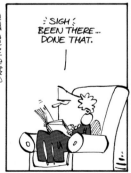

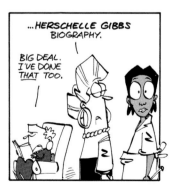

WHAT SEEMS TO BE THE **PROBLEM**, OFFICER?
WELL... OUR **PAY** IS **LOW**. I NEED **MONEY**, SO I HAVE TO ASK YOU FOR A **BRIBE**.
www.madamandeve.co.za
I UNDERSTAND. HERE YOU GO.
©RAPID PHASE · 2010
...FINALLY. AN **HONEST** COP.

HOW IS MY DRIVING? 099-867564
©RAPID PHASE · 2010 www.madamandeve.co.za
HOW IS MY BRIBING? 088-8350898
POLICE

WHAT ARE THOSE **METRO POLICE** DOING?
THEY'RE FIGURING OUT THE BEST PLACE TO PUT UP THEIR **ROADBLOCK**.
AHA! THIS IS THE **PERFECT** SPOT! RIGHT HERE!
©RAPID PHASE · 2010 www.madamandeve.co.za
ATM

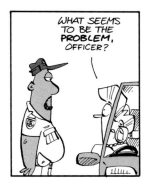

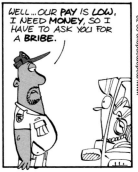

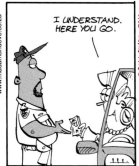

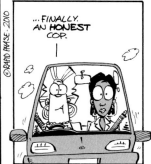

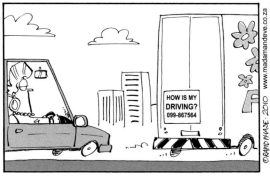

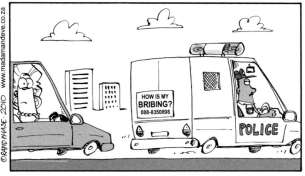

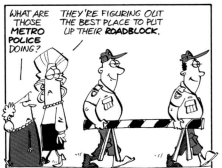

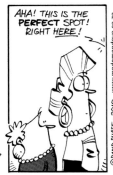

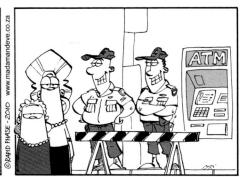

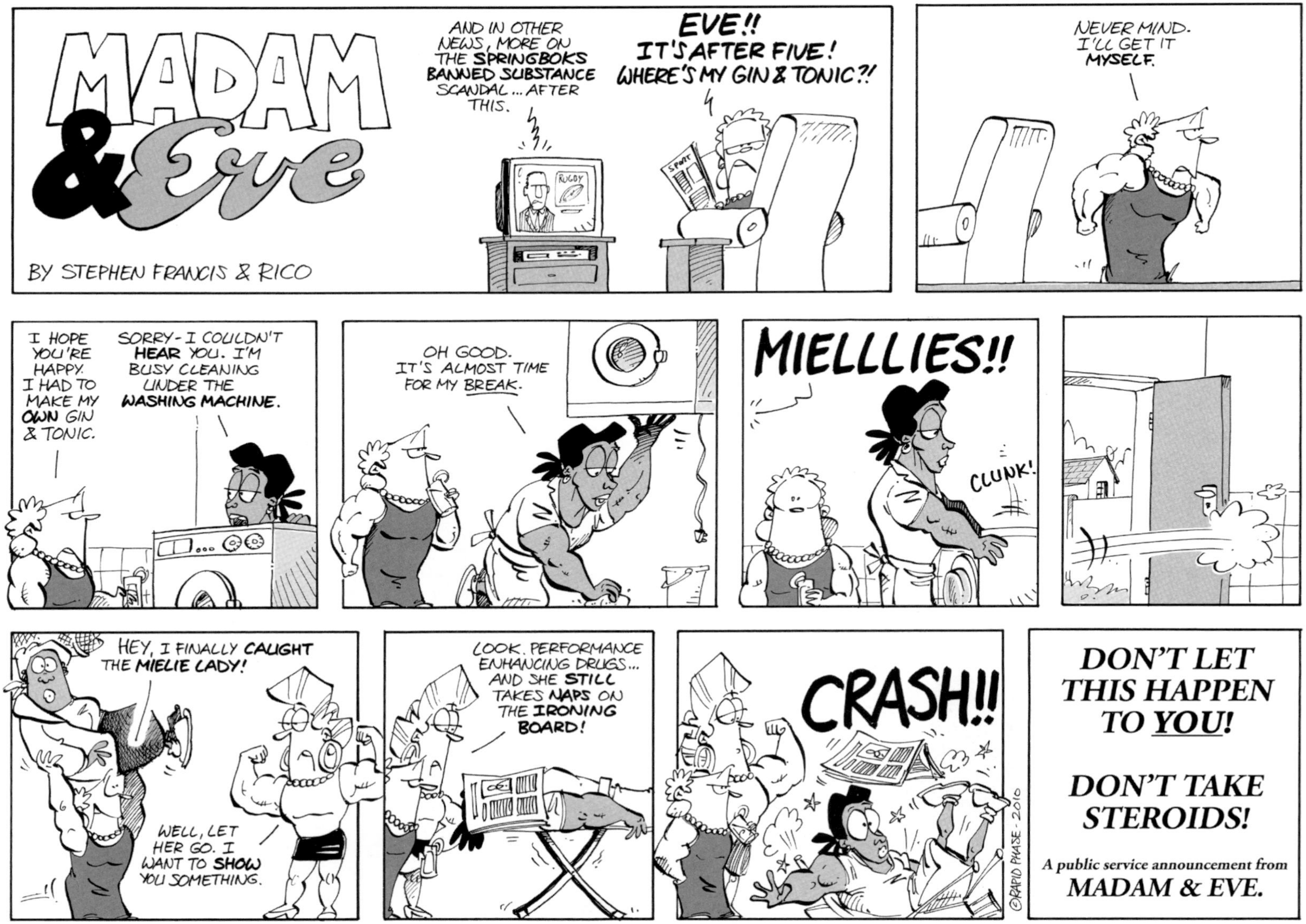
MADAM & Eve
BY STEPHEN FRANCIS & RICO
AND IN OTHER NEWS, MORE ON THE SPRINGBOKS BANNED SUBSTANCE SCANDAL... AFTER THIS.
RUGBY
EVE!! IT'S AFTER FIVE! WHERE'S MY GIN & TONIC?!
SPORT
NEVER MIND. I'LL GET IT MYSELF.
I HOPE YOU'RE HAPPY. I HAD TO MAKE MY OWN GIN & TONIC.
SORRY- I COULDN'T HEAR YOU. I'M BUSY CLEANING UNDER THE WASHING MACHINE.
OH GOOD. IT'S ALMOST TIME FOR MY BREAK.
MIELLLIES!!
CLUNK!
HEY, I FINALLY CAUGHT THE MIELIE LADY!
WELL, LET HER GO. I WANT TO SHOW YOU SOMETHING.
LOOK. PERFORMANCE ENHANCING DRUGS... AND SHE STILL TAKES NAPS ON THE IRONING BOARD!
CRASH!!
©RAPID PHASE · 2010
DON'T LET THIS HAPPEN TO YOU!
DON'T TAKE STEROIDS!
A public service announcement from MADAM & EVE.

KNOCK KNOCK! OPEN UP! IT'S THE CARTOON STRIP REGULATORY AUTHORITY!!
©RAPID PHASE · 2010
I'M SORRY TO INFORM YOU...THAT YOUR MOTHER HAS TESTED POSITIVE FOR A BANNED SUBSTANCE.
WHAT?! WHICH ONE?!
www.madamandeve.co.za
PERFORMANCE-ENHANCING HUMOUR STEROIDS.
SO THAT'S WHY THE CARTOON HAS BEEN SO FUNNY LATELY.
I MUST HAVE SWALLOWED THEM BY ACCIDENT! I SWEAR!

MY MOTHER'S BEEN TAKING PERFORMANCE-ENHANCING HUMOUR STEROIDS?!
DIDN'T YOU NOTICE HOW MUCH FUNNIER I'VE BEEN?
SO WHAT HAPPENS NOW?
I'M AFRAID TEMPORARY SUSPENSION.
TEMPORARY SUSPENSION?! HOW CAN YOU SUSPEND A CARTOON STRIP?!
©RAPID PHASE · 2010

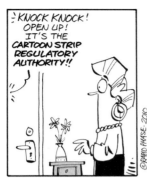

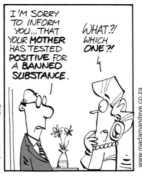

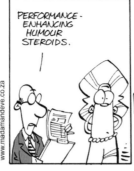

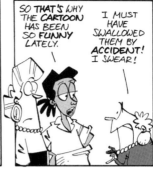

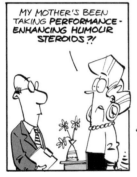

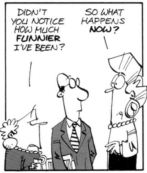

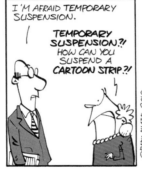

MADAM & EVE is temporarily suspended today.
One of the characters tested positive for performance-enhancing humour steroids.
THANKS A LOT, MOM!
IT WAS AN ACCIDENT! NO ONE CAN TELL ME NOT TO BE FUNNY!
©RAPID PHASE · 2010
TA-DA!
www.madamandeve.co.za
HEY! WHAT ABOUT MY RIGHT TO JOKE?!
THEY'RE REALLY STRICT.

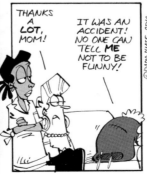

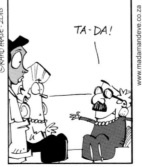

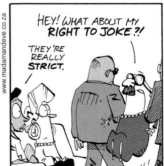

LET'S SEE... FRAUD... FRAUD... JOBS FOR PALS... FRAUD... FRAUD...
...FRAUD... ILLEGAL TENDERS... FRAUD... JOBS FOR PALS...
...FRAUD... FRAUD... CORRUPTION... FRAUD... FRAUD... FRAUD.
©RAPID PHASE 2010 www.madamandeve.co.za
HEY!! A BANK ROBBERY!!
MOM SAYS THE NEWS HAS BEEN BORING LATELY.

AH... NATURE! IT'S SO GOOD TO FINALLY GET AWAY FROM CELLPHONES, LAPTOPS AND ALL SOCIAL MEDIA!
©RAPID PHASE 2010
TWITTER TWITTER
TWEET TWEET
BLOG BLOG

CORRUPTION! CORRUPTION! CORRUPTION! I'M SO SICK OF CORRUPTION!
©RAPID PHASE 2010 www.madamandeve.co.za
CORRUPTION! IT'S LIKE... WEEDS! NO MATTER WHAT YOU DO, THEY KEEP POPPING UP!
PSST TWO HUNDRED BUCKS AND WE MOVE TO THE NEIGHBOUR'S GARDEN.
WHO SAID THAT?!
WHO SAID WHAT?

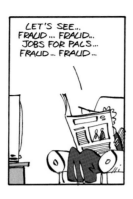

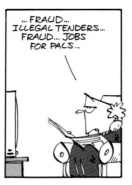

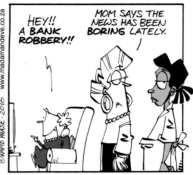

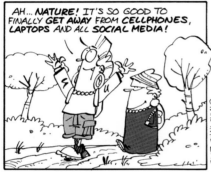

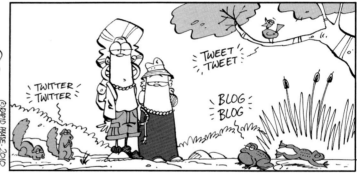

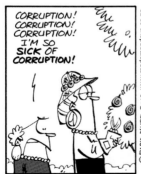

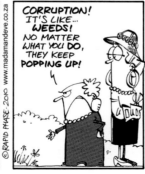

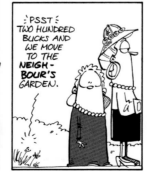

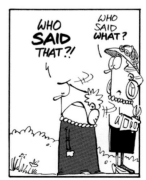

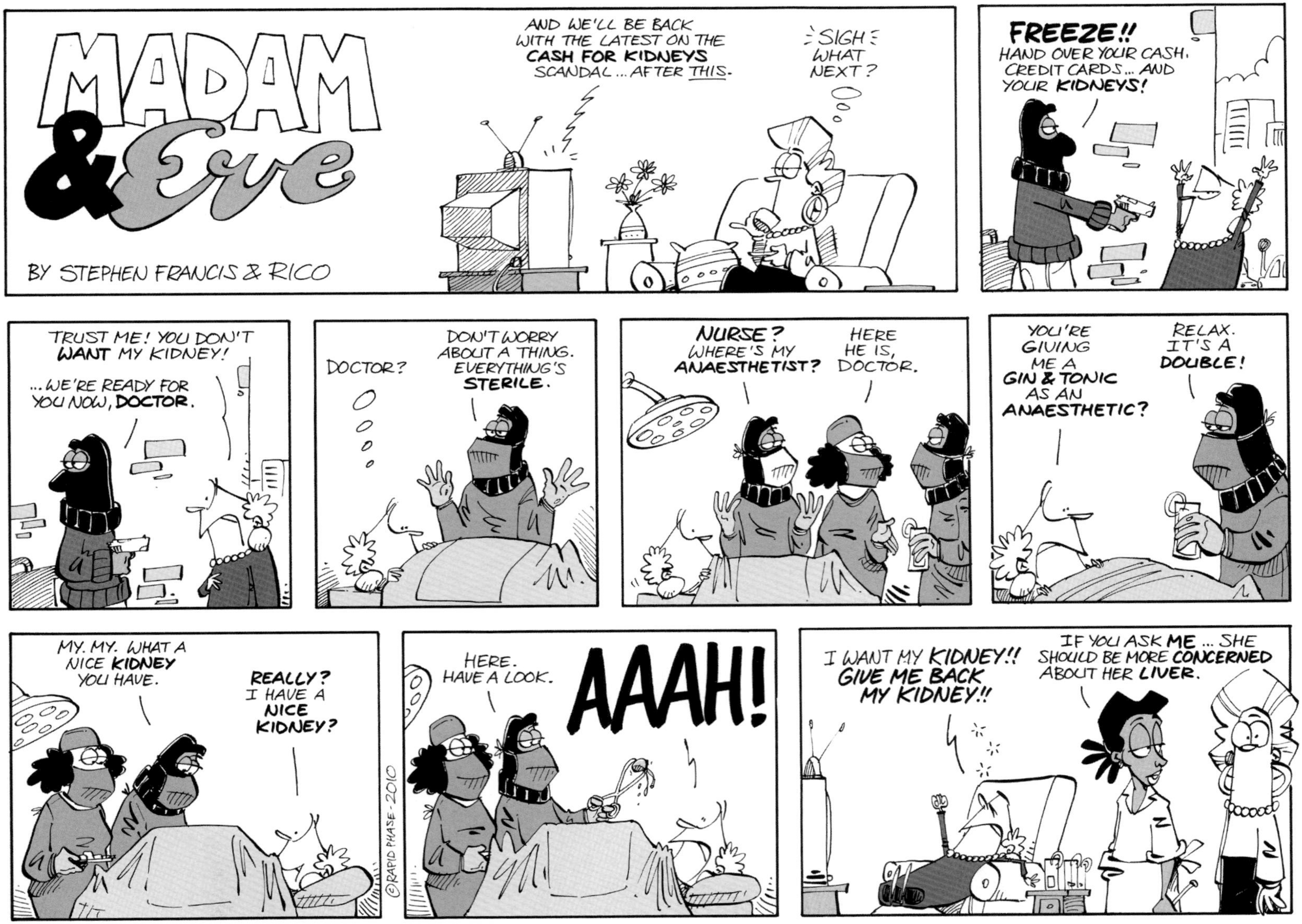
MADAM & Eve
BY STEPHEN FRANCIS & RICO
AND WE'LL BE BACK WITH THE LATEST ON THE CASH FOR KIDNEYS SCANDAL ... AFTER THIS.
SIGH WHAT NEXT?
FREEZE!! HAND OVER YOUR CASH, CREDIT CARDS... AND YOUR KIDNEYS!
TRUST ME! YOU DON'T WANT MY KIDNEY!
... WE'RE READY FOR YOU NOW, DOCTOR.
DOCTOR?
DON'T WORRY ABOUT A THING. EVERYTHING'S STERILE.
NURSE? WHERE'S MY ANAESTHETIST?
HERE HE IS, DOCTOR.
YOU'RE GIVING ME A GIN & TONIC AS AN ANAESTHETIC?
RELAX. IT'S A DOUBLE!
MY. MY. WHAT A NICE KIDNEY YOU HAVE.
REALLY? I HAVE A NICE KIDNEY?
©RAPID PHASE - 2010
HERE. HAVE A LOOK.
AAAH!
I WANT MY KIDNEY!! GIVE ME BACK MY KIDNEY!!
IF YOU ASK ME ... SHE SHOULD BE MORE CONCERNED ABOUT HER LIVER.

MOM! WATCH WHAT YOU'RE DOING! YOU KEEP DROPPING YOUR PASTA!
PLOP!
I CAN'T HELP IT! IT'S MORE SLIPPERY THAN IT LOOKS! THE CHEF BUNGLED THE RECIPE!
www.madamandeve.co.za
WHAT DID YOU ORDER?
©RAPID PHASE · 2010
THE VEAL AGLIOTTI.

THANDI! WHERE'S YOUR HOMEWORK?
I DIDN'T DO IT.
...BUT DON'T WORRY. I'LL GIVE MYSELF DETENTION LATER WHEN I GET HOME.
©RAPID PHASE · 2010
www.madamandeve.co.za
...OBVIOUSLY SOME PEOPLE HAVE NO FAITH IN SELF-REGULATION!
PRINCIPAL

LOOK AT THE SIZE OF THIS QUEUE!... JUST SO YOU CAN SIT ON FATHER CHRISTMAS'S LAP!
SANTA'S GROTTO
www.madamandeve.co.za
...MAYBE IF WE GAVE THE ELF TEN RANDS.
WHAT'S WRONG WITH YOU?! ARE YOU CRAZY?!
...I ALREADY HAD TO SLIP THE REINDEER TEN BUCKS JUST TO GET US PAST THE PEPPERMINT FOREST.
©RAPID PHASE · 2010
SIGH WHATEVER HAPPENED TO CHRISTMAS SPIRIT?
THE DAMN ELVES GOT GREEDY.

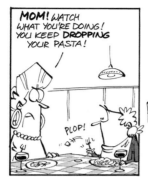

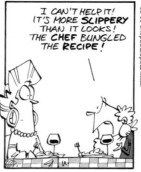

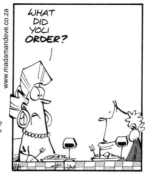

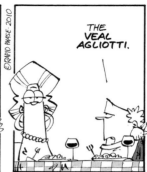

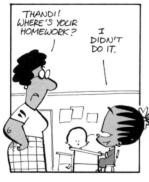

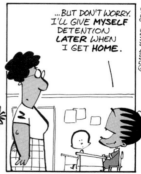

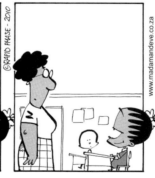

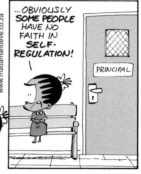

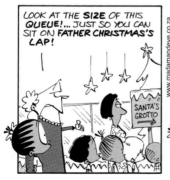

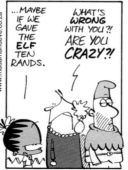

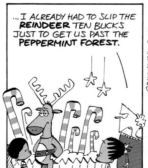

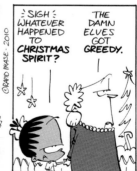

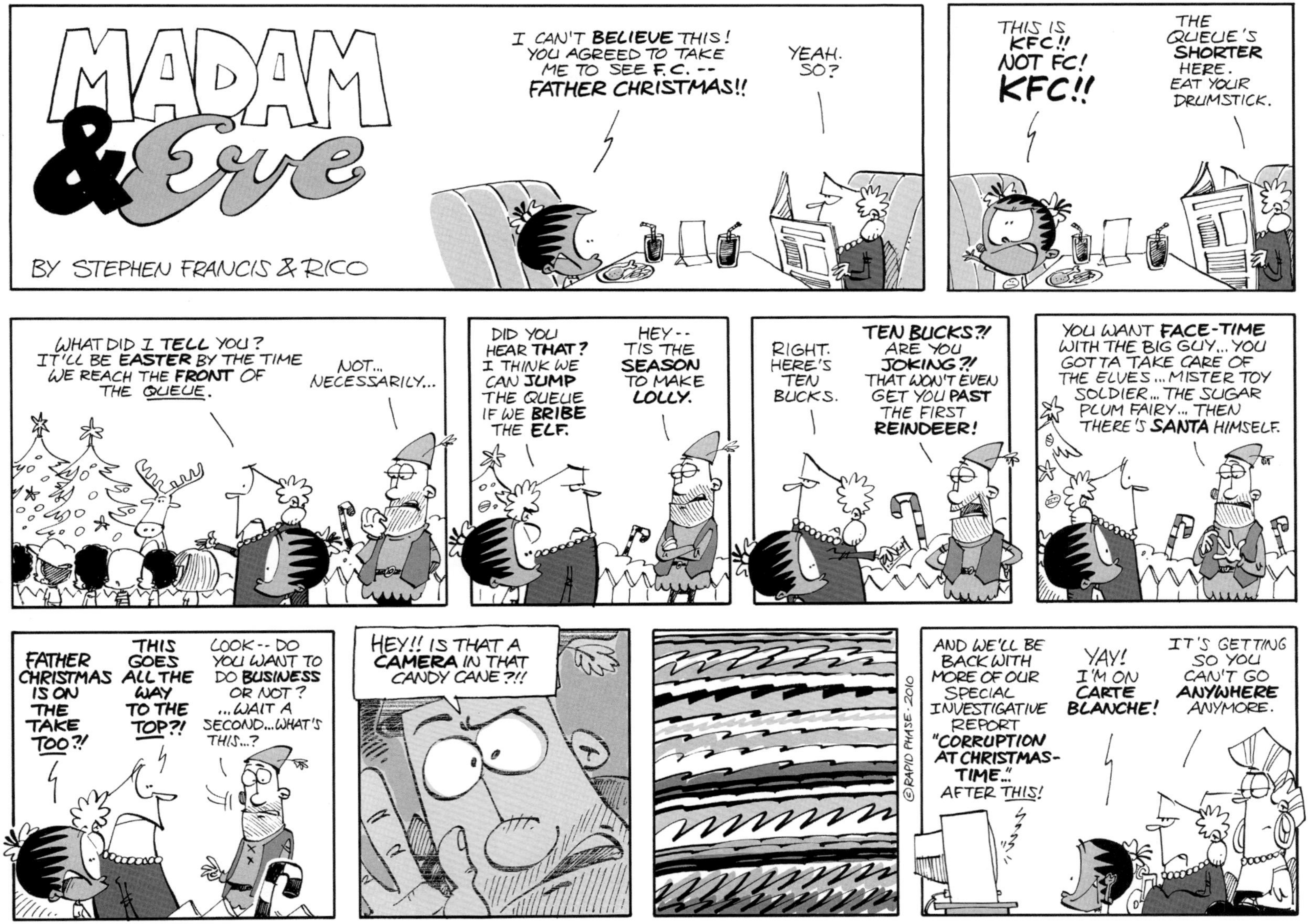
MADAM & Eve
BY STEPHEN FRANCIS & RICO
I CAN'T BELIEVE THIS! YOU AGREED TO TAKE ME TO SEE F.C. -- FATHER CHRISTMAS!!
YEAH. SO?
THIS IS KFC!! NOT FC! KFC!!
THE QUEUE'S SHORTER HERE. EAT YOUR DRUMSTICK.
WHAT DID I TELL YOU? IT'LL BE EASTER BY THE TIME WE REACH THE FRONT OF THE QUEUE.
NOT... NECESSARILY...
DID YOU HEAR THAT? I THINK WE CAN JUMP THE QUEUE IF WE BRIBE THE ELF.
HEY -- 'TIS THE SEASON TO MAKE LOLLY.
RIGHT. HERE'S TEN BUCKS.
TEN BUCKS?! ARE YOU JOKING?! THAT WON'T EVEN GET YOU PAST THE FIRST REINDEER!
YOU WANT FACE-TIME WITH THE BIG GUY... YOU GOTTA TAKE CARE OF THE ELVES... MISTER TOY SOLDIER... THE SUGAR PLUM FAIRY... THEN THERE'S SANTA HIMSELF.
FATHER CHRISTMAS IS ON THE TAKE TOO?!
THIS GOES ALL THE WAY TO THE TOP?!
LOOK -- DO YOU WANT TO DO BUSINESS OR NOT? ...WAIT A SECOND...WHAT'S THIS...?
HEY!! IS THAT A CAMERA IN THAT CANDY CANE?!!
© RAPID PHASE · 2010
AND WE'LL BE BACK WITH MORE OF OUR SPECIAL INVESTIGATIVE REPORT "CORRUPTION AT CHRISTMAS-TIME..." AFTER THIS!
YAY! I'M ON CARTE BLANCHE!
IT'S GETTING SO YOU CAN'T GO ANYWHERE ANYMORE.

HUH? WHAT'S THIS? "WELCOME TO WORLDWIDE MADAMS DOT COM."
"HO, HO, HO. PRESENTING THIS WEEK'S UPDATED ALPHABETISED "STINGY LIST"... OF MADAMS WHO HAVEN'T PAID A CHRISTMAS BONUS."
ABRAMS... ADELSKY... AGUMA... AMOOJEE... ANDERSON...
GASP!
I'VE BEEN WIKILEAKED!!
www.madamandeve.co.za
©RAPID PHASE · 2010

AAAAH!!
I'VE BEEN WIKILEAKED!!
WHO'S WIKILEAKING ME?!!
<IT'S AN ONLINE LIST. "MADAMS WHO DON'T PAY A CHRISTMAS BONUS.">
<BIG DEAL. KNOWN ABOUT THAT FOR YEARS.>
©RAPID PHASE · 2010
www.madamandeve.co.za

HEY EVERYONE!
WHAT HAPPENS IF YOU GET A HOLE IN YOUR WIKI?
YOUR WIKI LEAKS!!
IS IT ME OR HAS THE SILLY SEASON GONE BY QUICKLY THIS YEAR?
www.madamandeve.co.za
©RAPID PHASE · 2010

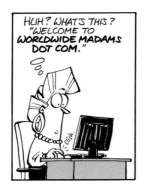

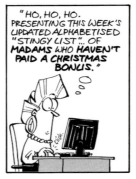

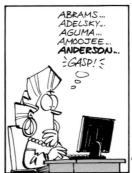

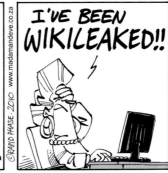

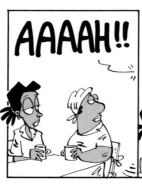

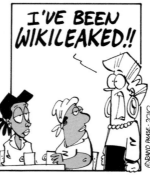

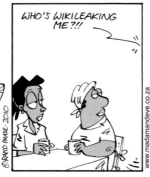

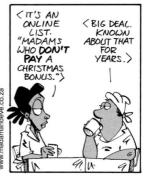

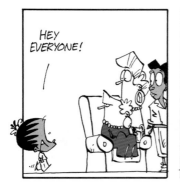

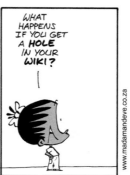

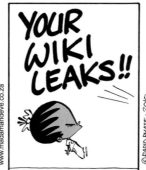

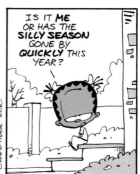

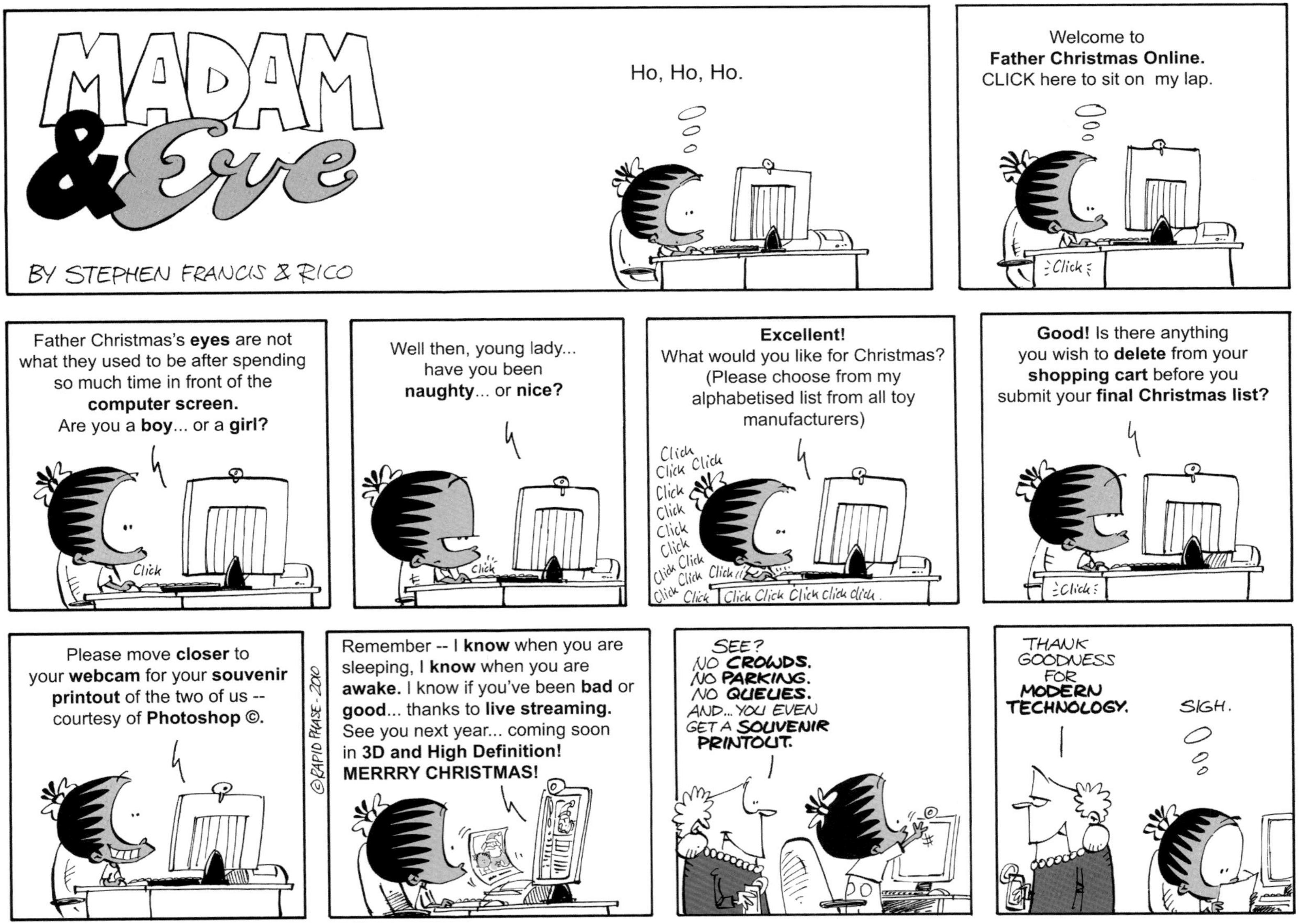

MADAM & Eve
BY STEPHEN FRANCIS & RICO
Ho, Ho, Ho.
Welcome to Father Christmas Online. CLICK here to sit on my lap.
Click
Father Christmas's eyes are not what they used to be after spending so much time in front of the computer screen. Are you a boy... or a girl?
Click
Well then, young lady... have you been naughty... or nice?
Click
Excellent! What would you like for Christmas? (Please choose from my alphabetised list from all toy manufacturers)
Click Click Click Click Click Click Click Click Click Click Click Click Click Click Click Click Click click click
Good! Is there anything you wish to delete from your shopping cart before you submit your final Christmas list?
Click
Please move closer to your webcam for your souvenir printout of the two of us -- courtesy of Photoshop ©.
©RAPID PHASE - 2010
Remember -- I know when you are sleeping, I know when you are awake. I know if you've been bad or good... thanks to live streaming. See you next year... coming soon in 3D and High Definition! MERRRY CHRISTMAS!
SEE? NO CROWDS. NO PARKING. NO QUEUES. AND... YOU EVEN GET A SOUVENIR PRINTOUT.
THANK GOODNESS FOR MODERN TECHNOLOGY.
SIGH.

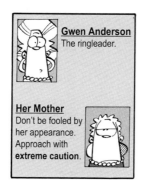

Gwen Anderson
The ringleader.
Her Mother
Don't be fooled by her appearance. Approach with extreme caution.
Eve Sisulu
Domestic worker. Often used as a decoy.
WE WAIT UNTIL THEY COME OUT OF THE BANK, THEN WE CORNER THEM. ANY QUESTIONS?
THIS SEEMS LIKE A LOT OF TROUBLE JUST TO COLLECT ONE CUSTOMER'S CHRISTMAS BONUS!
©RAPID PHASE - 2010
www.madamandeve.co.za
RIGHT! WHO SAID THAT?!!
HE'S NEW, SIR.

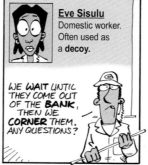

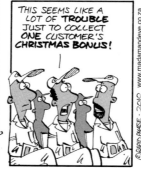

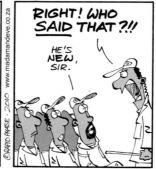

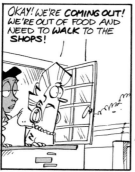

OKAY! WE'RE COMING OUT! WE'RE OUT OF FOOD AND NEED TO WALK TO THE SHOPS!
EAGLE'S NEST TO BASE! SIR...THEY'RE ALL UNDER A BLANKET! WE CAN'T TELL WHO'S WHO!
www.madamandeve.co.za
DAMN! THESE GUYS ARE GOOD! WE'LL GET 'EM NEXT TIME.
HOSTAGE NEGOTIATION?
©RAPID PHASE - 2010
DUSTBIN MEN CHRISTMAS BONUS COLLECTION.

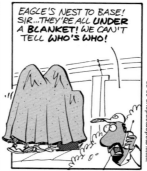

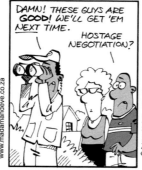

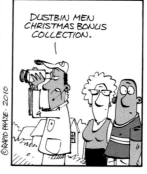

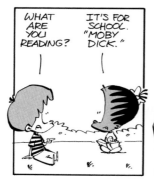

WHAT ARE YOU READING?
IT'S FOR SCHOOL. "MOBY DICK."
...THE STORY OF A MAN AND HIS RELENTLESS PURSUIT TO CAPTURE THE GREAT WHITE WHALE.
©RAPID PHASE - 2010
ODD. SOMEHOW THAT STORY HAS A FAMILIAR RING TO IT.
www.madamandeve.co.za
SIR? CAN'T WE FORGET COLLECTING OUR XMAS BONUS FROM GWEN ANDERSON THIS YEAR? THERE'S LOTS OF OTHER HOUSES.
SHE'S INSIDE. I JUST KNOW IT.

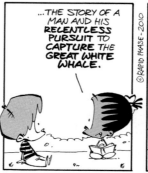

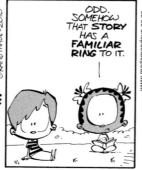

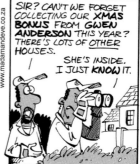

SCIENCE QUIZ:
QUESTION 1: DRAW A DIAGRAM ILLUSTRATING AN IRRESISTABLE FORCE MEETING AN IMMOVABLE OBJECT.
©RAPID PHASE - 2010
www.madamandeve.co.za
Dustbin men trying to collect Christmas Bonus.
Madam
Mother ANDERSON

HERE. PLEASE THANK ALL THE DUSTBIN MEN AND ACCEPT THIS AS A GENEROUS CHRISTMAS BONUS.
©RAPID PHASE - 2010
www.madamandeve.co.za
IT'S GETTING DARK. HE'S STILL STANDING THERE?
I THINK HE'S IN SHOCK.

LOOK AT THIS! NOT ONE EMPTY TABLE AT THIS RESTAURANT! THEY'RE ALL BOOKED FOR COMPANY CHRISTMAS PARTIES!
©RAPID PHASE - 2010
DON'T ASK.

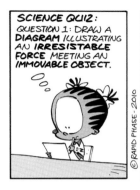

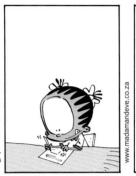

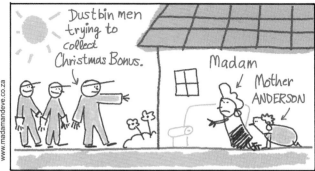

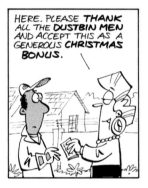

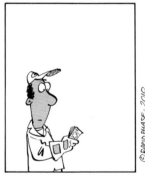

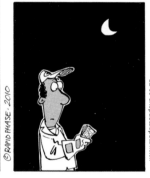

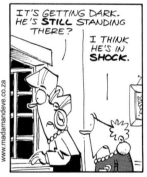

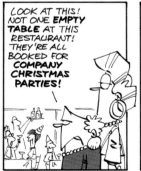

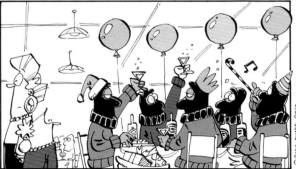

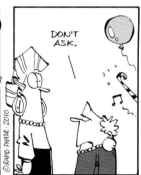

MORNING, MADAM. TODAY IS RECONCILIATION DAY.

HAPPY RECONCILIATION DAY!

www.madamandeve.co.za

WHAT ARE WE RECONCILING?

©RAPID PHASE - 2010

I BROKE YOUR FAVOURITE VASE THIS MORNING.

AND IN MORE WIKILEAKS NEWS -- ACCORDING TO REPORTS, IN 2007, JULIUS MALEMA MET SECRETLY WITH U.S. OFFICIALS, PROVIDING SENSITIVE INFORMATION...

OKAY. LET'S GET DOWN TO BUSINESS, JULIUS.

NOT SO FAST. THIS COULD BE A TRAP! LET'S HEAR THE CODE WORDS!

www.madamandeve.co.za

§ SIGH § ..."THEY SAY A WOMAN HAS A NICE TIME..."

-- IF SHE HAS BREAKFAST AND ASKS FOR TAXI FARE IN THE MORNING.

AMATEURS.

HEY! WHERE'S YOUR DISGUISE? I SAID TO WEAR A DISGUISE!

2007: JULIUS MEETS SECRETLY WITH U.S. DIPLOMATS.

§ SIGH § "THEY SAY A WOMAN HAS A NICE TIME..."

"...IF SHE HAS BREAKFAST AND ASKS FOR TAXI FARE IN THE MORNING."

CAN WE GET STARTED NOW, JULIUS? ...IS YOUR INTELLIGENCE RELIABLE?

HEY! DON'T GET PERSONAL! I'M SMARTER THAN I LOOK!

-- WAIT A MINUTE! YOU CALLED ME JULIUS! -- YOU KNOW WHO I AM?

OF COURSE I DO.

©RAPID PHASE - 2010   www.madamandeve.co.za

WELL YOU'RE NOT SUPPOSED TO! I'M A BLOODY SECRET AGENT!

THIS IS GOING TO BE HARDER THAN I THOUGHT.

WIKI-LEAKS! WIKI-LEAKS! WIKI ALL THE WAY! OH WHAT FUN IT IS TO LEAK A SECRET EVERY DAY!
JUST THINK... SOON THERE WON'T BE ANY MORE SECRETS! EVERYONE WILL KNOW EVERYTHING!
...INCLUDING OUR TEACHER.
www.madamandeve.co.za ©RAPID PHASE - 2010
SAY GOODBYE TO "MY DOG ATE MY HOMEWORK."
I DON'T EVEN HAVE A DOG.

TWITTER, TWITTER LITTLE STAR. HOW I WONDER WHERE YOU --
TWINKLE!! IT'S TWINKLE! NOT "TWITTER!" TWINKLE!!
©RAPID PHASE - 2010
JINGLE BLOGS JINGLE BLOGS JINGLE ALL THE WAY...

AND WHAT WOULD THE HOLIDAYS BE WITHOUT MY ANNUAL HOMEMADE CHRISTMAS FRUITCAKE?
UH-OH.
THERE! RIGHT ON THE GLASS COFFEE TABLE NEXT TO NELSON MANDELA'S NEW HARDCOVER.
©RAPID PHASE - 2010 www.madamandeve.co.za
CRASH!
MAYBE I USED TOO MANY NUTS.
AND NEXT TIME... WAIT FOR THE SOFTCOVER.

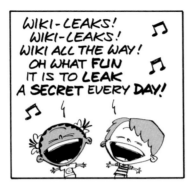

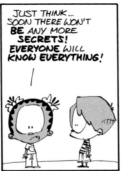

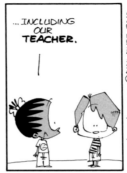

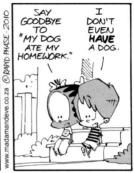

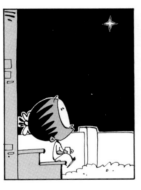

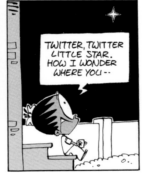

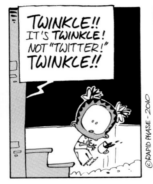

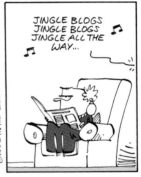

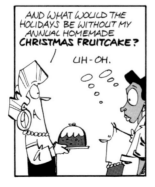

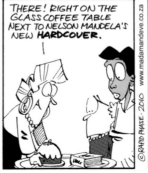

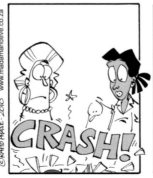

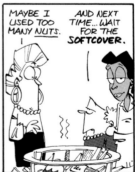

WHAT'S THAT FOR?
A GIN & TONIC WITH CRISPS. I'M LEAVING IT OUT FOR SANTA ON CHRISTMAS EVE.
www.madamandeve.co.za
INSTEAD OF MILK & COOKIES? HOW DO YOU EVEN KNOW FATHER CHRISTMAS WANTS A GIN & TONIC?!
THINK ABOUT IT. HE'S BEEN DRIVING ALONE THROUGH JOHANNESBURG LATE AT NIGHT IN AN UNLOCKED VEHICLE FILLED WITH EXPENSIVE GIFTS AND PRESENTS JUST SITTING IN THE BACK SEAT?
©RAPID PHASE-2010
... COME TO THINK OF IT, MAYBE I SHOULD MAKE IT A DOUBLE.
MOM!!

WHEN WILL SOMEBODY FIX THESE @☆#@# POTHOLES ?!!
©RAPID PHASE-2010

ARE YOU ENJOYING THE PRESENT I GAVE YOU, MOM?
ABSOLUTELY!
DO YOU EVEN KNOW WHAT IT IS?
OF COURSE! IT'S A FOOTREST... IN THE SHAPE OF A HOMEMADE CHRISTMAS FRUITCAKE.
©RAPID PHASE-2010
WRONG! IT IS A HOMEMADE FRUITCAKE! THERE IS NO FOOTREST!
THERE IS NO FOOTREST?
www.madamandeve.co.za
... IT'S KIND OF A ZEN THING?
I WOULDN'T TALK! YOU THOUGHT IT WAS A DOOR STOP!

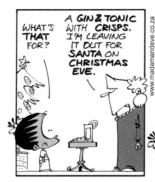

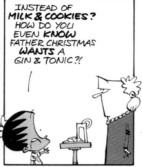

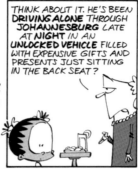

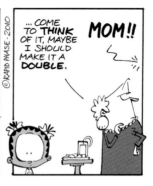

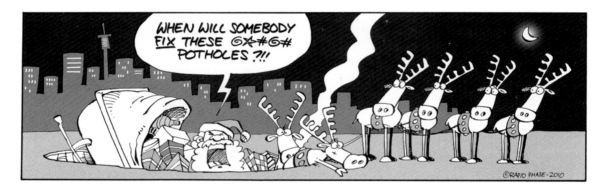

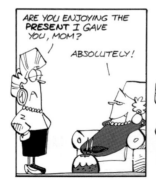

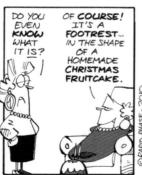

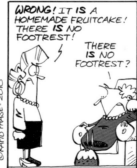

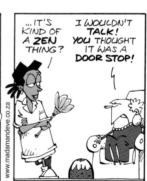

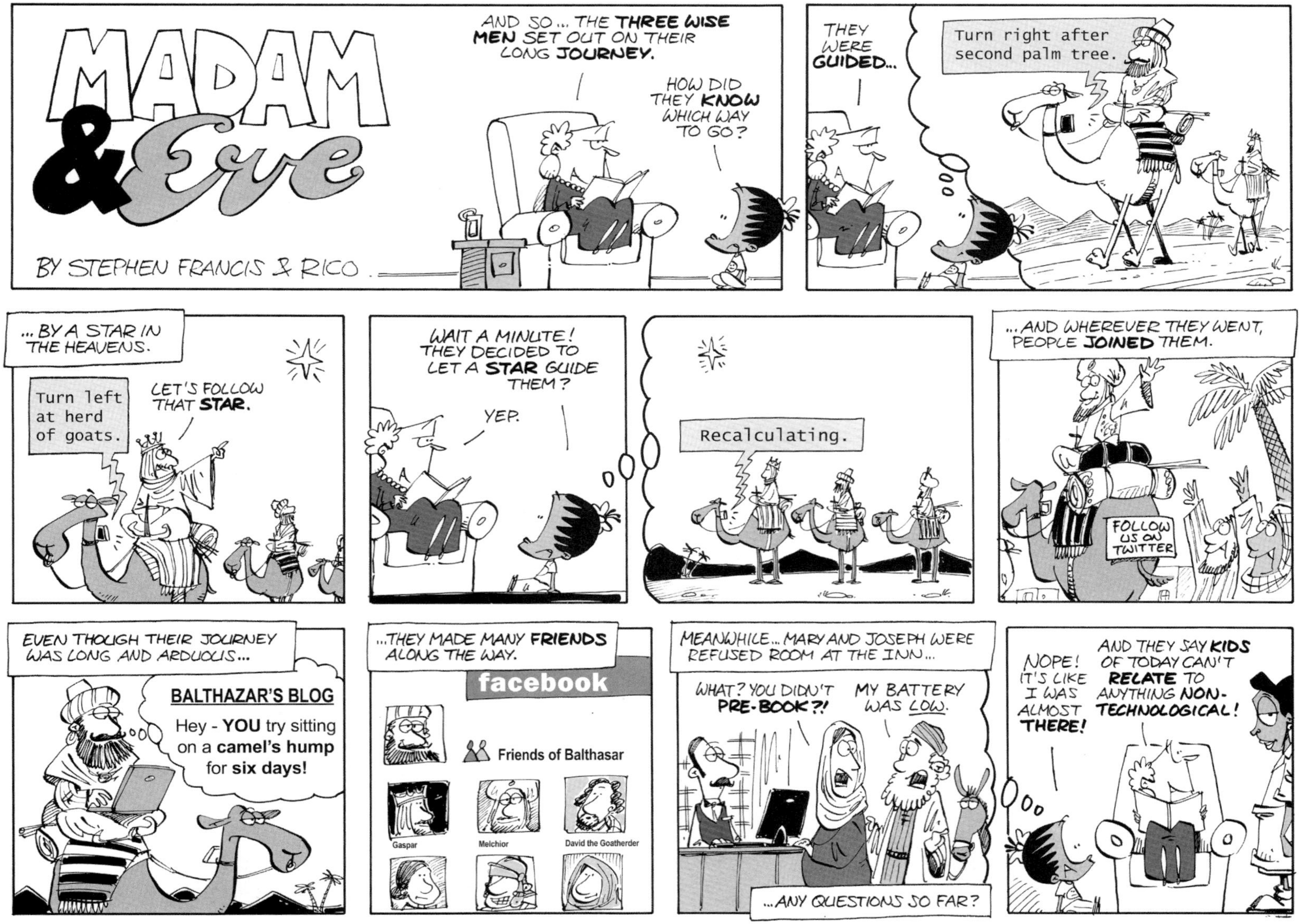

MADAM & Eve
BY STEPHEN FRANCIS & RICO
AND SO... THE THREE WISE MEN SET OUT ON THEIR LONG JOURNEY.
HOW DID THEY KNOW WHICH WAY TO GO?
THEY WERE GUIDED...
Turn right after second palm tree.
...BY A STAR IN THE HEAVENS.
Turn left at herd of goats.
LET'S FOLLOW THAT STAR.
WAIT A MINUTE! THEY DECIDED TO LET A STAR GUIDE THEM?
YEP.
Recalculating.
...AND WHEREVER THEY WENT, PEOPLE JOINED THEM.
FOLLOW US ON TWITTER
EVEN THOUGH THEIR JOURNEY WAS LONG AND ARDUOUS...
BALTHAZAR'S BLOG
Hey - YOU try sitting on a camel's hump for six days!
...THEY MADE MANY FRIENDS ALONG THE WAY.
facebook
Friends of Balthasar
Gaspar
Melchior
David the Goatherder
MEANWHILE... MARY AND JOSEPH WERE REFUSED ROOM AT THE INN...
WHAT? YOU DIDN'T PRE-BOOK?!
MY BATTERY WAS LOW.
...ANY QUESTIONS SO FAR?
NOPE! IT'S LIKE I WAS ALMOST THERE!
AND THEY SAY KIDS OF TODAY CAN'T RELATE TO ANYTHING NON-TECHNOLOGICAL!

TIC TIC TIC
www.madamandeve.co.za
RUMBLE!
©RAPID PHASE - 2011
WHOOSH!
POST HOLIDAY EMAIL DOWNLOAD **AVALANCHE.**
SOMEBODY HELP ME OUT OF HERE!

I CAN'T BELIEVE IT! **POST HOLIDAY EMAIL AVALANCHE!** AND THEY'RE STILL COMING!
WHAT DO THEY **DO?** WAIT UNTIL THE **HOLIDAYS** -- THEN PRESS **"SEND?"**
©RAPID PHASE - 2011
LOOK AT THE **BRIGHT** SIDE! YOU **WON** THE **UK LOTTERY.**
www.madamandeve.co.za
ALL **EIGHT** OF THEM.
EVE! GET THE DUST PAN!
EVE'S LEFT THE BUILDING!

EEEEDITH!! **EDITHHH ANDERSONNN!!**
HUH?
©RAPID PHASE - 2010 www.madamandeve.co.za
TONIGHT... YOU WILL BE VISITED BY **THREE SPIRITS.** I AM THE **GHOST OF CHRISTMAS PAST!** THIS... IS THE **GHOST OF CHRISTMAS PRESENT...**
ARE YOU CRAZY?! YOU'RE TOO **LATE!** IT'S ALREADY WAY **PAST NEW YEARS!**
... AND **THIS**... IS THE **GHOST OF CHRISTMAS AFRICAN TIME.**

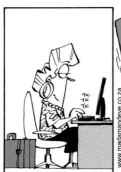

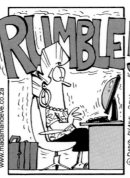

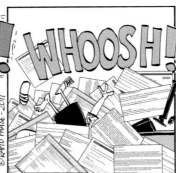

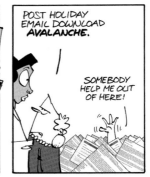

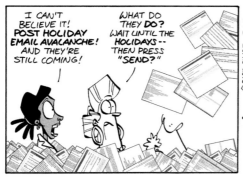

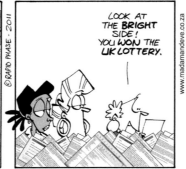

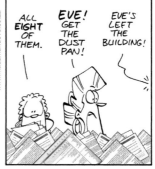

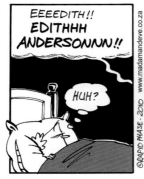

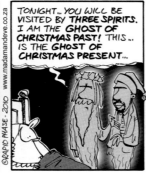

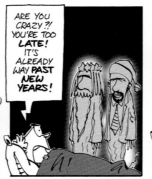

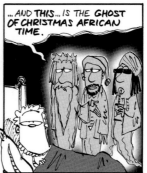

MEN WORKING

MEN NETWORKING

www.madamandeve.co.za

OPERATORS ARE STANDING BY TO TAKE YOUR ORDER.

COME ON... COME ON... PICK IT UP...

THIS COULD BE IT! I CAN FEEL IT!

WHAT'S SHE DOING? I CAN'T SEE!

GET READY! SHE'S REACHING FOR THE PHONE!

©RAPID PHASE - 2011

TWEET!

MIELLLLLLLLLLLLLLLLLLLLLL
LLLLLLLLLLLLLLLLLLLLLLLLL
LLLLLLLLLLLLLLLLLLLLLLLLL
LLLLLLLLLLLLLLLLLLLLLLLLL
LLLLLLLLLLLLLLLLLLLLLLLLL
LLLLLLLLLLLLLLLLLLLLLIES!!!

©RAPID PHASE - 2011

COOL. YOU'RE BEING TWEETED BY THE MIELIE LADY.

www.madamandeve.co.za

HEY LOOK. EXACTLY 140 CHARACTERS.

WHERE'S MY KATTY?!

AND WE'LL BE BACK... WITH MORE NEWS HEADLINES... AFTER THIS.
CORRUPTION! CORRUPTION! CORRUPTION!
WHO DO WE HAVE TO BRIBE TO GET RID OF ALL THIS CORRUPTION?!
www.madamandeve.co.za
©RAPID PHASE · 2010

Please Help
NO MONEY NO FOOD AND ENTOURAGE TO SUPPORT
www.madamandeve.co.za
©RAPID PHASE · 2011

HEY! I KNOW YOU! YOU'RE ZAKUMI ...THE 2010 WORLD CUP MASCOT!
SIGH I USED TO BE.
THEY PROMISED ME EVERYTHING! ZAKUMI THIS... ZAKUMI THAT! THEY SAID I'D BE BIGGER THAN GARFIELD!
©RAPID PHASE · 2011
AS SOON AS THE WORLD CUP ENDED, THEY HAD NO MORE USE FOR ME! ...TOSSED ASIDE LIKE AN EMPTY FOOTBALL STADIUM! SEPP BLATTER WON'T EVEN TAKE MY CALLS!
www.madamandeve.co.za
SOB!!
SOMEBODY REDEPLOY ME!!
DO YOU HAVE ANY MINISTERIAL EXPERIENCE?

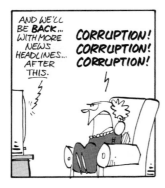

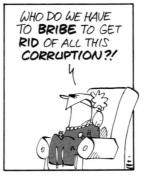

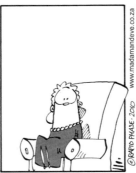

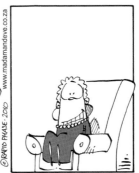

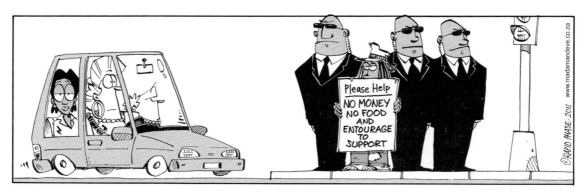

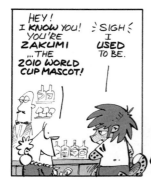

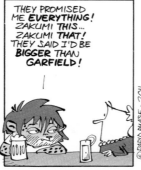

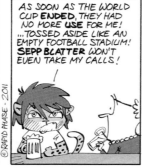

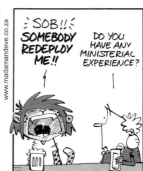

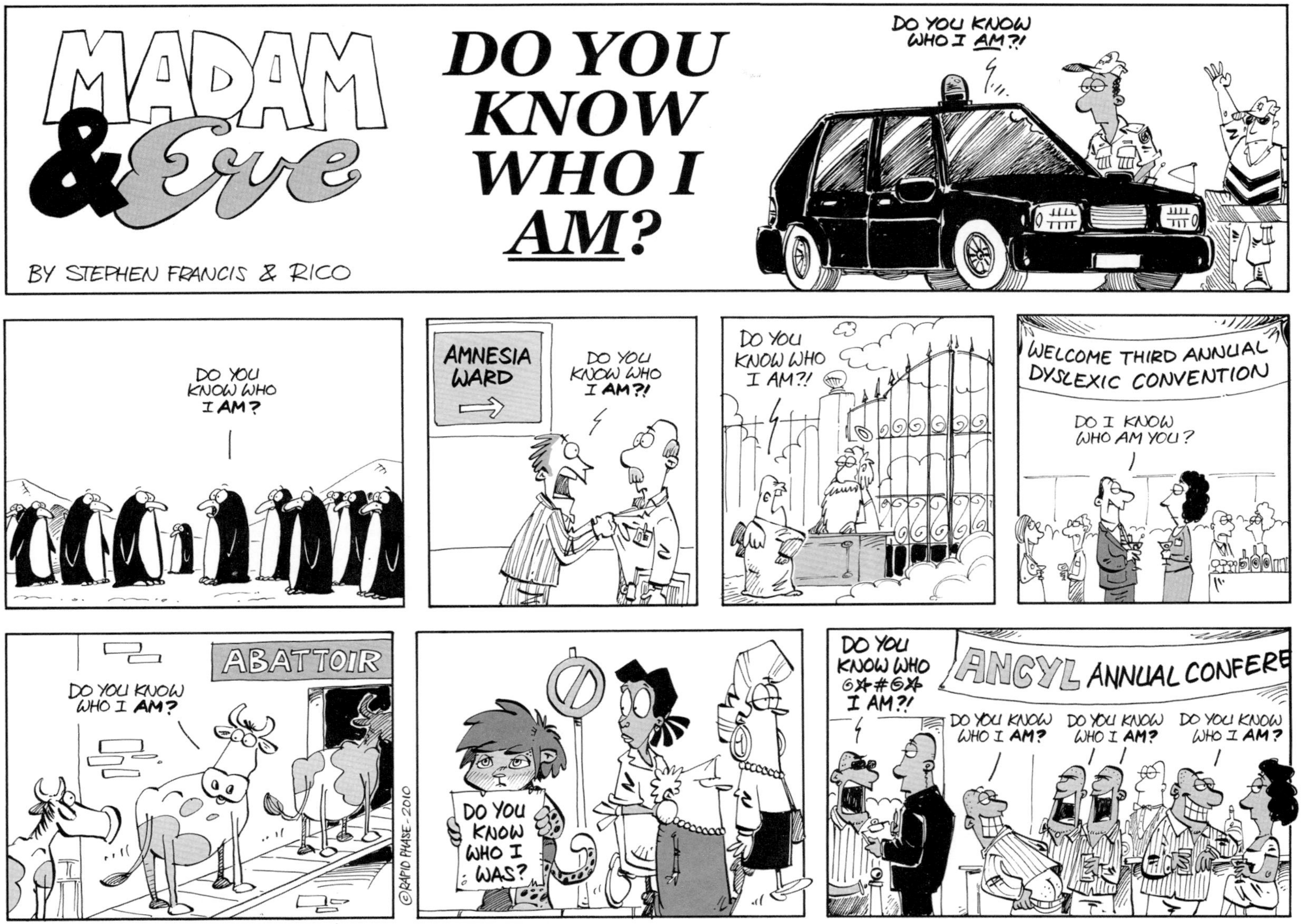
MADAM & Eve
BY STEPHEN FRANCIS & RICO
DO YOU KNOW WHO I AM?
DO YOU KNOW WHO I AM?!
DO YOU KNOW WHO I AM?
AMNESIA WARD
DO YOU KNOW WHO I AM?!
DO YOU KNOW WHO I AM?!
WELCOME THIRD ANNUAL DYSLEXIC CONVENTION
DO I KNOW WHO AM YOU?
ABATTOIR
DO YOU KNOW WHO I AM?
©RAPID PHASE - 2010
DO YOU KNOW WHO I WAS?
ANCYL ANNUAL CONFERE
DO YOU KNOW WHO @*#@* I AM?!
DO YOU KNOW WHO I AM?
DO YOU KNOW WHO I AM?
DO YOU KNOW WHO I AM?

OKAY! THIS IS NOW GETTING OUT OF HAND!
DO YOU KNOW WHO I AM?
NO WORK. NO FOOD. NO MONEY.
©RAPID PHASE · 2011
www.madamandeve.co.za

DUELLING EGOS
DO YOU KNOW WHO I AM?
NO. DO YOU KNOW WHO I AM?
DO YOU KNOW WHO I AM?
DO YOU KNOW WHO I AM?
DO YOU KNOW WHO I AM?
DO YOU KNOW WHO I AM?
www.madamandeve.co.za

COMING UP... MORE NEWS ABOUT THE HUGE MUNICIPAL BILLING CRISIS IN JOHANNESBURG...
MADAM!! IT'S A MUNICIPAL BILLING CRISIS!!
www.madamandeve.co.za
I REPEAT! IT'S THE MUNICIPALITY! YOUR 1.1 MILLION RAND WATER BILL IS NOT THE GARDENER'S FAULT!!
©RAPID PHASE · 2011
OKAY. LET HIM UP.
WHEW

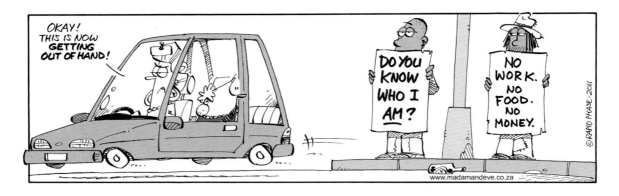

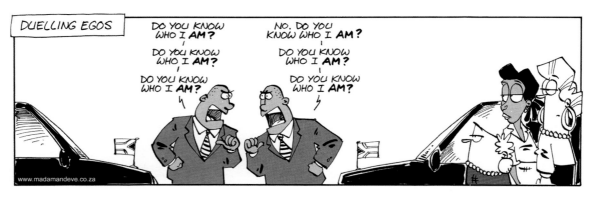

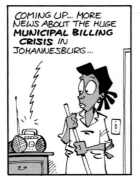

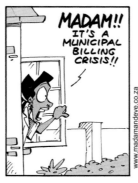

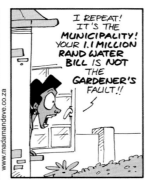

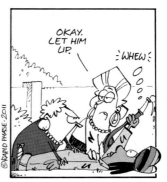

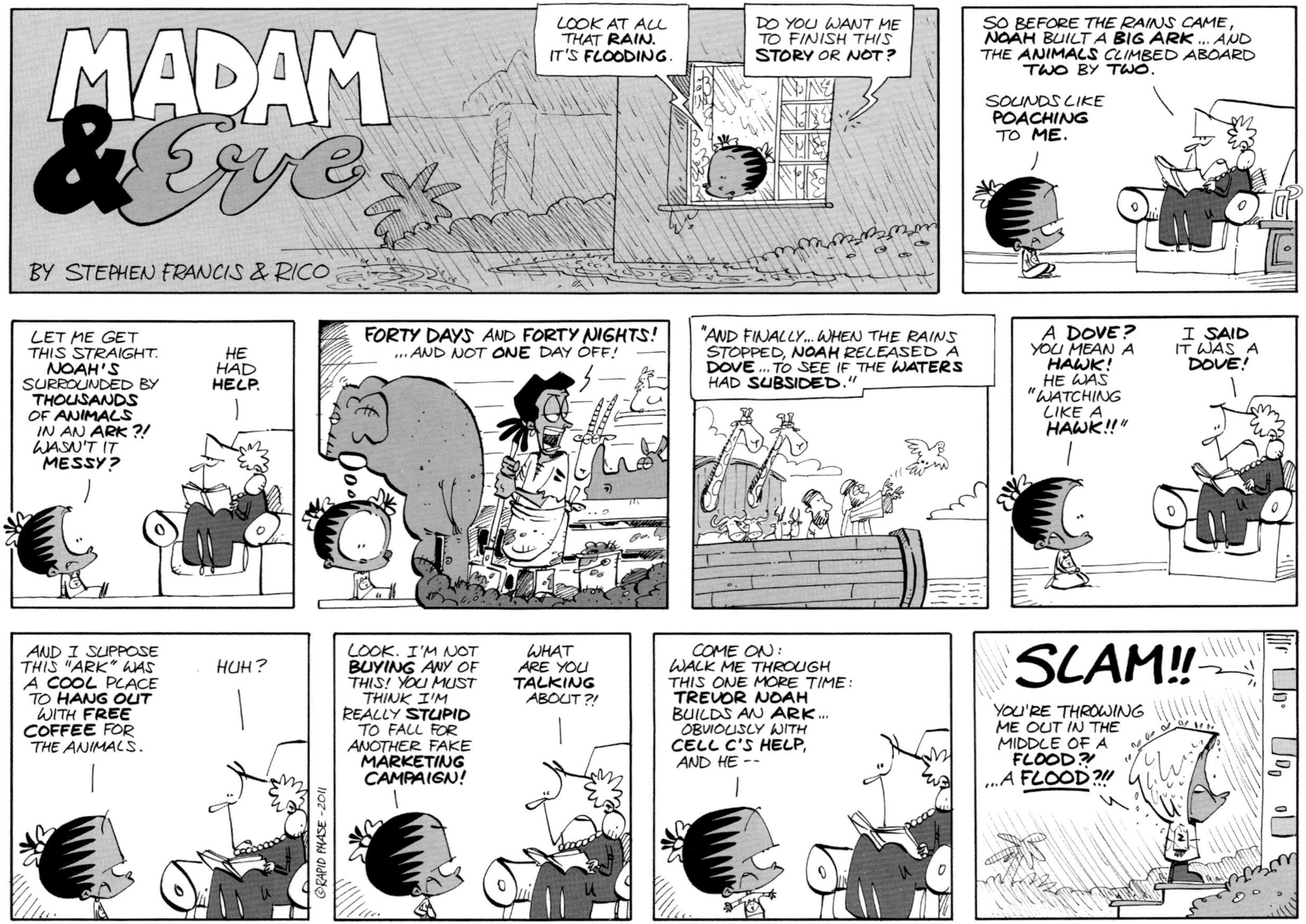
MADAM & Eve
BY STEPHEN FRANCIS & RICO
LOOK AT ALL THAT RAIN. IT'S FLOODING.
DO YOU WANT ME TO FINISH THIS STORY OR NOT?
SO BEFORE THE RAINS CAME, NOAH BUILT A BIG ARK ... AND THE ANIMALS CLIMBED ABOARD TWO BY TWO.
SOUNDS LIKE POACHING TO ME.
LET ME GET THIS STRAIGHT. NOAH'S SURROUNDED BY THOUSANDS OF ANIMALS IN AN ARK?! WASN'T IT MESSY?
HE HAD HELP.
FORTY DAYS AND FORTY NIGHTS! ...AND NOT ONE DAY OFF!
"AND FINALLY... WHEN THE RAINS STOPPED, NOAH RELEASED A DOVE ... TO SEE IF THE WATERS HAD SUBSIDED."
A DOVE? YOU MEAN A HAWK! HE WAS "WATCHING LIKE A HAWK!!"
I SAID IT WAS A DOVE!
AND I SUPPOSE THIS "ARK" WAS A COOL PLACE TO HANG OUT WITH FREE COFFEE FOR THE ANIMALS.
HUH?
©RAPID PHASE - 2011
LOOK. I'M NOT BUYING ANY OF THIS! YOU MUST THINK I'M REALLY STUPID TO FALL FOR ANOTHER FAKE MARKETING CAMPAIGN!
WHAT ARE YOU TALKING ABOUT?!
COME ON: WALK ME THROUGH THIS ONE MORE TIME: TREVOR NOAH BUILDS AN ARK... OBVIOUSLY WITH CELL C'S HELP, AND HE --
SLAM!!
YOU'RE THROWING ME OUT IN THE MIDDLE OF A FLOOD?! ...A FLOOD?!!

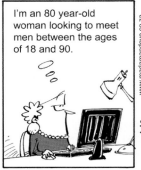

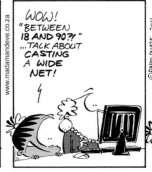

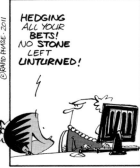

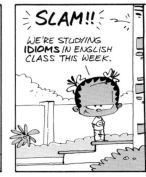

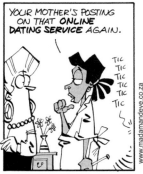

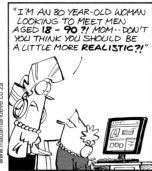

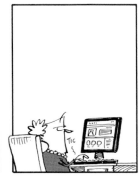

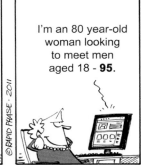

I'm an 80 year-old woman looking to meet men between the ages of 18 and 90.
www.madamandeve.co.za
WOW! "BETWEEN 18 AND 90?!" ...TALK ABOUT CASTING A WIDE NET!
©RAPID PHASE · 2011
HEDGING ALL YOUR BETS! NO STONE LEFT UNTURNED!
SLAM!!
WE'RE STUDYING IDIOMS IN ENGLISH CLASS THIS WEEK.

YOUR MOTHER'S POSTING ON THAT ONLINE DATING SERVICE AGAIN.
TIC TIC TIC TIC TIC TIC
www.madamandeve.co.za
"I'M AN 80 YEAR-OLD WOMAN LOOKING TO MEET MEN AGED 18 - 90 ?! MOM-- DON'T YOU THINK YOU SHOULD BE A LITTLE MORE REALISTIC?!"
TIC
©RAPID PHASE · 2011
I'm an 80 year-old woman looking to meet men aged 18 - 95.

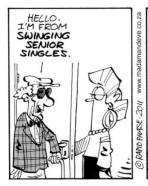

HELLO. I'M FROM SWINGING SENIOR SINGLES.
www.madamandeve.co.za
©RAPID PHASE · 2011
MOM! YOUR INTERNET DATE IS HERE!
FOXY MAMA!
STUD MUFFIN!
DON'T WAIT UP.
"STUD MUFFIN?"

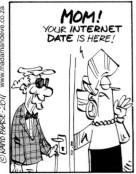

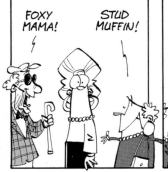

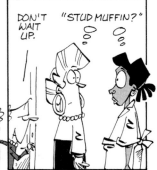

HOW'S YOUR MOTHER'S SECOND **SENIOR INTERNET DATE** GOING?
SO FAR SO GOOD...
WELL. SHALL WE SIT DOWN AND **RELAX**, EDITH?
YOU... USE A **WALKER?**
www.madamandeve.co.za ©RAPID PHASE · 2011
WALKER? IT'S A **PORTABLE DRINKS TABLE!** YOU SAID YOU LIKE **GIN & TONICS?**
TSHIKA! TSHIKA! TSHIKA!
THIS GUY'S SMOOTH.
SMOOTH? HE'S ALREADY IN LIKE FLYNN.

I DON'T KNOW, DOCTOR. IT'S THIS NEW **TECHNOLOGICAL AGE** WE'RE IN. THERE ARE NO **BOUNDARIES** ANY MORE!
GO ON.
WHATEVER HAPPENED TO **PRIVACY**... OR **HUMAN CONTACT?** EVERYONE'S EITHER **BLOGGING** OR **TWEETING.** EVEN MY OWN MOTHER.
TWEET!
©RAPID PHASE · 2011
WHAT WAS **THAT?**
NOTHING. PLEASE GO ON.
LET'S SEE...
Therapy session today with Gwen Anderson. Mildly obsessive and paranoid.
Had banana for breakfast.

Washing **dishes** at the moment. Can't wait to start dusting the **lounge!**
TIC TIC TIC
©RAPID PHASE · 2010
So much to do! My **tea break** will just have to **wait!**
TIC TIC TIC
Laundry to the left of me. **Clotheslines** to the right of me. I'll be busy for **HOURS!**
TIC TIC TIC
www.madamandeve.co.za
FOLLOWING **EVE ON TWITTER?**
SHE'S WORKING REALLY **HARD.** MAYBE WE SHOULD GIVE HER A **RAISE.**
TWEET!

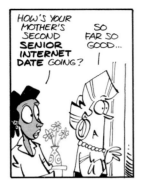

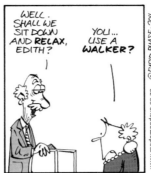

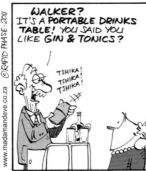

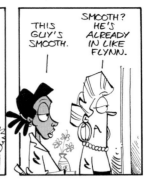

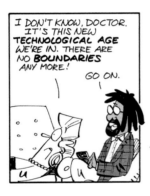

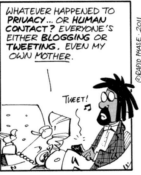

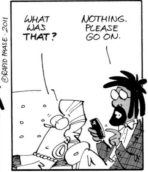

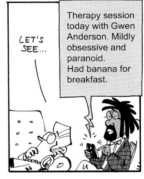

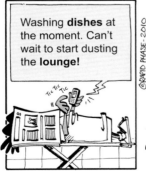

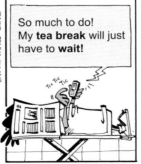

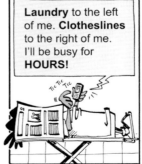

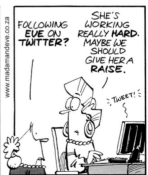

WHAT ARE YOU DOING?
WRITING MADIBA A GET-WELL CARD.
©RAPID PHASE - 2011
ROSES ARE RED, VIOLETS ARE BLUE, GET WELL SOON, MADIBA...
www.madamandeve.co.za
BECAUSE WE LOVE YOU AND YOU SHOWED US THE WAY AND BROUGHT US TOGETHER AND YOU'RE THE BEST AND WE CAN'T EVEN CONSIDER A WORLD WITHOUT YOU AND...
YOU'RE GOING TO NEED A BIGGER CARD.

THANDI SISULU WILL NOW ADDRESS THE CLASS ON THE SUBJECT OF VOLCANOES.
I ALREADY DID!
EVERYONE -- CHECK YOUR CELLPHONE MESSAGES. I JUST SENT TEXT WITH A MULTIMEDIA MMS ATTACHMENT!
©RAPID PHASE - 2011
GOODBYE "SHOW AND TELL." HELLO, "SHOW AND TWEET!" COOL, HUH?
SOMETIMES TEACHERS DON'T APPRECIATE THINKING OUTSIDE THE TECHNOLOGY BOX.
PRINCIPAL

GIMME A BREAK! "SHOOT THE BOER, KILL THE FARMER" IS JUST A STRUGGLE SONG!
HELL-OH! IT'S INCITING VIOLENCE!
THERE'S NO LEGAL PRECEDENT!
www.madamandeve.co.za
©RAPID PHASE - 2011

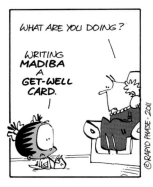

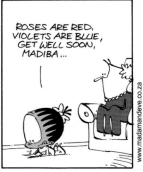

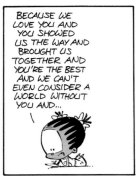

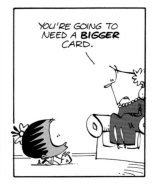

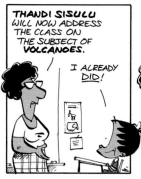

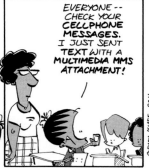

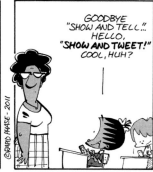

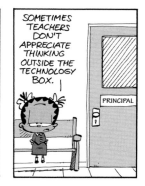

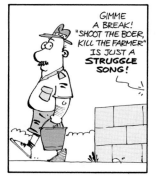

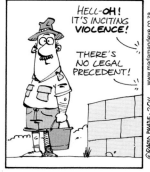

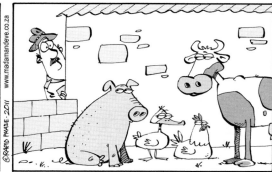

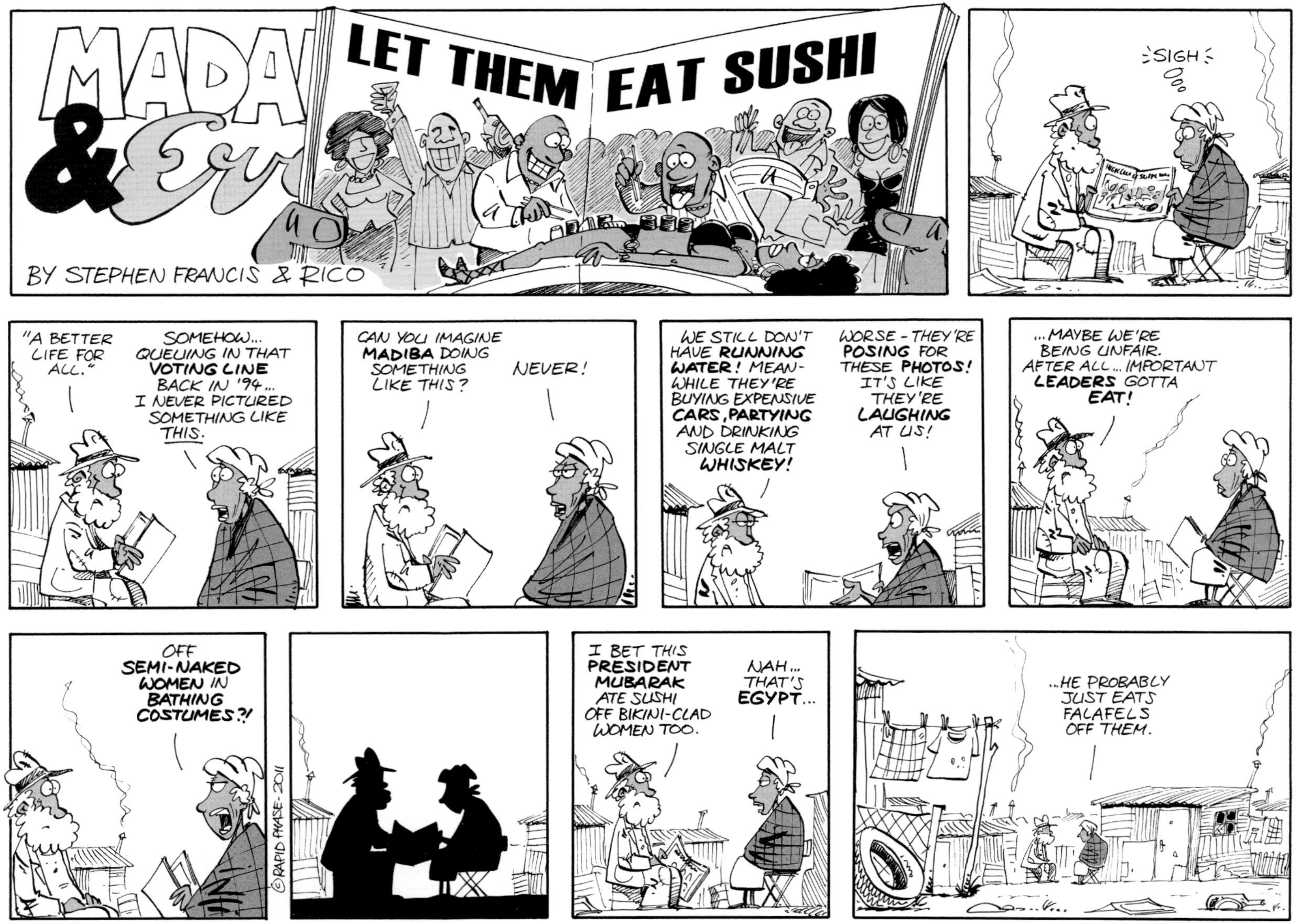

MADAM & Eve
LET THEM EAT SUSHI
BY STEPHEN FRANCIS & RICO
SIGH
"A BETTER LIFE FOR ALL."
SOMEHOW... QUEUING IN THAT VOTING LINE BACK IN '94... I NEVER PICTURED SOMETHING LIKE THIS.
CAN YOU IMAGINE MADIBA DOING SOMETHING LIKE THIS?
NEVER!
WE STILL DON'T HAVE RUNNING WATER! MEANWHILE THEY'RE BUYING EXPENSIVE CARS, PARTYING AND DRINKING SINGLE MALT WHISKEY!
WORSE - THEY'RE POSING FOR THESE PHOTOS! IT'S LIKE THEY'RE LAUGHING AT US!
...MAYBE WE'RE BEING UNFAIR. AFTER ALL... IMPORTANT LEADERS GOTTA EAT!
OFF SEMI-NAKED WOMEN IN BATHING COSTUMES?!
© RAPID PHASE - 2011
I BET THIS PRESIDENT MUBARAK ATE SUSHI OFF BIKINI-CLAD WOMEN TOO.
NAH... THAT'S EGYPT...
...HE PROBABLY JUST EATS FALAFELS OFF THEM.

HI. WE'RE HERE TO TALK TO OUR LOCAL **GOVERNMENT REPRESENTATIVE** ABOUT FIXING A POTHOLE.
THAT WOULD BE **COUNCILMAN VUSI**, YOUR ELECTED LEADER.
©RAPID PHASE-2011 www.madamandeve.co.za
WHO THE HELL IS COUNCIL-MAN VUSI?
IN THE LAST ELECTION, THE **ANC** HAD A **MAJORITY**, SO PRESIDENT ZUMA DEPLOYED A TRUSTED **COMRADE** TO RUN THE PROVINCE...
...WHO IN TURN DEPLOYED **ANOTHER** TRUSTED **COMRADE** WHO IN TURN DEPLOYED A TRUSTED **RELATIVE** TO OVERSEE YOUR AREA. ...THAT WOULD BE **COUNCILMAN VUSI**.
IMPRESSIVE CREDENTIALS. WHERE IS HE?
TODAY'S FRIDAY. TRY THE OFFICE **JACUZZI**.

HOW DID IT GO? IS **LOCAL GOVERN-MENT** GOING TO FIX OUR POTHOLE?
≷SIGH≶ NO ONE WAS **AVAILABLE**. BUT THEY **PROMISED** TO GET BACK TO US BY THE END OF THE DAY.
RING! RING!
THAT COULD BE THEM NOW!
©RAPID PHASE-2011
HUH? IT'S AN SMS. "PLEASE CALL COUNCILMAN VUSI."
OUR **LOCAL GOVERNMENT REPRESENT-ATIVE** SENT US A **"PLEASE CALL ME"** MESSAGE?!!
www.madamandeve.co.za
WAIT--THERE'S MORE: "CALLS CHARGED AT R2.50 PER MINUTE. TWO FOR ONE SPECIAL AT JOE'S PIZZA EVERY MONDAY."
I'VE HEARD OF THEM. DO THEY **DELIVER?**

COUNCILMAN VUSI -- THERE'S A **GWEN ANDERSON** TO SEE YOU ABOUT A POTHOLE PROBLEM.
DIDN'T YOU TELL HER I'M HAVING **LUNCH?**
YES, BUT SHE'S VERY **DETERMINED**.
www.madamandeve.co.za ©RAPID PHASE-2011
THESE PEOPLE THINK WE HAVE AN **UNLIMITED BUDGET!** ...WANT SOME **SUSHI?**
TRY THE EEL.
HEY! DO YOU MIND?

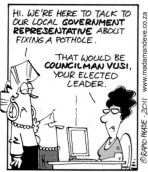

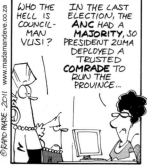

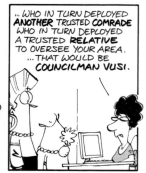

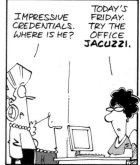

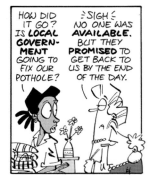

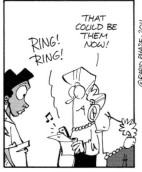

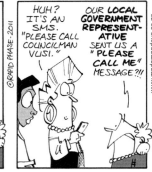

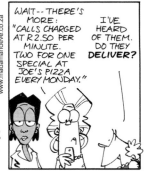

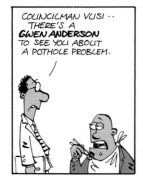

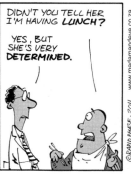

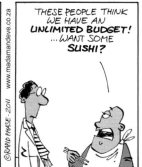

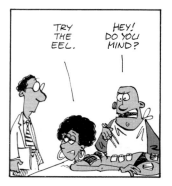

IS COUNCILMAN VUSI FREE YET?
SORRY. HE'S STILL AT LUNCH.
SIR -- ONE OF YOUR CONSTITUENTS IS IN RECEPTION.
GOTCHA.
©RAPID PHASE - 2011 www.madamandeve.co.za
"CONSTITUENT." WHAT THE G#✲&#✲ IS A CONSTITUENT?
IT'S A CITIZEN RESIDING IN THE AREA THAT YOU REPRESENT.
HEY! I'M JUST THINKING OUT LOUD HERE, OK?!

COUNCILMAN VUSI... I NEED HELP WITH A 1.1 MILLION RAND WATER BILL.
DON'T WORRY, Ms ANDERSON, COUNCILMAN VUSI IS ON THE CASE!
www.madamandeve.co.za
AND I HOPE I CAN COUNT ON YOUR VOTE IN THE NEXT LOCAL ELECTIONS. MY MOTTO: "A BETTER LIFE FOR ME."
©RAPID PHASE - 2011
UH, SIR... IT'S ALL. "A BETTER LIFE FOR ALL."
DAMMIT! I ALWAYS DO THAT.
IT CAN HAPPEN TO ANYBODY, SIR.

PHEW! THE PHONES ARE RINGING OFF THE HOOK! I'D HATE TO MEET THE PERSON RESPONSIBLE FOR THIS MUNICIPAL BILLING CRISIS.
RING! RING! RING! RING! RING! RING! RING! RING!
©RAPID PHASE - 2011
ACTUALLY, COUNCILMAN VUSI... THEY'RE YOUR CONSTITUENTS.
THERE'S THAT WORD AGAIN.
www.madamandeve.co.za
ARE YOU SAYING I'M RESPONSIBLE FOR THE PEOPLE IN THIS AREA? SINCE WHEN?
UH, SINCE THE LAST ELECTION, SIR.
SORRY. I'M GOING TO NEED MORE PROOF.
SOMEBODY BRING THE COUNCILMAN A MAP AND A COMPASS!

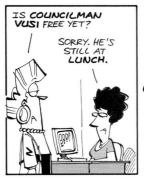

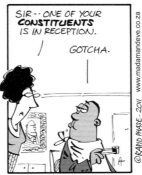

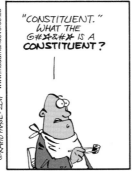

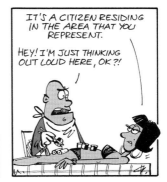

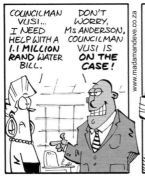

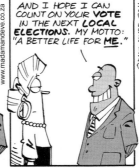

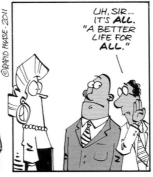

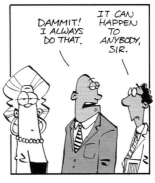

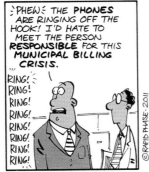

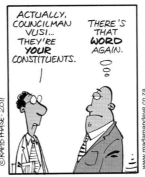

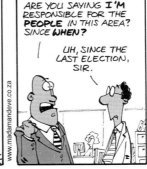

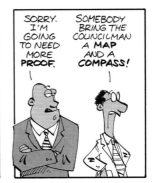

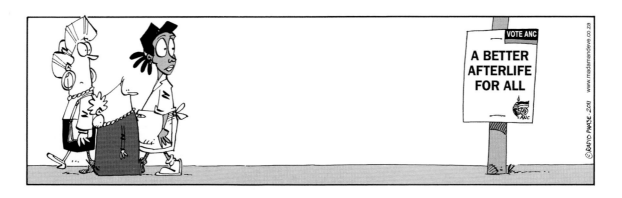

VOTE ANC
A BETTER AFTERLIFE FOR ALL
ANC
© RAPID PHASE · 2011 www.madamandeve.co.za

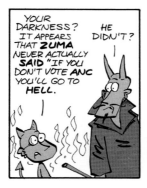

YOUR DARKNESS? IT APPEARS THAT ZUMA NEVER ACTUALLY SAID "IF YOU DON'T VOTE ANC YOU'LL GO TO HELL.
HE DIDN'T?
NO... BUT HE DID SAY "IF YOU DON'T VOTE ANC ... YOU'RE CHOOSING THE MAN WITH THE FORK."
UH HUH. WHAT'S THIS? ...CHOPPED LIVER?
www.madamandeve.co.za
FRANKLY, SIR... ZUMA SHOULDN'T BE SAYING THESE THINGS. DIDN'T HE SIGN A NON-DISCLOSURE AGREEMENT?
MAYBE HE FOUND A LOOPHOLE. ...GO PULL THE ZUMA-POLOKWANE CONTRACT.
© RAPID PHASE · 2011
...AND WHO SHOULD I HAVE CHECK IT, SIR?
THERE'S TEN MILLION LAWYERS DOWN HERE! PICK ONE!!

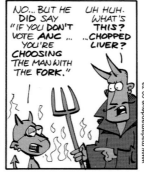

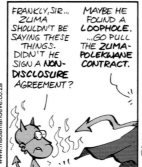

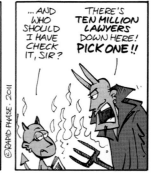

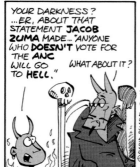

YOUR DARKNESS? ...ER, ABOUT THAT STATEMENT JACOB ZUMA MADE... "ANYONE WHO DOESN'T VOTE FOR THE ANC WILL GO TO HELL."
WHAT ABOUT IT?
© RAPID PHASE · 2011
WELL, IT'S CAUSING PROBLEMS HERE IN PURGATORY. MANY OF US HERE ALREADY ARE SUPPORTERS OF THE ANC.
WHAT? SINCE WHEN?!
LET'S SEE... SINCE THE ARMS DEAL... TRAVELGATE... THE SABC... THE SUSHI THING...
WHAT ABOUT MY SON? IS HE AN ANC SUPPORTER?
www.madamandeve.co.za
NO, SIR. HE'S STILL A BIG FAN OF COPE.
SIGH I'LL GET BACK TO YOU.

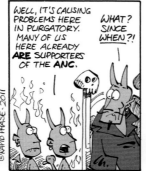

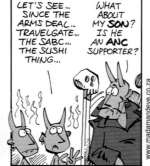

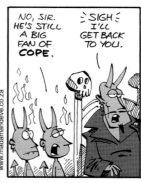

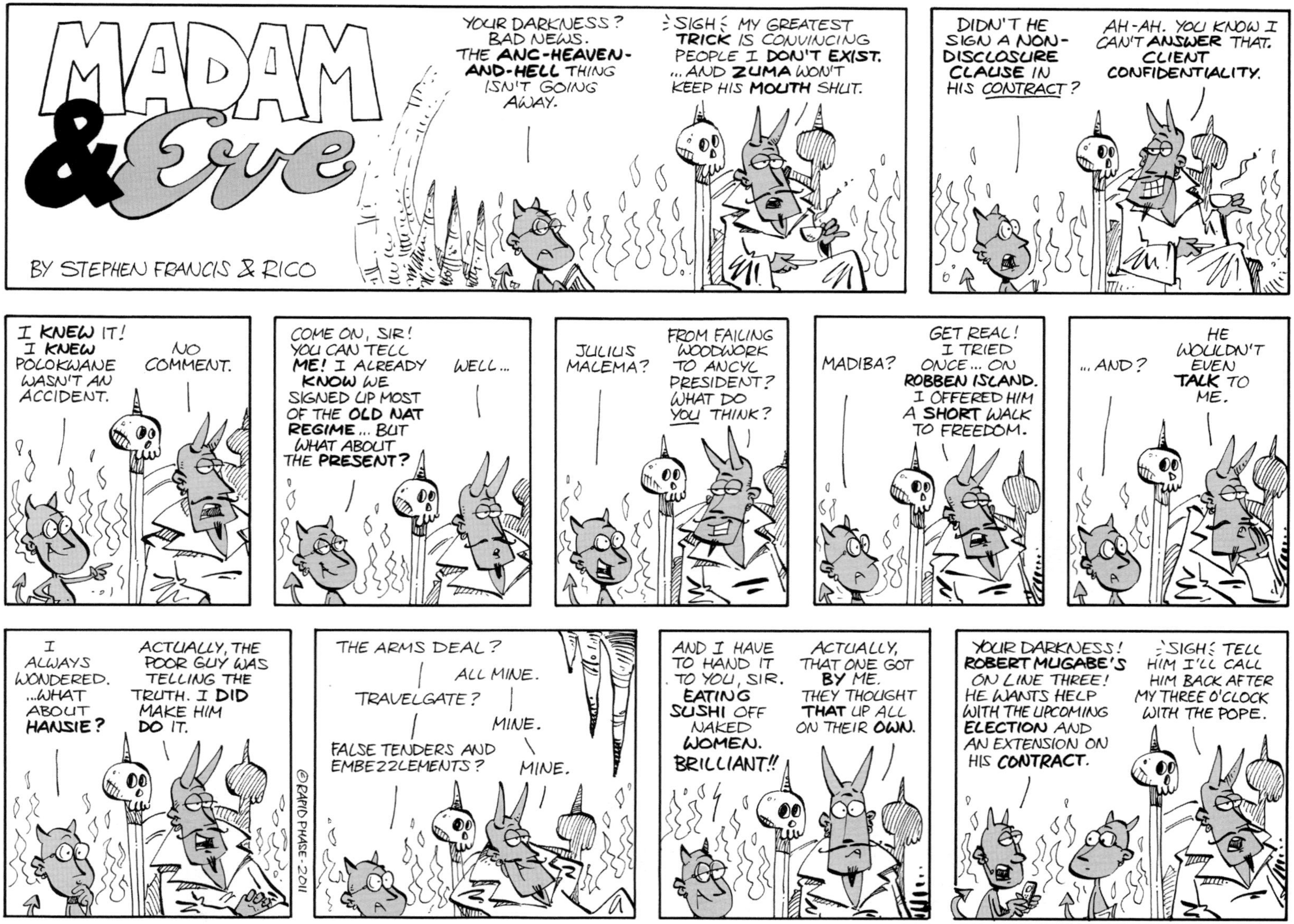
MADAM & Eve
BY STEPHEN FRANCIS & RICO
YOUR DARKNESS? BAD NEWS. THE ANC-HEAVEN-AND-HELL THING ISN'T GOING AWAY.
:SIGH: MY GREATEST TRICK IS CONVINCING PEOPLE I DON'T EXIST. ...AND ZUMA WON'T KEEP HIS MOUTH SHUT.
DIDN'T HE SIGN A NON-DISCLOSURE CLAUSE IN HIS CONTRACT?
AH-AH. YOU KNOW I CAN'T ANSWER THAT. CLIENT CONFIDENTIALITY.
I KNEW IT! I KNEW POLOKWANE WASN'T AN ACCIDENT.
NO COMMENT.
COME ON, SIR! YOU CAN TELL ME! I ALREADY KNOW WE SIGNED UP MOST OF THE OLD NAT REGIME... BUT WHAT ABOUT THE PRESENT?
WELL...
JULIUS MALEMA?
FROM FAILING WOODWORK TO ANCYL PRESIDENT? WHAT DO YOU THINK?
MADIBA?
GET REAL! I TRIED ONCE... ON ROBBEN ISLAND. I OFFERED HIM A SHORT WALK TO FREEDOM.
...AND?
HE WOULDN'T EVEN TALK TO ME.
I ALWAYS WONDERED. ...WHAT ABOUT HANSIE?
ACTUALLY, THE POOR GUY WAS TELLING THE TRUTH. I DID MAKE HIM DO IT.
© RAPID PHASE · 2011
THE ARMS DEAL?
ALL MINE.
TRAVELGATE?
MINE.
FALSE TENDERS AND EMBEZZLEMENTS?
MINE.
AND I HAVE TO HAND IT TO YOU, SIR. EATING SUSHI OFF NAKED WOMEN. BRILLIANT!!
ACTUALLY, THAT ONE GOT BY ME. THEY THOUGHT THAT UP ALL ON THEIR OWN.
YOUR DARKNESS! ROBERT MUGABE'S ON LINE THREE! HE WANTS HELP WITH THE UPCOMING ELECTION AND AN EXTENSION ON HIS CONTRACT.
:SIGH: TELL HIM I'LL CALL HIM BACK AFTER MY THREE O'CLOCK WITH THE POPE.

DAMN! I WISH ZUMA WOULD KEEP HIS MOUTH SHUT! THIS WHOLE "ANC HEAVEN AND HELL" THING IS GETTING OUT OF HAND. TAKE A MEMO.
YES, YOUR DARKNESS.
©RAPID PHASE · 2011
"FROM NOW ON, ALL LESSER DEMONS WILL BE APOLITICAL. I DON'T WANT TO HEAR OF ANY HELP, SUPPORT OR ENCOURAGEMENT FOR THE ANC!"
www.madamandeve.co.za
DOES THAT INCLUDE JULIUS MALEMA, SIR?
NOT TO THROW A SPANNER IN THE WORKS OR ANYTHING, ...BUT HE'S PRETTY POPULAR DOWN HERE.
SIGH
LET ME THINK ABOUT IT.

YOUR DARKNESS? IT APPEARS THAT ZUMA NEVER ACTUALLY SAID "IF YOU DON'T VOTE ANC YOU'LL GO TO HELL.
HE DIDN'T?
NO... BUT HE DID SAY "IF YOU DON'T VOTE ANC ... YOU'RE CHOOSING THE MAN WITH THE FORK."
UH HUH. WHAT'S THIS? ...CHOPPED LIVER?
www.madamandeve.co.za
FRANKLY, SIR... ZUMA SHOULDN'T BE SAYING THESE THINGS. DIDN'T HE SIGN A NON-DISCLOSURE AGREEMENT?
MAYBE HE FOUND A LOOPHOLE. ...GO PULL THE ZUMA-POLEKWANE CONTRACT.
©RAPID PHASE · 2011
...AND WHO SHOULD I HAVE CHECK IT, SIR?
THERE'S TEN MILLION LAWYERS DOWN HERE! PICK ONE!!

ONE LARGE MARGHERITA PIZZA WITH ANCHOVIES! IT'S ON ITS WAY!
TWO LARGE QUATTRO STAGIONI PIZZAS WITH EXTRA CHILI? NO PROBLEM! THEY'RE ON THEIR WAY!
©RAPID PHASE · 2011
SIR-- YOU CAN'T KEEP PROMISING CUSTOMERS PIZZAS! WE DON'T DELIVER!
www.madamandeve.co.za
WE DON'T?
ZUMA's
Pizza

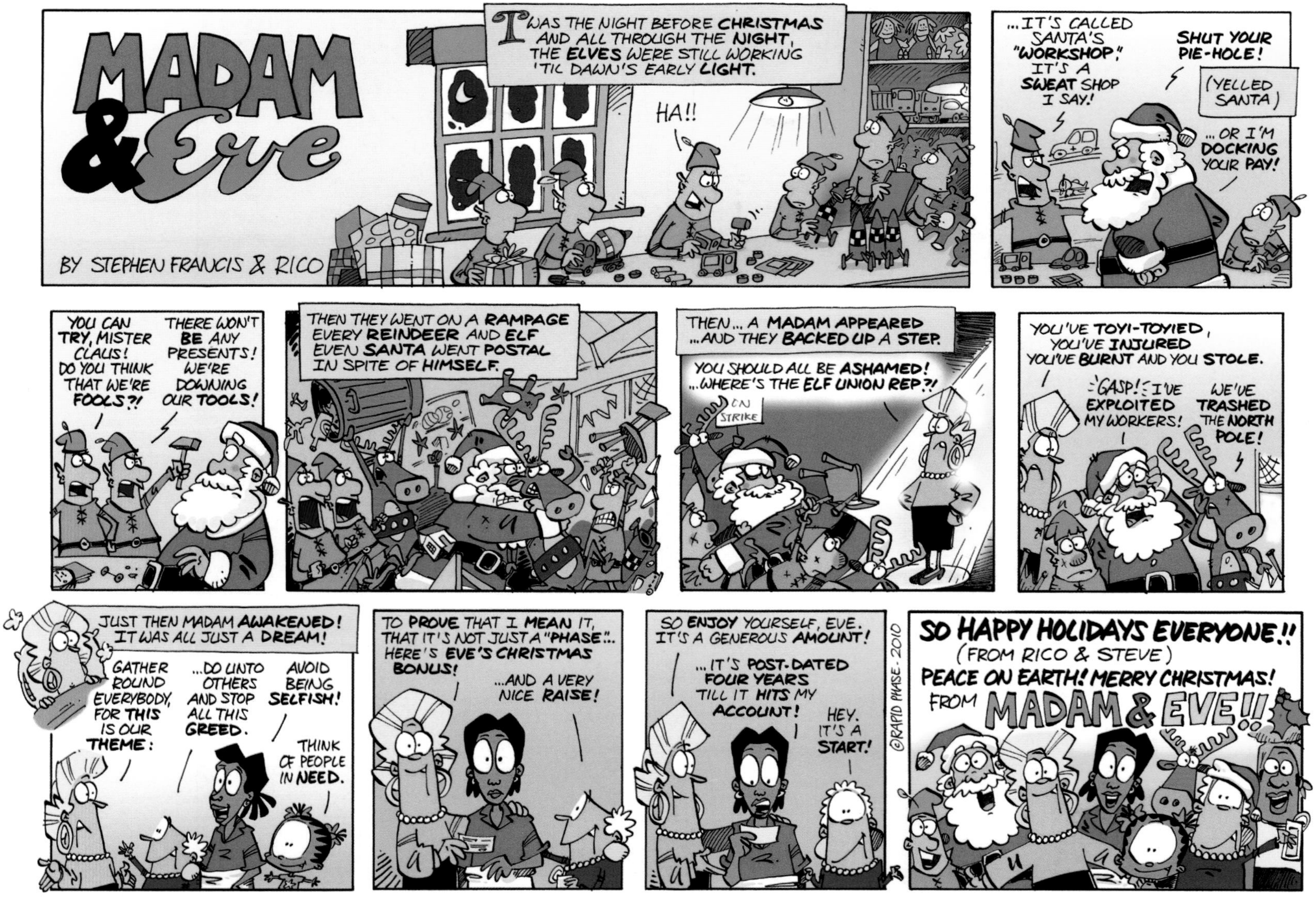
MADAM & Eve
BY STEPHEN FRANCIS & RICO
'TWAS THE NIGHT BEFORE CHRISTMAS AND ALL THROUGH THE NIGHT, THE ELVES WERE STILL WORKING 'TIL DAWN'S EARLY LIGHT.
HA!!
...IT'S CALLED SANTA'S "WORKSHOP," IT'S A SWEAT SHOP I SAY!
SHUT YOUR PIE-HOLE!
(YELLED SANTA)
...OR I'M DOCKING YOUR PAY!
YOU CAN TRY, MISTER CLAUS! DO YOU THINK THAT WE'RE FOOLS?!
THERE WON'T BE ANY PRESENTS! WE'RE DOWNING OUR TOOLS!
THEN THEY WENT ON A RAMPAGE EVERY REINDEER AND ELF EVEN SANTA WENT POSTAL IN SPITE OF HIMSELF.
THEN... A MADAM APPEARED ...AND THEY BACKED UP A STEP.
YOU SHOULD ALL BE ASHAMED! ...WHERE'S THE ELF UNION REP?!
ON STRIKE
YOU'VE TOYI-TOYIED, YOU'VE INJURED YOU'VE BURNT AND YOU STOLE.
GASP! I'VE EXPLOITED MY WORKERS!
WE'VE TRASHED THE NORTH POLE!
JUST THEN MADAM AWAKENED! IT WAS ALL JUST A DREAM!
GATHER ROUND EVERYBODY, FOR THIS IS OUR THEME:
...DO UNTO OTHERS AND STOP ALL THIS GREED.
AVOID BEING SELFISH!
THINK OF PEOPLE IN NEED.
TO PROVE THAT I MEAN IT, THAT IT'S NOT JUST A "PHASE"... HERE'S EVE'S CHRISTMAS BONUS!
...AND A VERY NICE RAISE!
SO ENJOY YOURSELF, EVE. IT'S A GENEROUS AMOUNT!
...IT'S POST-DATED FOUR YEARS TILL IT HITS MY ACCOUNT!
HEY. IT'S A START!
©RAPID PHASE - 2010
SO HAPPY HOLIDAYS EVERYONE!!
(FROM RICO & STEVE)
PEACE ON EARTH! MERRY CHRISTMAS!
FROM MADAM & EVE!!

©RAPID PHASE · 2010
Puff! Puff! Puff!
www.madamandeve.co.za
NICE **TREADMILL WORKOUT**, MOM. WHAT **MOTIVATIONAL MUSIC** ARE YOU LISTENING TO ON YOUR iPOD?
Puff! Puff!
Click
MIELLLIES!! MIELLLIES!!
Puff. Puff. Puff.

Plink! Plink! Plink!
Plink! Plink! Plink! Plink! Plink!
MOM! IT'S **HAILING**! **DO** SOMETHING!
Plink! Plink! Plink! Plink! Plink! Plink! Plink! Plink!
www.madamandeve.co.za
©RAPID PHASE · 2010
Plink! Plink! Plink! Plink!

FISH
www.madamandeve.co.za
GRRR.
©RAPID PHASE · 2011
ZOO
I THINK I'VE BEEN SPENDING FAR TOO MUCH TIME WITH **GOGO**.

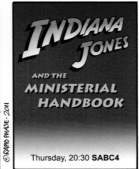

INDIANA JONES

AND THE

MINISTERIAL HANDBOOK

Thursday, 20:30 **SABC4**

©RAPID PHASE - 2011

WHAT'S THAT?

IT'S A COOL NEW SOUTH AFRICAN PLAYSTATION **GAME.**

CHOMP! CHOMP! CHOMP! CHOMP!

CAN I PLAY? WHAT'S THE OBJECT OF THE GAME?

I'M NOT SURE, BUT I THINK YOU'RE SUPPOSED TO **GOBBLE UP** AS MANY **COMPANIES** AND AS MUCH **REAL ESTATE** AS POSSIBLE.

©RAPID PHASE - 2011

GUPMAN

CHOMP! CHOMP! CHOMP! CH

EVE SAYS SHE'S SUFFERING FROM AN **IRON** DEFICIENCY.

©RAPID PHASE - 2011

THANKS DAVE G.

IMPOSSIBLE. I JUST **BOUGHT** HER A **NEW ONE** LAST WEEK.

THAT'S WHAT I **THOUGHT.**

www.madamandeve.co.za

65

DA
TOILET STORY
ANC
©RAPID PHASE - 2011

RENT A CURTAIN
Only 10 Rand
"RENT A CURTAIN?" WHY WOULD ANYONE WANT TO RENT A CURTAIN?
OPEN AIR TOILETS →
www.madamandeve.co.za
©RAPID PHASE - 2011
YOU HAVE TO ADMIT. SHE'S ALWAYS THINKING OUTSIDE THE BOX.

WHAT SEEMS TO BE THE PROBLEM, OFFICER?
SNIFF-SNIFF I SMELL ALCOHOL...
www.madamandeve.co.za
HEH-HEH THAT'S MY PERFUME. "EAU DE GIN & TONIQUE BY GILBEY."
"EAU DE GIN & TONIQUE?"
©RAPID PHASE - 2010
IT'S FRENCH.
OKAY. YOU MAY GO. --AND IT'S A GOOD THING YOU'RE NOT DRIVING...
OTHERWISE YOU'D BE WEARING "EAU DE SUSPEND YOUR DRIVER'S LICENCE."
I THINK HE'S ON TO YOU.

IF YOU ASK ME, THIS "VIP THING" HAS REALLY GOT OUT OF HAND.
©RAPID PHASE · 2010
www.madamandeve.co.za

Hello, my friend.
I am a wealthy member of a Nigerian royal family.
Unfortunately, the government has frozen my entire fortune in my bank account. If you provide me with your...
www.madamandeve.co.za
©RAPID PHASE · 2010
LIKE I'M GOING TO FALL FOR THAT ONE! NICE TRY! ... AND HASTA LA VISTA, BABY!
Click!
I DON'T UNDERSTAND IT, YOUR HIGHNESS. NO ONE SEEMS INTERESTED IN HELPING US OR MAKING MILLIONS OF DOLLARS!
KEEP TRYING.

www.madamandeve.co.za
CATCH OF THE DAY
©RAPID PHASE · 2011
JOE'S FISH MARKET
CATCH OF THE DAY

HEE-HEE! HEY, CHECK OUT THIS YOU TUBE VIDEO.
WHAT IS IT?
THIS WOMAN WAS TEXTING WHILE WALKING... AND SHE FELL INTO A PUBLIC FOUNTAIN!
©RAPID PHASE · 2011
www.madamandeve.co.za
WHAT A MORON!
REALLY? LET'S SEE!
BONK!!

EAT PRAY LOVE
©RAPID PHASE · 2011
AWAKE CHASE KATTY
MIELLLIES!
www.madamandeve.co.za
ANNOY STOEP SLAM
DRINK TEA BREAK

HEY!! THAT GUY JUST STOLE MY CELLPHONE OFF OUR TABLE!!
WAIT, MOM. HE'S COMING BACK!
SORRY- HERE! WHAT WAS I THINKING? THIS PHONE DOESN'T EVEN HAVE INTERNET ACCESS.
©RAPID PHASE · 2011
www.madamandeve.co.za
THIS IS SO HUMILI-ATING.
I'M OVERDUE FOR AN UPGRADE, OKAY?!

STOP
©RAPID PHASE - 2010
www.madamandeve.co.za

YOU KNOW... SOMETIMES I THINK WE'RE TOO ACCEPTING WHEN IT COMES TO CRIME.
WHAT MAKES YOU SAY THAT?
LA MODE
©RAPID PHASE - 2011
BALACLAVA AUTUMN FASHION PREVIEW

HI.
©RAPID PHASE - 2010
DO YOU KNOW THERE'S A TOKOLOSH IN MY CHAIR?
NO, BUT WE'LL TRY AND FAKE IT.
OH, THERE'S A TOKOLOSH IN MY CHAIR! THERE'S A TOKOLOSH IN MY CHAIR!
HOW DO YOU LIVE WITH THESE PEOPLE?
THE SILLY SEASON ARRIVED EARLY THIS YEAR.

EVE!! HURRY!
CLICK
©RAPID PHASE · 2011 www.madamandeve.co.za
SMACK!
AND DON'T THINK I'M NOT KEEPING SCORE. WE SAID TEN BUCKS A MOSQUITO.
PROTECTED BY SWAT.
CLICK

SIR?... WE HAVE A CODE YELLOW. TWO WOMEN PUSHED OUR BANK'S REVOLVING SECURITY DOOR AT THE SAME TIME. NOW THEY'RE STUCK!
MANAGER
SO? WHY IS THAT A CODE YELLOW?
THEY'VE DONE IT BEFORE.
MANAGER
©RAPID PHASE · 2011
SO? WHY IS THAT A CODE YELLOW?
YOU MIGHT WANT TO TAKE A LOOK AT THE WOMEN, SIR.
MANAGER
CALL SECURITY!! THIS IS A CODE RED! CODE RED!!
RATTLE! RATTLE! RATTLE!

WHERE'S THANDI AND HER FRIENDS?
THEY SAID THEY WERE GOING INTO THE KITCHEN TO JAM.
"JAM?!" I DIDN'T KNOW THEY WERE IN A BAND.
THEY'RE NOT.
©RAPID PHASE · 2011 www.madamandeve.co.za
JAM

GIVE ME YOUR MONEY!
SPROING!
©RAPID PHASE 2010
www.madamandeve.co.za
"HIJACK IN A BOX." I'M CURRENTLY LOOKING FOR INVESTORS.
YOU'RE MAKING A BIG MISTAKE! OUR FOCUS GROUP LOVED IT!!

I WAS JUST WONDERING.
www.madamandeve.co.za
ARE YOU A "GLASS HALF-EMPTY" OR A "GLASS HALF-FULL" KIND OF PERSON?
I'D SAY SHE'S A "GLASS HALF-EMPTY BUT OPTIMISTIC ABOUT GETTING AN IMMINENT REFILL" KIND OF PERSON.
©RAPID PHASE 2010
EVERYONE'S A @#☆#@☆ PHILOSOPHER.

NO THANK YOU! -- WHAT AM I SUPPOSED TO DO WITH SUPER-GLUE AND PLASTIC HANGERS?!
www.madamandeve.co.za
©RAPID PHASE 2010
GALLERY OPENING

WHAT'S THAT?
BRILLIANT IDEA. WHENEVER IT'S TIME FOR MY COCKTAIL, I SIMPLY SMS **EVE** AN ATTACHED IMAGE OF A **GIN & TONIC**.
EVE GETS THE MESSAGE AND I DON'T HAVE TO **SHOUT** ANYMORE.
RING! RING!
©RAPID PHASE - 2011
www.madamandeve.co.za
RING! RING! RING! RING!
EVE!! ANSWER YOUR G#☆D# PHONE!!
RING! RING! RING! RING!

TIC TIC TIC
TIC TIC TIC TIC TIC TIC
SCREECH!!
www.madamandeve.co.za
MADAM!! **TEXTING** WHILE DRIVING IS **DANGEROUS!!**
I KNOW! WHEW THAT WAS A **CLOSE** ONE.
...WAIT TILL I TELL MOM!!
TIC TIC TIC TIC TIC TIC TIC TIC

YES!! WHAT AN **AMAZING DAY!** I'LL NEVER **FORGET** IT!!
©RAPID PHASE - 2011
SOUTH AFRICAN POLICE SERVICE -- I **LOVE** YOU! FROM NOW ON... THE **SKY'S** THE **LIMIT!**
www.madamandeve.co.za
IT'S NICE TO SEE A TRAFFIC COP SO POSITIVE AND MOTIVATED! WHAT HAPPENED? DID HE GET A **PROMOTION?**
EVEN BETTER. HE JUST GOT HIS **BRIBER'S LICENCE**.

LOOK! TO YOUR RIGHT! A LION!
CLICK CLICK CLICK
www.madamandeve.co.za
STRAIGHT AHEAD! BEHIND THAT BUSH! A RHINO!
CLICK CLICK CLICK
©RAPID PHASE · 2010
YOU'RE VERY LUCKY! THE ANIMALS ARE ALL OUT TODAY!
CLICK CLICK CLICK
I WANT MY MONEY BACK.
EVE'S WIRE ANIMAL GAME PARK

BRACE YOURSELVES! THIS ONE'S GOING TO BE STEEP.
©RAPID PHASE · 2011
AAAAAH
www.madamandeve.co.za
THESE SUBURBAN SPEED BUMPS ARE GETTING HIGHER AND HIGHER.
CLUNK!!

LOOK AT THIS: EVE'S ALWAYS LEAVING US LITTLE NOTES. WE'RE OUT OF SPRAY STARCH, SO SHE STICKS A NOTE UNDER THE SPRAY STARCH CAN.
www.madamandeve.co.za
WE'RE OUT OF SELLOTAPE ... SO SHE SELLOTAPES A NOTE TO THE GROCERY CUPBOARD.
©RAPID PHASE · 2011
THWAK! TWONG!!
WE NEED MORE TOILET BOWL FRESHENER.

NO WORK NO FOOD
DANGER POTHOLE
SHABBY ROAD

HAVE A HAPPY DAY YOURSELVES.
©RAPID PHASE - 2011

WHAT ARE YOU DOING WITH MY GOOD SCISSORS?
CHECK IT OUT.
SNIP! SNIP! SNIP! SNIP! SNIP! SNIP!
ENTOURAGE PAPER DOLLS.
©RAPID PHASE - 2011
SLAM!!
I CAN'T HELP IT! WHEN MY MUSE CALLS, I HAVE TO LISTEN!

HERE YOU GO. KNOCK YOURSELF OUT.
...WHAT?
©RAPID PHASE · 2011
ALL WEEK I'VE BEEN LISTENING TO YOU TELL ME YOU WANT TO SEE YOU TUBE. WELL, HERE IT IS.
www.madamandeve.co.za
U2!! NOT YOU TUBE! I WANT TO SEE U2!!
YOU WANT TO GO SEE A GERMAN SUBMARINE?
GENERATION GAP?
GENERATION CHASM.

UNBELIEVABLE.
JUST LOOK AT ALL THOSE WHITE PEOPLE.
www.madamandeve.co.za
WHITE PEOPLE... AS FAR AS THE EYE CAN SEE...
WHAT'S THAT? A RUGBY MATCH?
©RAPID PHASE · 2011
...LAST SUNDAY'S U2 CONCERT.

LOOK MADAM! AFTER YEARS OF TRYING, I'M FINALLY IN THE GUINNESS BOOK OF RECORDS!!
"WORLD'S LONGEST TEA BREAK: EVE SISULU, SOUTH AFRICA."
Guinness Book of Records
EVE'S IN THE GUINNESS BOOK OF RECORDS!! WORLD'S LONGEST TEA BREAK! EVE'S IN THE GUINNESS BOOK OF RECORDS! WORLD'S LONGEST --
©RAPID PHASE · 2011
www.madamandeve.co.za
GET BACK HERE!!

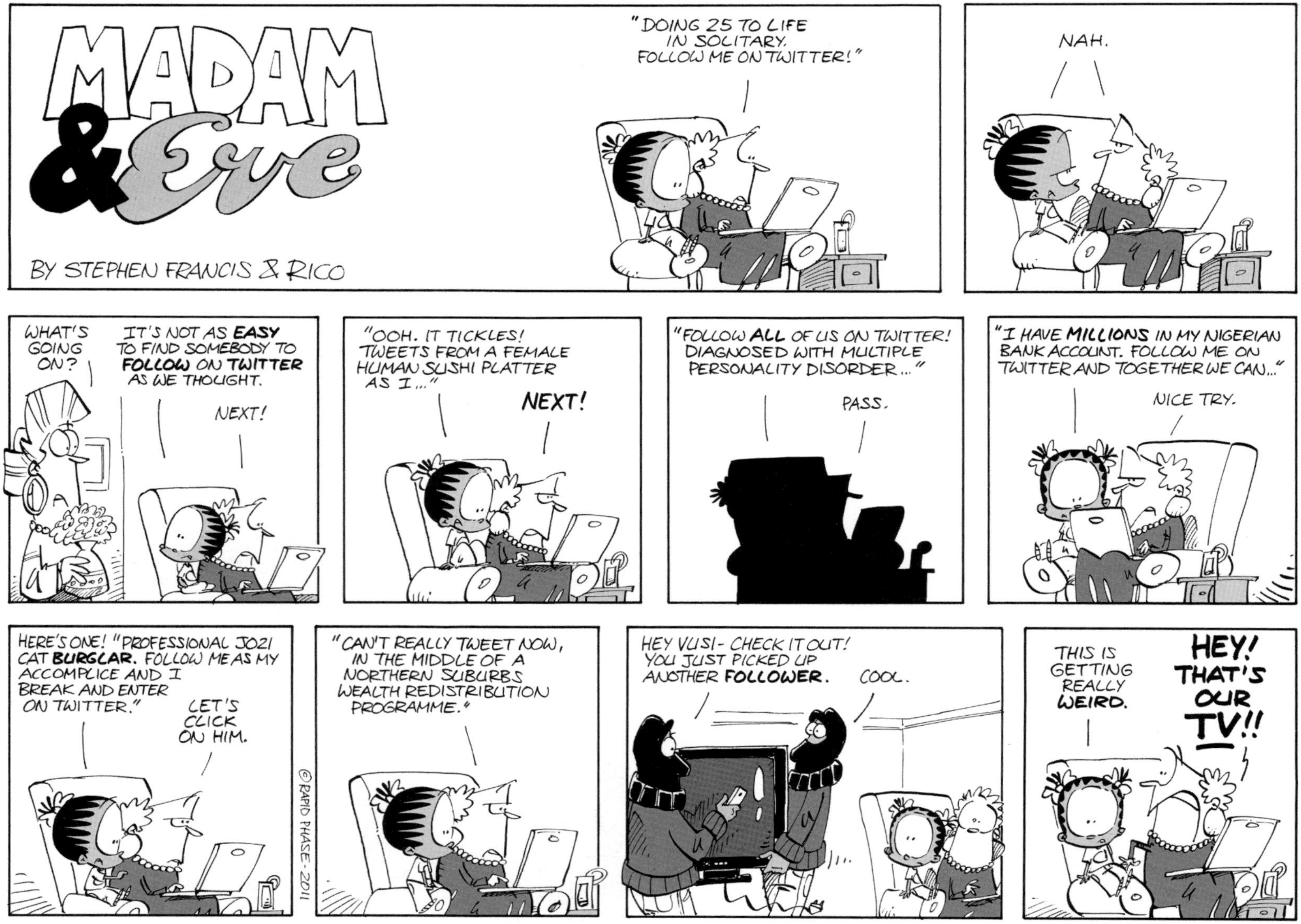
MADAM & Eve
BY STEPHEN FRANCIS & RICO
"DOING 25 TO LIFE IN SOLITARY. FOLLOW ME ON TWITTER!"
NAH.
WHAT'S GOING ON?
IT'S NOT AS EASY TO FIND SOMEBODY TO FOLLOW ON TWITTER AS WE THOUGHT.
NEXT!
"OOH. IT TICKLES! TWEETS FROM A FEMALE HUMAN SUSHI PLATTER AS I..."
NEXT!
"FOLLOW ALL OF US ON TWITTER! DIAGNOSED WITH MULTIPLE PERSONALITY DISORDER..."
PASS.
"I HAVE MILLIONS IN MY NIGERIAN BANK ACCOUNT. FOLLOW ME ON TWITTER AND TOGETHER WE CAN..."
NICE TRY.
HERE'S ONE! "PROFESSIONAL JOZI CAT BURGLAR. FOLLOW ME AS MY ACCOMPLICE AND I BREAK AND ENTER ON TWITTER."
LET'S CLICK ON HIM.
© RAPID PHASE - 2011
"CAN'T REALLY TWEET NOW, IN THE MIDDLE OF A NORTHERN SUBURBS WEALTH REDISTRIBUTION PROGRAMME."
HEY VUSI- CHECK IT OUT! YOU JUST PICKED UP ANOTHER FOLLOWER.
COOL.
THIS IS GETTING REALLY WEIRD.
HEY! THAT'S OUR TV!!

DOCTOR... IS IT NARCISSISTIC TO ASK PEOPLE TO FOLLOW ME ON TWITTER?
YES.
www.madamandeve.co.za
DO YOU EVER FOLLOW ME ON TWITTER?
DON'T BE PARANOID.
BUT YES... I DO FOLLOW YOU ON TWITTER.
REALLY?
©RAPID PHASE·2011
WOW! MY THERAPIST FOLLOWS ME ON TWITTER!
...FOR 400 BUCKS AN HOUR. WAIT UNTIL SHE GETS THE BILL.

GASP! MY PSYCHIATRIST SENT ME A HUGE BILL! HE'S BEEN FOLLOWING ME ON TWITTER FOR 400 BUCKS AN HOUR!
...AND MY LAWYER TOO! "FOLLOWING CLIENT ON TWITTER AND PERUSING TWEETS." R1200 AN HOUR!!
©RAPID PHASE·2011 www.madamandeve.co.za
HERE'S ONE FROM THE POLICE. THEY SAY THEY'LL STOP FOLLOWING ME ON TWITTER IF I BUY THEM A COOLDRINK!
THEY WANT A BRIBE TO STOP FOLLOWING YOU?
I'M TWEETING MY LAWYER.
Follow Madam & Eve on Twitter: http://twitter.com/madamevecartoon

MARK-- THERE MUST BE SOME MISTAKE! YOU SENT ME THIS HUGE LEGAL BILL... JUST FOR FOLLOWING ME ON TWITTER?
www.madamandeve.co.za
MEGAN! WHERE'S THE ANDERSON-TWITTER FILE?!
©RAPID PHASE·2011
SEE? RIGHT HERE: DID YOU... OR DID YOU NOT INSTRUCT ME TO FOLLOW YOU ON TWITTER?
NOT FOR 1200 BUCKS AN HOUR!! FOR FREE! FOR FUN!!
..."FREE?" ..."FUN?"
I'LL EXPLAIN LATER.
Follow Madam & Eve on Twitter: http://twitter.com/madamevecartoon

MARK! HOW CAN YOU CHARGE ME 1200 BUCKS AN HOUR JUST TO FOLLOW ME ON TWITTER?!
HEY! I'M YOUR LAWYER! I'VE GOT YOUR BACK IN CYBER-SPACE!
www.madamandeve.co.za
©RAPID PHASE - 2011
LET'S SAY... ONE OF YOUR TWITTER FOLLOWERS CROSSES THE LINE LEGALLY...
WHAT? YOU SEND THEM A LAWYER'S LETTER?
WELL... ACTUALLY I SEND THEM A LAWYER'S TWEET.
A "LAWYER'S TWEET?" IS THAT CHEAPER?
WAY MORE EXPENSIVE! DO YOU HAVE ANY IDEA HOW HARD IT IS TO SOUND THREATENING IN ONLY 140 CHARACTERS OR LESS?
Follow Madam & Eve on Twitter:
http://twitter.com/madamevecartoon

DO YOU THINK EVE HAS DIFFICULTY WORKING BECAUSE OF AAD?
www.madamandeve.co.za
NO. SHE HAS DIFFICULTY WORKING BECAUSE OF ATB.
©RAPID PHASE - 2011
ATB? WHAT'S ATB?
ALWAYS ON TEA BREAK.

CHOMP. CHOMP.
CHOMP! CHOMP! GULP.
CHOMP CHOMP CHOMP
CHOMP! CHOMP! CHOMP!
www.madamandeve.co.za
©RAPID PHASE - 2011
HA-HA. VERY FUNNY!

AND WE'LL BE BACK WITH MORE ON THE JIMMY MANYI RACISM DEBATE... AFTER THIS...
WOW.
...A RACISM SCANDAL WITHOUT WHITE PEOPLE.
WE'RE SITTING THIS ONE OUT ON THE SIDELINES.
©RAPID PHASE · 2011 www.madamandeve.co.za

CLASS- WHO CAN GIVE ME AN EXAMPLE OF A "COLLECTIVE NOUN?"
A HERD OF SPRINGBOK!
A SWARM OF BEES!
A BLOCK OF FLATS.
VERY GOOD.
AN OVERSUPPLY OF COLOURED PEOPLE!
WELL EXCUSE ME FOR KEEPING UP WITH CURRENT EVENTS!
PRINCIPAL
www.madamandeve.co.za ©RAPID PHASE · 2011

IF YOU ASK ME, WE HAVE AN OVERSUPPLY OF TEA BREAKS IN THIS HOUSE.
YEBO.
...TO MATCH THE UNDERSUPPLY OF WAGE INCREASES.
www.madamandeve.co.za ©RAPID PHASE · 2011

THEY'RE TALKING ABOUT SOME GUY ON THE NEWS... BHEKI SILLY.
CELE.
www.madamandeve.co.za
AS IN ...BUY AND CELE.
MOM!!
...BUT WHAT DOES HE **DO**?
HE'S THE **LEASE** COMMISSIONER. --I MEAN **POLICE** COMMISSIONER.
©RAPID PHASE - 2011
MOM!!
WHAT?! SLIP OF THE TONGUE!

DUDUZANE, I'M VERY BUSY... WHAT IS IT?
IT'S THE **MEDIA**, DAD. WHY DO THEY CONSPIRE AGAINST ME AND THE **GUPTA** BROTHERS?
...BECAUSE I'VE WORKED HARD TO BECOME SOUTH AFRICA'S YOUNGEST **BILLIONAIRE.** BEING THE **PRESIDENT'S SON** HAS **NOTHING** TO DO WITH IT!!
©RAPID PHASE - 2011
IN FACT, DO YOU KNOW HOW **MANY** COMPANIES I AM A **DIRECTOR** OF?!
NO.
www.madamandeve.co.za
NEITHER DO I. IT KEEPS CHANGING. I WOKE UP THIS MORNING--THEY APPOINTED ME TO **TWO MORE!**
AND GET A LIST OF YOUR LEASED CARS! THERE'S A BRAND-NEW **PORSCHE** PARKING US IN DOWNSTAIRS ALL WEEK!

MISTER PRESIDENT. YOUR **SON** IS HERE TO SEE YOU.
SEND HIM IN.
DAD! --YOU WON'T BELIEVE THIS! THE **GUPTA BROTHERS** APPOINTED ME TO THE BOARD OF YET **ANOTHER** COMPANY!
CONGRATULATIONS.
www.madamandeve.co.za
NO!! YOU DON'T UNDERSTAND! I DON'T **WANT** IT! I HAVE TOO MUCH **RESPONSIBILITY** AS IT IS!
ATTENDING ALL THOSE **BOARD MEETINGS?**
©RAPID PHASE - 2011
...TAKING CARE OF ALL THE **PORSCHES** THEY GAVE ME!
IS THAT RED ONE **YOURS?** YOU PARKED ME IN AGAIN.

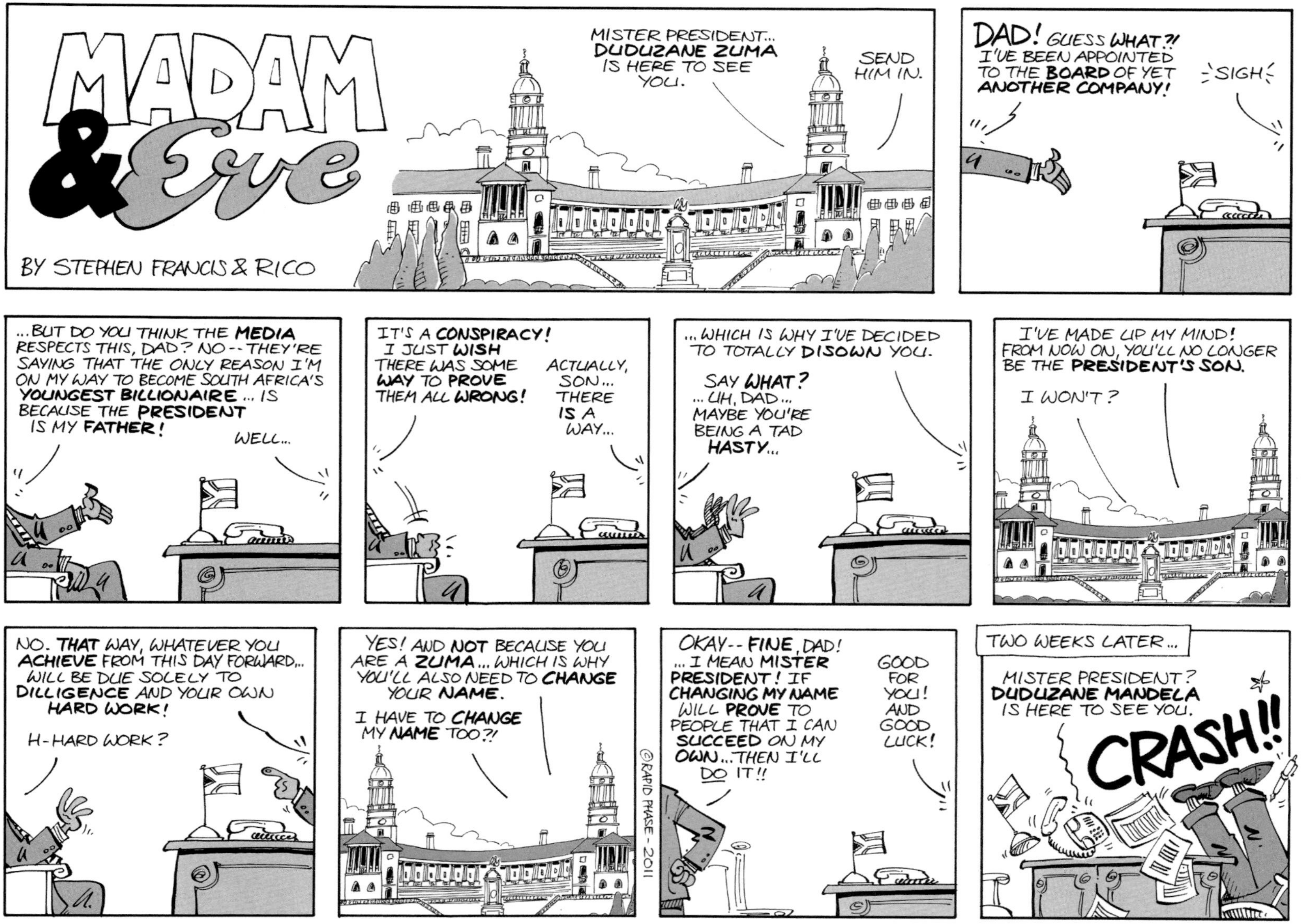

MADAM & Eve
BY STEPHEN FRANCIS & RICO
MISTER PRESIDENT... DUDUZANE ZUMA IS HERE TO SEE YOU.
SEND HIM IN.
DAD! GUESS WHAT?! I'VE BEEN APPOINTED TO THE BOARD OF YET ANOTHER COMPANY!
SIGH
...BUT DO YOU THINK THE MEDIA RESPECTS THIS, DAD? NO -- THEY'RE SAYING THAT THE ONLY REASON I'M ON MY WAY TO BECOME SOUTH AFRICA'S YOUNGEST BILLIONAIRE ... IS BECAUSE THE PRESIDENT IS MY FATHER!
WELL...
IT'S A CONSPIRACY! I JUST WISH THERE WAS SOME WAY TO PROVE THEM ALL WRONG!
ACTUALLY, SON... THERE IS A WAY...
...WHICH IS WHY I'VE DECIDED TO TOTALLY DISOWN YOU.
SAY WHAT? ...UH, DAD... MAYBE YOU'RE BEING A TAD HASTY...
I'VE MADE UP MY MIND! FROM NOW ON, YOU'LL NO LONGER BE THE PRESIDENT'S SON.
I WON'T?
NO. THAT WAY, WHATEVER YOU ACHIEVE FROM THIS DAY FORWARD... WILL BE DUE SOLELY TO DILLIGENCE AND YOUR OWN HARD WORK!
H-HARD WORK?
YES! AND NOT BECAUSE YOU ARE A ZUMA ... WHICH IS WHY YOU'LL ALSO NEED TO CHANGE YOUR NAME.
I HAVE TO CHANGE MY NAME TOO?!
© RAPID PHASE - 2011
OKAY-- FINE, DAD! ...I MEAN MISTER PRESIDENT! IF CHANGING MY NAME WILL PROVE TO PEOPLE THAT I CAN SUCCEED ON MY OWN... THEN I'LL DO IT!!
GOOD FOR YOU! AND GOOD LUCK!
TWO WEEKS LATER...
MISTER PRESIDENT? DUDUZANE MANDELA IS HERE TO SEE YOU.
CRASH!!

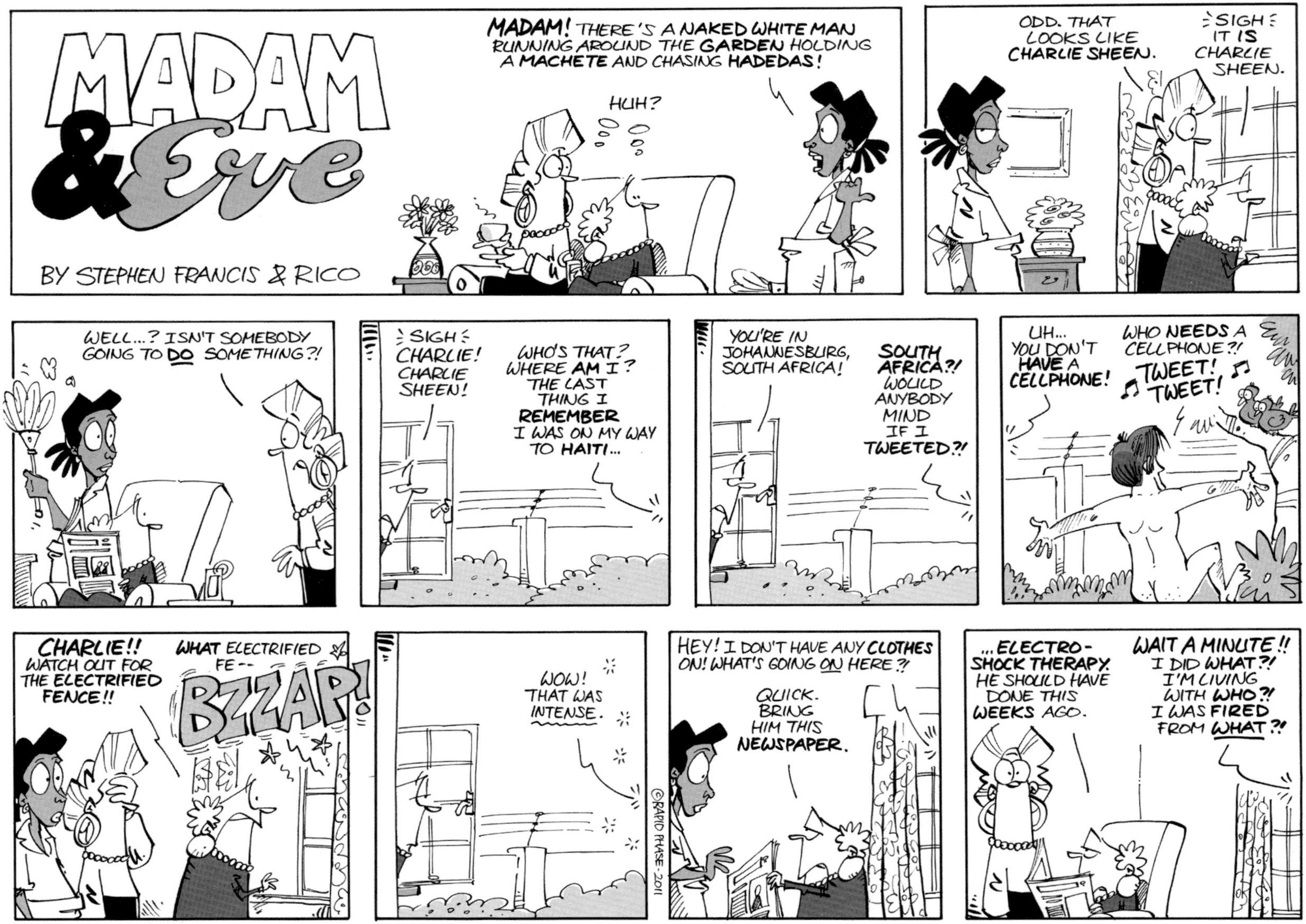
MADAM & Eve
BY STEPHEN FRANCIS & RICO
MADAM! THERE'S A NAKED WHITE MAN RUNNING AROUND THE GARDEN HOLDING A MACHETE AND CHASING HADEDAS!
HUH?
ODD. THAT LOOKS LIKE CHARLIE SHEEN.
SIGH IT IS CHARLIE SHEEN.
WELL...? ISN'T SOMEBODY GOING TO DO SOMETHING?!
SIGH CHARLIE! CHARLIE SHEEN!
WHO'S THAT? WHERE AM I? THE LAST THING I REMEMBER I WAS ON MY WAY TO HAITI...
YOU'RE IN JOHANNESBURG, SOUTH AFRICA!
SOUTH AFRICA?! WOULD ANYBODY MIND IF I TWEETED?!
UH... YOU DON'T HAVE A CELLPHONE!
WHO NEEDS A CELLPHONE?!
TWEET! TWEET!
CHARLIE!! WATCH OUT FOR THE ELECTRIFIED FENCE!!
WHAT ELECTRIFIED FE--
BZZAP!
WOW! THAT WAS INTENSE.
©RAPID PHASE·2011
HEY! I DON'T HAVE ANY CLOTHES ON! WHAT'S GOING ON HERE?!
QUICK. BRING HIM THIS NEWSPAPER.
...ELECTRO-SHOCK THERAPY. HE SHOULD HAVE DONE THIS WEEKS AGO.
WAIT A MINUTE!! I DID WHAT?! I'M LIVING WITH WHO?! I WAS FIRED FROM WHAT?!

COOL!
HUH? THAT'S WEIRD!
WHAT ARE YOU DOING?
FOLLOWING CHARLIE SHEEN ON TWITTER.
© RAPID PHASE · 2011 www.madamandeve.co.za
HEY! MY CELLPHONE!!

AND IN OTHER NEWS... CONTROVERSIAL ACTOR CHARLIE SHEEN HAS DECIDED TO SPEND SEVERAL WEEKS "CHILLING" IN SOUTH AFRICA, NOW THAT HE'S BEEN FIRED FROM HIS POPULAR TV SHOW.
IN A RARE MOMENT OF CLARITY, SHEEN SAID HE DECIDED TO VISIT THIS COUNTRY... AFTER READING ABOUT THE NEW SOUTH AFRICAN PARTY TREND OF EATING SUSHI OFF EXPOSED NAKED STOMACHS.
© RAPID PHASE · 2011 www.madamandeve.co.za
SHEEN SAYS HE'S NEVER TRIED IT BEFORE... BUT ADMITS THAT IT "SURE SOUNDS LIKE SOMETHING HE'D REALLY ENJOY.
FRANKLY... I'M A TAD DISAPPOINTED.

Free Muti →
YOU LEFT YOUR SCHOOL BOOKS IN THE LOUNGE. YOU SHOULD PICK THEM UP BEFORE THEY GET LOST.
© RAPID PHASE · 2011 www.madamandeve.co.za
TOLD YOU WE SHOULD HAVE WAITED UNTIL AFTER HER SECOND GIN & TONIC.

THEY SAY THE LIBYAN GOVERNMENT HAS BILLIONS OF RANDS SECRETLY INVESTED RIGHT HERE IN SOUTH AFRICA.
www.madamandeve.co.za
REALLY? WHERE?
NO ONE KNOWS.
©RAPID PHASE 2011
SO KEEP YOUR EYES OPEN.
- COMING SOON -
McGaddafi's

I DON'T BELIEVE IT! McGADDAFI'S?!
DIDN'T I TELL YOU THE LIBYAN GOVERNMENT HAS BILLIONS SECRETLY INVESTED IN SOUTH AFRICA?!
McGaddafi's
GRAND OPENING
©RAPID PHASE 2011
LOOK! IT'S-- UH... IT'S...
www.madamandeve.co.za
RONALD McGADDAFI!!
HIYA KIDS!

CAN I HELP YOU?
YES.
www.madamandeve.co.za
...THREE BIG MUAMMARS, THREE TRIPOLI SHAKES AND AN ORDER OF REBEL NUGGETS.
©RAPID PHASE 2011
WOULD YOU LIKE THE REBEL NUGGETS REGULAR OR EXTRA CRISPY?
EXTRA CRISPY.
I CAN'T BELIEVE WE'RE DOING THIS.
HEY! IT'S NOT BAD!
McGaddafi's

SEE THAT HOTEL? THEY SAY IT'S OWNED BY LIBYAN INVESTMENTS.
SERIOUSLY?
www.madamandeve.co.za
©RAPID PHASE · 2011
I WONDER WHAT ELSE THEY'VE PUT THEIR MONEY INTO HERE?
PLANET GADDAFI
LIBYAN LIFE
Mr Oil Price
LFC
LIBYAN FRIED CHICKEN

AND IN INTERNATIONAL NEWS... MUAMMAR GADDAFI SAYS THAT "ANY WESTERN POWERS ATTACKING LIBYA WILL END UP IN THE DUSTBIN OF HISTORY."
DING! DONG!
©RAPID PHASE · 2011
WHO COULD THAT BE?
www.madamandeve.co.za
...IT'S THE DUSTBIN OF HISTORY MEN. THEY WANT THEIR BONUS.

TOLL ROAD
Please deposit R5
©RAPID PHASE · 2011
www.madamandeve.co.za

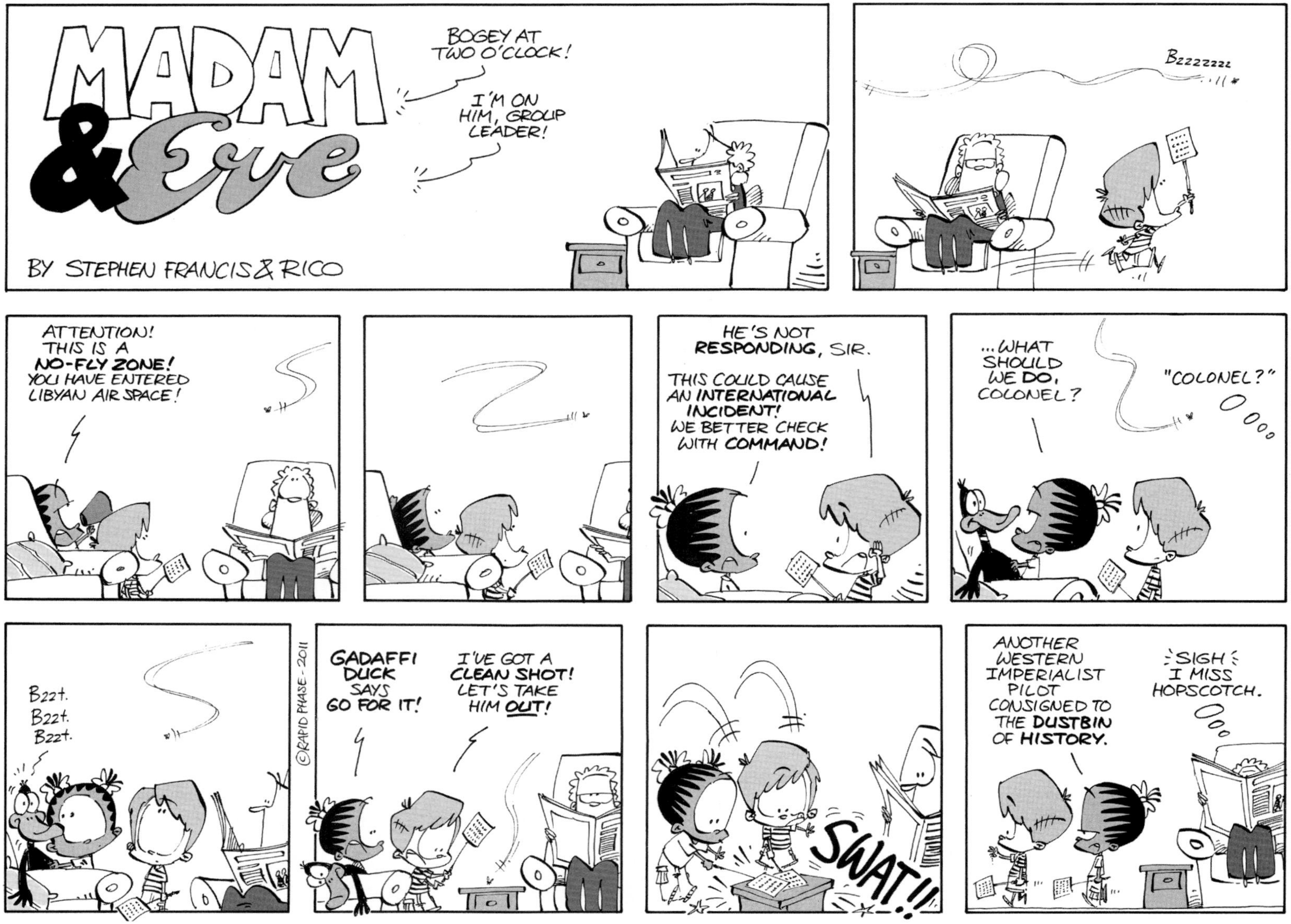
MADAM & Eve
BY STEPHEN FRANCIS & RICO
BOGEY AT TWO O'CLOCK!
I'M ON HIM, GROUP LEADER!
Bzzzzzzz
ATTENTION! THIS IS A NO-FLY ZONE! YOU HAVE ENTERED LIBYAN AIR SPACE!
HE'S NOT RESPONDING, SIR.
THIS COULD CAUSE AN INTERNATIONAL INCIDENT! WE BETTER CHECK WITH COMMAND!
...WHAT SHOULD WE DO, COLONEL?
"COLONEL?"
Bzzt. Bzzt. Bzzt.
©RAPID PHASE - 2011
GADAFFI DUCK SAYS GO FOR IT!
I'VE GOT A CLEAN SHOT! LET'S TAKE HIM OUT!
SWAT!!
ANOTHER WESTERN IMPERIALIST PILOT CONSIGNED TO THE DUSTBIN OF HISTORY.
SIGH I MISS HOPSCOTCH.

SIGH
IT MUST BE NICE TO BE A BIRD! NO WORRIES... NO CARES...
NO POLITICS. NO GREED. NO RACISM...
www.madamandeve.co.za ©RAPID PHASE-2011
BONK!
WHAT A MORON.

ONE SEVENTH OF YOUR LIFE IS SPENT ON WEDNESDAYS.
www.madamandeve.co.za
THINK ABOUT IT.
©RAPID PHASE-2011
THE EARLY MORNING PHILOSOPHER.
I'M GOING BACK TO BED.

MOM!! COME OUT! YOU CAN'T STAY IN YOUR ROOM ALL MORNING!!
©RAPID PHASE-2011
WHY NOT?! JUST LOOK AT THE HEADLINES! NUCLEAR RADIATION! HIT LISTS! RACISM! AXE MURDERERS!
HEY LOOK! WALMART'S COMING TO SOUTH AFRICA!
www.madamandeve.co.za
MOM!!
GO AWAY.

AND IN OTHER NEWS, **POLICE** ARE STILL TRYING TO VERIFY THE ALLEGED **HIT LIST** FOUND IN **RADOVAN KREJCIR'S** BEDFORDVIEW MANSION.
©RAPID PHASE-2011 www.madamandeve.co.za
HIT LIST? WHERE DOES SOMEONE KEEP A "HIT LIST" IN THEIR OWN **HOUSE?**
Eggs Milk Butter
HITLIST
1. Cyril Beeka
NAH.
IT'S POSSIBLE.

AARGH!
HERE I COME! AND YOU'RE NEXT ON MY HIT LIST!
N-NO! **KEEP AWAY!!**
SOMEBODY! **HELP!!**
WILL YOU TWO HOLD IT DOWN?! WHAT KIND OF **GAME** ARE YOU PLAYING!?
AARGH!
THE KREJCIR FROM THE BLACK LAGOON.
©RAPID PHASE-2011 www.madamandeve.co.za
SLAM!!
NOBODY APPRECIATES CHILDHOOD ORIGINALITY ANY MORE.

WHAT ARE YOU DOING?
WRITING MY OWN **HIT LIST.**
©RAPID PHASE-2011
1. BRUNO MARS
2. RIHANNA
3. ADELE
4. KATY PERRY
5. KANYE WEST...
WHO **ARE** THESE PEOPLE?!
www.madamandeve.co.za
MY FAVOURITE **HITS** ON THE **RADIO.**

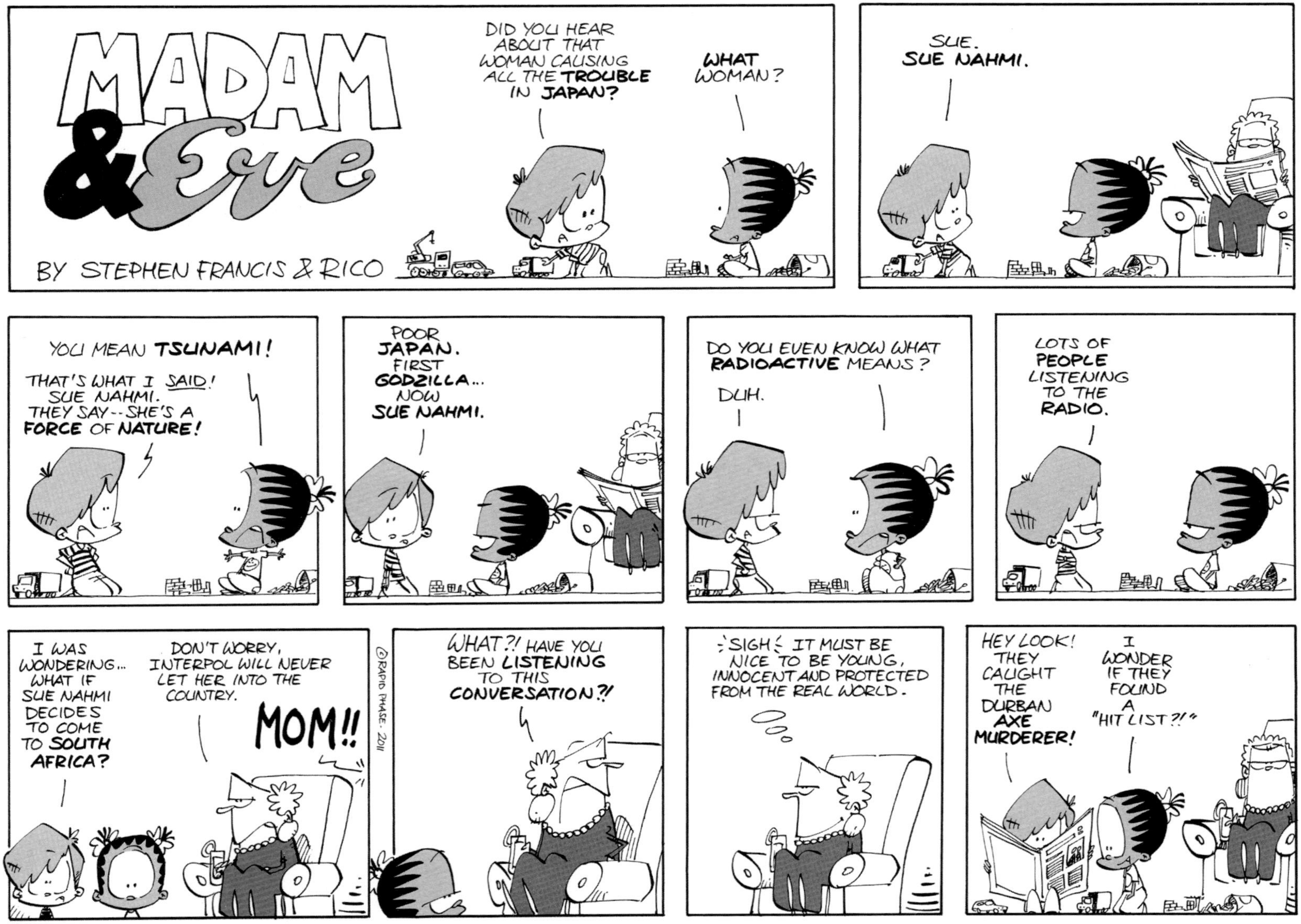
MADAM & Eve
BY STEPHEN FRANCIS & RICO
DID YOU HEAR ABOUT THAT WOMAN CAUSING ALL THE TROUBLE IN JAPAN?
WHAT WOMAN?
SUE. SUE NAHMI.
YOU MEAN TSUNAMI!
THAT'S WHAT I SAID! SUE NAHMI. THEY SAY--SHE'S A FORCE OF NATURE!
POOR JAPAN. FIRST GODZILLA... NOW SUE NAHMI.
DO YOU EVEN KNOW WHAT RADIOACTIVE MEANS?
DUH.
LOTS OF PEOPLE LISTENING TO THE RADIO.
I WAS WONDERING... WHAT IF SUE NAHMI DECIDES TO COME TO SOUTH AFRICA?
DON'T WORRY, INTERPOL WILL NEVER LET HER INTO THE COUNTRY.
MOM!!
©RAPID PHASE. 2011
WHAT?! HAVE YOU BEEN LISTENING TO THIS CONVERSATION?!
SIGH IT MUST BE NICE TO BE YOUNG, INNOCENT AND PROTECTED FROM THE REAL WORLD.
HEY LOOK! THEY CAUGHT THE DURBAN AXE MURDERER!
I WONDER IF THEY FOUND A "HIT LIST?!"

... MAYBE WE SHOULD TRY A DIFFERENT POLICE STATION.
©RAPID PHASE - 2011

CAN I HELP YOU?
YES, OFFICER. I WANT TO FILE A COMPLAINT ABOUT A CORRUPT POLICEMAN.
POLICE
RIGHT. SO WHAT'S THE COMPLAINT?
©RAPID PHASE - 2011
FORGET IT, OFFICER VUSI.
HEY! I'M WEARING A BALACLAVA! HOW DID YOU KNOW WHO I AM?!
www.madamandeve.co.za
YOU'RE WEARING YOUR NAME TAG.
YOU IDIOT. NO WONDER PEOPLE DON'T RESPECT US.

THIS IS RIDICULOUS! IS CORRUPTION THAT WIDESPREAD?! WE'RE COPS! DO WE HAVE TO HIDE BEHIND BALACLAVAS IN OUR OWN POLICE STATION?!
©RAPID PHASE - 2011 www.madamandeve.co.za
WELL, I SAY... THE HELL WITH THIS! I'M TAKING MINE OFF RIGHT NOW!
IT'S HIM!
HE TOOK MY WALLET!
STOP THIEF!
HE'S THE ONE WHO STOLE MY CAR!
ARREST THAT GUY!!
DON'T LET HIM ESCAPE!

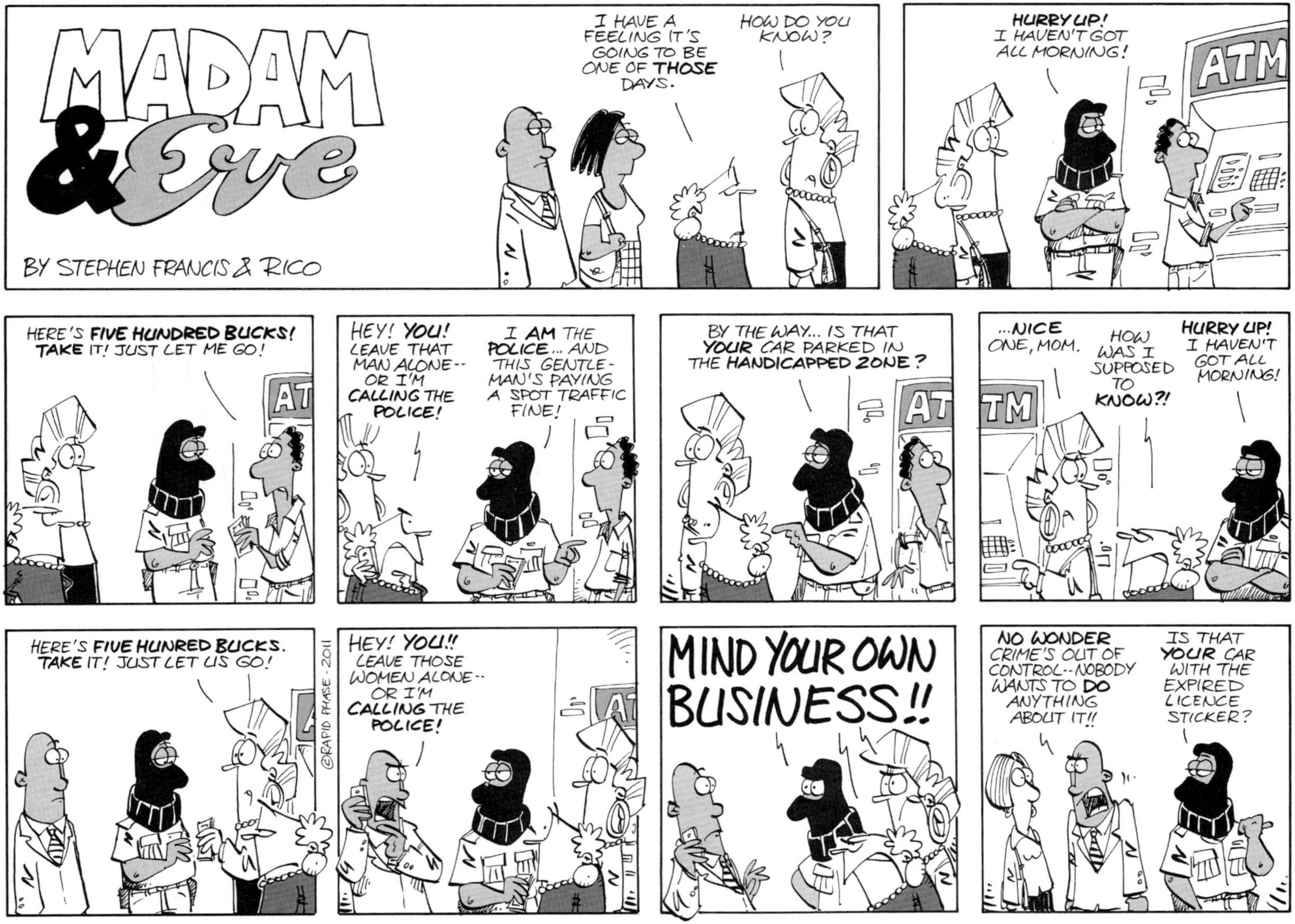

MADAM & Eve
BY STEPHEN FRANCIS & RICO
I HAVE A FEELING IT'S GOING TO BE ONE OF **THOSE** DAYS.
HOW DO YOU KNOW?
HURRY UP! I HAVEN'T GOT ALL MORNING!
ATM
HERE'S **FIVE HUNDRED BUCKS! TAKE** IT! JUST LET ME GO!
HEY! **YOU!** LEAVE THAT MAN ALONE-- OR I'M **CALLING** THE **POLICE!**
I **AM** THE **POLICE**... AND THIS GENTLEMAN'S PAYING A SPOT TRAFFIC FINE!
BY THE WAY... IS THAT **YOUR** CAR PARKED IN THE **HANDICAPPED ZONE**?
...**NICE** ONE, MOM.
HOW WAS I SUPPOSED TO **KNOW?!**
HURRY UP! I HAVEN'T GOT ALL MORNING!
HERE'S **FIVE HUNRED BUCKS. TAKE** IT! JUST LET US GO!
©RAPID PHASE · 2011
HEY! **YOU!!** LEAVE THOSE WOMEN ALONE-- OR I'M **CALLING** THE **POLICE!**
MIND YOUR OWN BUSINESS!!
NO WONDER CRIME'S OUT OF CONTROL--NOBODY WANTS TO **DO** ANYTHING ABOUT IT!!
IS THAT **YOUR** CAR WITH THE EXPIRED LICENCE STICKER?

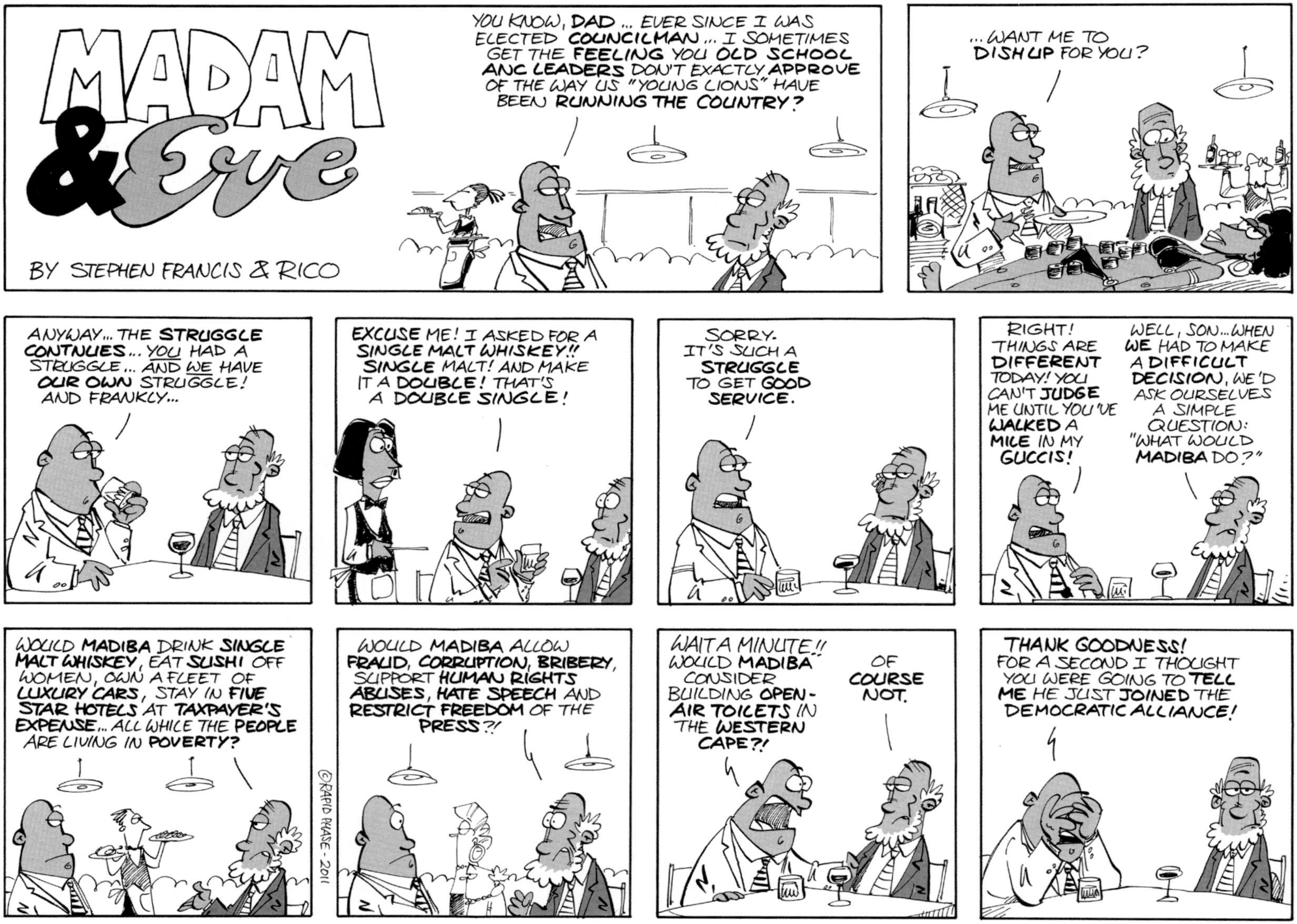
MADAM & Eve
BY STEPHEN FRANCIS & RICO
YOU KNOW, DAD ... EVER SINCE I WAS ELECTED COUNCILMAN ... I SOMETIMES GET THE FEELING YOU OLD SCHOOL ANC LEADERS DON'T EXACTLY APPROVE OF THE WAY US "YOUNG LIONS" HAVE BEEN RUNNING THE COUNTRY?
...WANT ME TO DISH UP FOR YOU?
ANYWAY... THE STRUGGLE CONTINUES... YOU HAD A STRUGGLE... AND WE HAVE OUR OWN STRUGGLE! AND FRANKLY...
EXCUSE ME! I ASKED FOR A SINGLE MALT WHISKEY!! SINGLE MALT! AND MAKE IT A DOUBLE! THAT'S A DOUBLE SINGLE!
SORRY. IT'S SUCH A STRUGGLE TO GET GOOD SERVICE.
RIGHT! THINGS ARE DIFFERENT TODAY! YOU CAN'T JUDGE ME UNTIL YOU'VE WALKED A MILE IN MY GUCCIS!
WELL, SON...WHEN WE HAD TO MAKE A DIFFICULT DECISION, WE'D ASK OURSELVES A SIMPLE QUESTION: "WHAT WOULD MADIBA DO?"
WOULD MADIBA DRINK SINGLE MALT WHISKEY, EAT SUSHI OFF WOMEN, OWN A FLEET OF LUXURY CARS, STAY IN FIVE STAR HOTELS AT TAXPAYER'S EXPENSE... ALL WHILE THE PEOPLE ARE LIVING IN POVERTY?
©RAPID PHASE - 2011
WOULD MADIBA ALLOW FRAUD, CORRUPTION, BRIBERY, SUPPORT HUMAN RIGHTS ABUSES, HATE SPEECH AND RESTRICT FREEDOM OF THE PRESS?!
WAIT A MINUTE!! WOULD MADIBA CONSIDER BUILDING OPEN-AIR TOILETS IN THE WESTERN CAPE?!
OF COURSE NOT.
THANK GOODNESS! FOR A SECOND I THOUGHT YOU WERE GOING TO TELL ME HE JUST JOINED THE DEMOCRATIC ALLIANCE!

HALT! OR I'LL SHOOT!
YOU HALT! OR I'LL SHOOT!
QUIET!! --WHAT THE HELL ARE YOU TWO PLAYING?!
"COPS AND ROBBERS!"
YOU'RE BOTH WEARING BALACLAVAS! WHO'S THE COP... AND WHO'S THE CRIMINAL?
OUR POINT EXACTLY!
THESE DAYS, IT'S A GREY AREA!
© RAPID PHASE · 2011
FREEZE!!
YOU FREEZE!!
FREEZE!!
YOU FREEZE!!
FREEZE!!
YOU FREEZE!!

QUIET!!
I ASKED YOU TEN MINUTES AGO... AND YOU SAID YOU WERE FINISHED PLAYING!
WE WERE!
...BUT WE REBOOTED.
© RAPID PHASE · 2011 www.madamandeve.co.za
SLAM!!
MAYBE I SHOULD CHOOSE MY WORDS MORE CAREFULLY.

LOOKS LIKE RAIN.
HOW CAN YOU TELL?
© RAPID PHASE · 2011 www.madamandeve.co.za

COMING UP... TODAY'S TOP STORIES...
... CORRUPTION INVESTIGATIONS, ILLEGAL TENDERS, SERVICE DELIVERY PROTESTS...
... MISSING GOVERNMENT FUNDS... TAXPAYER-FUNDED OVERSEAS JUNKETS, NEPOTISM AND POLICE CORRUPTION.
©RAPID PHASE · 2011
BUT FIRST... THE ANCYL ACCUSES HELEN ZILLE OF DANCING LIKE A MONKEY.

THERE'S A CURRENT POLITICAL DEBATE GOING AROUND THAT WHITE WOMEN DANCE LIKE MONKEYS... WOULD YOU MIND SHOWING US?
HOOHOOHOO!! HOOHOO!!
AAAAAH!!!
www.madamandeve.co.za
©RAPID PHASE · 2011
MOM!!
WHAT?! THEY ASKED FOR IT!

FLOAT LIKE A BUTTERFLY.
©RAPID PHASE · 2011
STING LIKE A BEE.
DANCE LIKE A MONKEY.
Helen & Julius
A wacky new romantic comedy!
Coming soon to SABC!

Sawubona!
This email will bring you good luck and good fortune within one hour! If you follow instructions!
Send this email immediately to ten of your friends... and VOTE ANC!! Do not break this chain, or you will affect MADIBA's health!
www.madamandeve.co.za
©RAPID PHASE - 2011
Comrade McBride forgot to vote ANC and broke the chain -- and look what happened to him! So keep MADIBA healthy! Be sure to --
CLICK!
HEY! I WAS READING THAT!

STOP STRUGGLING!! YOU'RE ALMOST OUT THE DOOR!
SLAM!!
SIGH.
www.madamandeve.co.za
©RAPID PHASE - 2011
Y'KNOW... SOMETIMES I MISS THE STRUGGLE.
ME TOO.

HEY! LOOK AT THIS! YESTERDAY WAS NATIONAL CLEAVAGE DAY! ... AND WE MISSED IT!
©RAPID PHASE - 2011
www.madamandeve.co.za
OH, WELL.
NO BIG DEAL.
MAYBE NEXT YEAR.

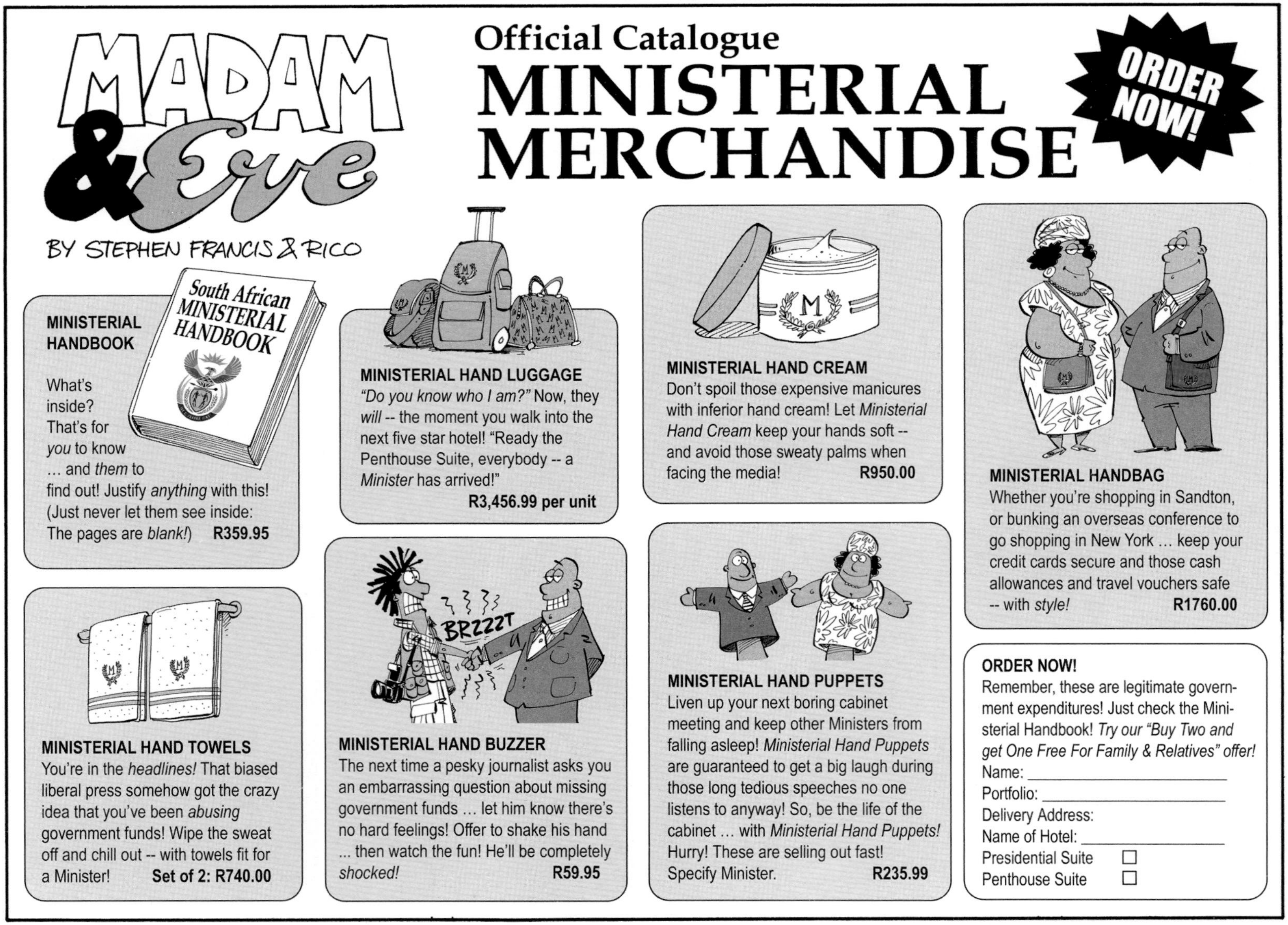
MADAM &Eve
BY STEPHEN FRANCIS & RICO
Official Catalogue
MINISTERIAL MERCHANDISE
ORDER NOW!
MINISTERIAL HANDBOOK
South African MINISTERIAL HANDBOOK
What's inside? That's for *you* to know ... and *them* to find out! Justify *anything* with this! (Just never let them see inside: The pages are *blank!*) **R359.95**
MINISTERIAL HAND LUGGAGE
"Do you know who I am?" Now, they *will* -- the moment you walk into the next five star hotel! "Ready the Penthouse Suite, everybody -- a *Minister* has arrived!" **R3,456.99 per unit**
MINISTERIAL HAND CREAM
Don't spoil those expensive manicures with inferior hand cream! Let *Ministerial Hand Cream* keep your hands soft -- and avoid those sweaty palms when facing the media! **R950.00**
MINISTERIAL HANDBAG
Whether you're shopping in Sandton, or bunking an overseas conference to go shopping in New York ... keep your credit cards secure and those cash allowances and travel vouchers safe -- with *style!* **R1760.00**
MINISTERIAL HAND TOWELS
You're in the *headlines!* That biased liberal press somehow got the crazy idea that you've been *abusing* government funds! Wipe the sweat off and chill out -- with towels fit for a Minister! **Set of 2: R740.00**
BRZZZT
MINISTERIAL HAND BUZZER
The next time a pesky journalist asks you an embarrassing question about missing government funds ... let him know there's no hard feelings! Offer to shake his hand ... then watch the fun! He'll be completely *shocked!* **R59.95**
MINISTERIAL HAND PUPPETS
Liven up your next boring cabinet meeting and keep other Ministers from falling asleep! *Ministerial Hand Puppets* are guaranteed to get a big laugh during those long tedious speeches no one listens to anyway! So, be the life of the cabinet ... with *Ministerial Hand Puppets!* Hurry! These are selling out fast! Specify Minister. **R235.99**
ORDER NOW!
Remember, these are legitimate government expenditures! Just check the Ministerial Handbook! *Try our "Buy Two and get One Free For Family & Relatives" offer!*
Name: ____________________
Portfolio: ____________________
Delivery Address:
Name of Hotel: ____________________
Presidential Suite ☐
Penthouse Suite ☐

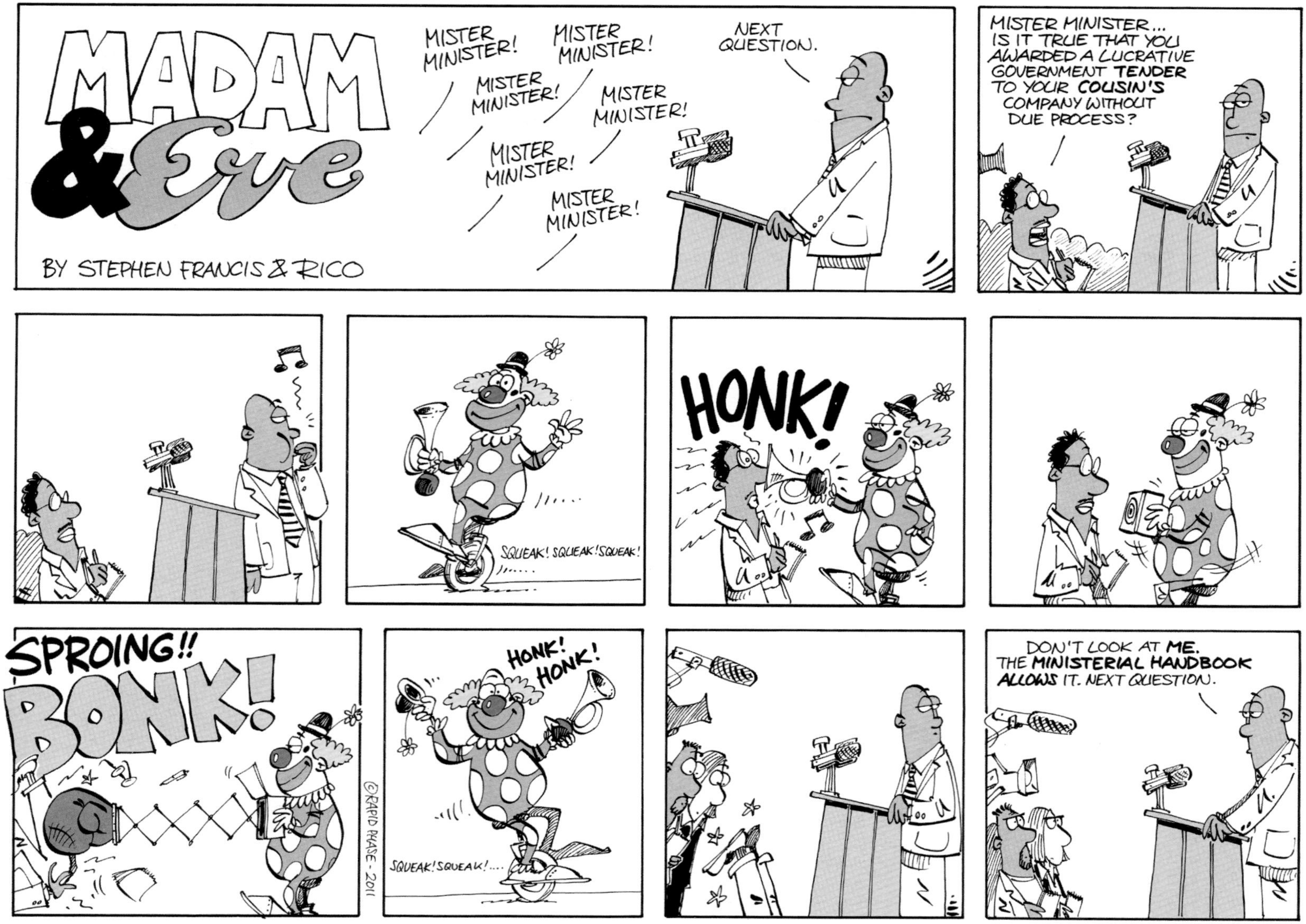

MADAM & Eve
BY STEPHEN FRANCIS & RICO
MISTER MINISTER!
MISTER MINISTER!
MISTER MINISTER!
MISTER MINISTER!
MISTER MINISTER!
MISTER MINISTER!
MISTER MINISTER!
NEXT QUESTION.
MISTER MINISTER... IS IT TRUE THAT YOU AWARDED A LUCRATIVE GOVERNMENT **TENDER** TO YOUR **COUSIN'S** COMPANY WITHOUT DUE PROCESS?
SQUEAK! SQUEAK! SQUEAK!
HONK!
SPROING!!
BONK!
©RAPID PHASE - 2011
HONK! HONK!
SQUEAK! SQUEAK!...
DON'T LOOK AT **ME.** THE **MINISTERIAL HANDBOOK ALLOWS** IT. NEXT QUESTION.

ARE YOU *CRAZY?!* DIDN'T YOU GET THE MEMO FROM *LUTHULI HOUSE?!*

WE'RE SUPPOSED TO BE *TIGHTENING OUR BELTS!* NO MORE EXTRAVAGANT SUSHI PARTIES UNTIL AFTER THE ELECTIONS!

WHAT DO YOU THINK? I'M *STUPID?!*

...SAUSAGE ROLLS.

≈WHEW≈ YOU HAD ME WORRIED THERE FOR A SECOND.

VOTE ANC

VOTE DA

SQUAWK! SQUAWK! SQUAWK! SQUAWK!! SQUAWK!! SQUAWK!!

VOTE ANC

VOTE DA

SHUT THE @#*@ UP!!

VOTE ANC

VOTE DA

VOTE ANC

POLITICS.

VOTE DA

OKAY..
1 x PORTABLE DVD PLAYER & HEADPHONES...
CHECK.
1 x NANDO'S FULL CHICKEN MEAL, MILD...
CHECK.
1 x BOTTLE, WHISKEY, SINGLE MALT...
CHECK.
1 x ELECTRIC BLANKET & GOOSEDOWN PILLOW...
CHECK!
HEY! YOU FORGOT MY CORKSCREW! HOW AM I SUPPOSED TO OPEN THE MERLOT?!
WHAT'S GOING ON?
©RAPID PHASE - 2011 www.madamandeve.co.za
TO HIGHLIGHT THE PLIGHT OF THE POOR ... COUNCILMAN VUSI WILL BE SPENDING ONE NIGHT IN A TOWNSHIP WITHOUT WATER OR ELECTRICITY.
HOW DO I LOOK?
LUMPY.

IN A FEW MOMENTS, I, COUNCILMAN VUSI, WILL EMBARK ON A JOURNEY OF DISCOVERY! SPENDING ONE NIGHT IN AS MANY SQUATTER CAMPS AS I CAN BEFORE ELECTION DAY.
SO I DON'T INCONVENIENCE MY SQUATTER, I'LL BE STAYING IN MY OWN PORTABLE SHACK DWELLING... WHICH I HAVE CHRISTENED SHACK ZULU!
INSIDE "SHACK ZULU", I WILL BE LIVING IN POVERTY... EXCEPT FOR A SMALL BATTERY-POWERED MICROWAVE AND A FLAT-SCREEN TV WITHOUT HIGH DEFINITION!
HURRY UP, SIR. YOU'RE LOSING THEM.
©RAPID PHASE - 2011 www.madamandeve.co.za
AT THIS TIME, I'D LIKE TO THANK THE SPONSORS OF MY TRIP... BUBBLE-MASTER INFLATABLE JACUZZIS...
THAT'S IT! WAKE UP THE DRIVER! WE'RE LEAVING!

HI! COUNCILMAN VUSI! ...SPENDING ONE NIGHT IN YOUR SQUATTER CAMP TO OBSERVE POVERTY FIRST HAND!
PHOTO OP! SMILE!
Click!
©RAPID PHASE - 2011 www.madamandeve.co.za
NOW... I'LL GO BACK INSIDE MY PORTABLE SHACK, EAT A MEAGRE DINNER AND SLEEP ON THE GROUND BELOW THE POVERTY LINE!
YOU VOTE FOR HIM, I'LL KILL YOU.
SLAM!!

SAVE THE RHINO
SAVE THE WHALES
OF COURSE! ...THAT'S IT!
YOU WANTED TO SEE ME, COUNCIL-MAN VUSI?
YES! I'VE JUST COME UP WITH MY NEW CAMPAIGN FOR THE UPCOMING LOCAL ELECTIONS!
LET THOSE OTHER IDIOTS PROMISE SERVICE DELIVERY. I'M RUNNING ON AN ENVIRONMENTAL PLATFORM!
©RAPID PHASE · 2011
www.madamandeve.co.za
WELL?
VOTE ANC
A better life for OWLS
HOO?
CAN I GET BACK TO YOU, SIR?

Re-elect Councilman Vusi!
ANC: A BETTER LIFE FOR AL.
UH... COUNCILMAN VUSI? YOU MISSPELLED A WORD ON OUR NEW BATCH OF ELECTION POSTERS!
NO, I DIDN'T.
©RAPID PHASE · 2011
www.madamandeve.co.za
SIR, IT SHOULD READ "ANC - A BETTER LIFE FOR ALL"... NOT AL. ...A BETTER LIFE FOR ALL!
...MEET MY COUSIN AL. HIS CONSTRUCTION COMPANY APPLIES FOR LOTS OF GOVERNMENT TENDERS.

PIKI TUP
©RAPID PHASE · 2011
LEAVIT THERE

...THE QUEEN IS BUSY PREPARING FOR THE UPCOMING ROYAL WEDDING...
©RAPID PHASE · 2011 www.madamandeve.co.za
NAH.

COMING UP... A SPECIAL REPORT ON THIS WEEK'S ROYAL WEDDING.
©RAPID PHASE · 2011 www.madamandeve.co.za
SHE TAKES THIS STUFF VERY SERIOUSLY.

AND WE'LL BE BACK... WITH MORE ON THE ROYAL WEDDING... AFTER THIS.
I WONDER WHAT IT WOULD BE LIKE IF WE IN SOUTH AFRICA HAD A QUEEN OR A KING?
ARE YOU JOKING? WE'D BE MUCH BETTER OFF!
©RAPID PHASE · 2011 www.madamandeve.co.za
...THEN ONLY ONE FAMILY WOULD BE SPENDING ALL THE TAXPAYER'S MONEY!
MOM!!

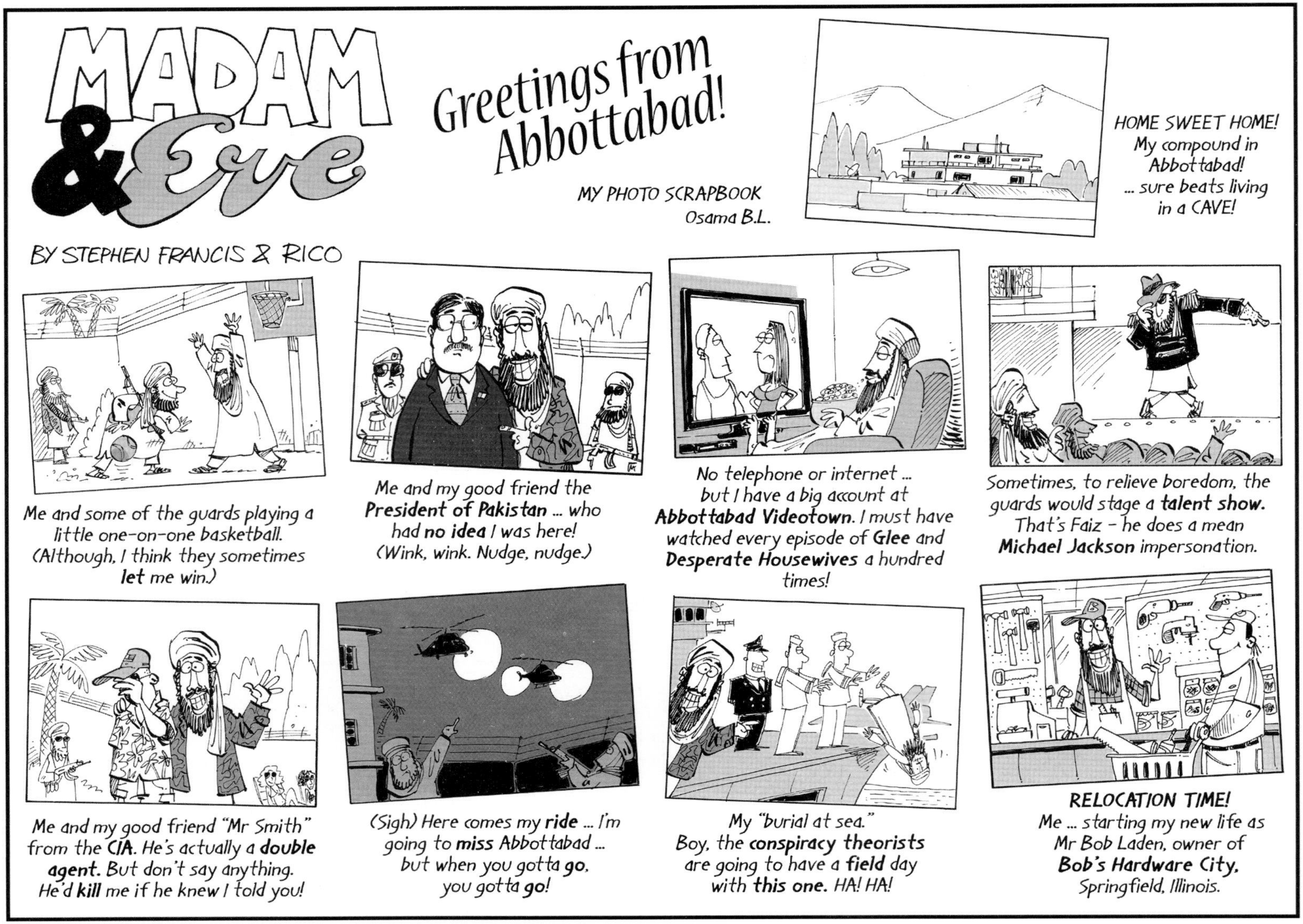
MADAM & Eve
BY STEPHEN FRANCIS & RICO
Greetings from Abbottabad!
MY PHOTO SCRAPBOOK
Osama B.L.
HOME SWEET HOME!
My compound in Abbottabad!
... sure beats living in a CAVE!
Me and some of the guards playing a little one-on-one basketball. (Although, I think they sometimes let me win.)
Me and my good friend the President of Pakistan ... who had no idea I was here! (Wink, wink. Nudge, nudge.)
No telephone or internet ... but I have a big account at Abbottabad Videotown. I must have watched every episode of Glee and Desperate Housewives a hundred times!
Sometimes, to relieve boredom, the guards would stage a talent show. That's Faiz – he does a mean Michael Jackson impersonation.
Me and my good friend "Mr Smith" from the CIA. He's actually a double agent. But don't say anything. He'd kill me if he knew I told you!
(Sigh) Here comes my ride ... I'm going to miss Abbottabad ... but when you gotta go, you gotta go!
My "burial at sea." Boy, the conspiracy theorists are going to have a field day with this one. HA! HA!
RELOCATION TIME!
Me ... starting my new life as Mr Bob Laden, owner of Bob's Hardware City, Springfield, Illinois.

HIS BIG MISTAKE : JOINING TWITTER

TWEET! AH. SITTING IN A HOT TUB IN **ABBOTTABAD**, DRINKING RED BULL! LET THE FOOLS LOOK FOR ME IN **CAVES!** HAHA!

©RAPID PHASE - 2011

©RAPID PHASE - 2011

AND WE'LL BE BACK WITH MORE NEWS ON THE **OSAMA BIN LADEN** RAID ... AFTER <u>THIS</u>.

www.madamandeve.co.za

THE COMPOUND WAS STORMED BY **NAVY SEALS?**

THAT'S WHAT THEY SAY.

WHERE'S EVE?

SHE TOOK TODAY OFF.

©RAPID PHASE - 2011

SHE **TOOK** THE DAY OFF ?! HOW CAN SHE TAKE THE DAY OFF ?!

...WE JUST HAD THE **EASTER WEEKEND, PASSOVER, FAMILY DAY, FREEDOM DAY** AND **WORKERS' DAY!**

SHE <u>KNOWS</u>.

www.madamandeve.co.za

... SHE SAID SHE NEEDS A **BREAK** AFTER ALL THOSE HOLIDAYS.

103

VOTE for Councilman Vusi!
A TRADITIONAL LEADER
MY NEW CAMPAIGN STRATEGY.
YOU'RE A "TRADITIONAL LEADER?"
YEP.
www.madamandeve.co.za
©RAPID PHASE - 2011
...THE TRADITION OF VOTING FOR THE SAME PEOPLE OVER AND OVER AGAIN, EVEN THOUGH WE DON'T DELIVER.
I LIKE IT.
MAY THE FORCE BE WITH YOU!
YEAH... THE FORCE OF HABIT.

AND WE'LL BE BACK WITH MORE ON THE DELIVERY PROTESTS... AFTER THIS.
I DON'T UNDERSTAND. IF PEOPLE ARE UNHAPPY WITH SERVICE DELIVERY... WHY DO THEY KEEP VOTING FOR THE SAME POLITICIANS?
... SIMPLE.
...PEOPLE AUTOMATICALLY DO THE SAME THING AGAIN AND AGAIN WITHOUT THINKING! IT BECOMES A HABIT.
©RAPID PHASE - 2011
www.madamandeve.co.za
EVE!! IT'S AFTER FIVE! WHERE'S MY GIN & TONIC?!!

COUNCILMAN VUSI, THE ELECTION'S AROUND THE CORNER. WE NEED SOMETHING CATCHY FOR YOUR NEW BILLBOARD!
©RAPID PHASE - 2011
ANY IDEAS?
HERE'S A BOOK OF FAMOUS QUOTATIONS! PICK ONE FROM SOMEBODY INTELLIGENT.
www.madamandeve.co.za
"The definition of insanity: Doing the same thing over and over and expecting a different result."
Albert Einstein
RE-ELECT COUNCILMAN VUSI

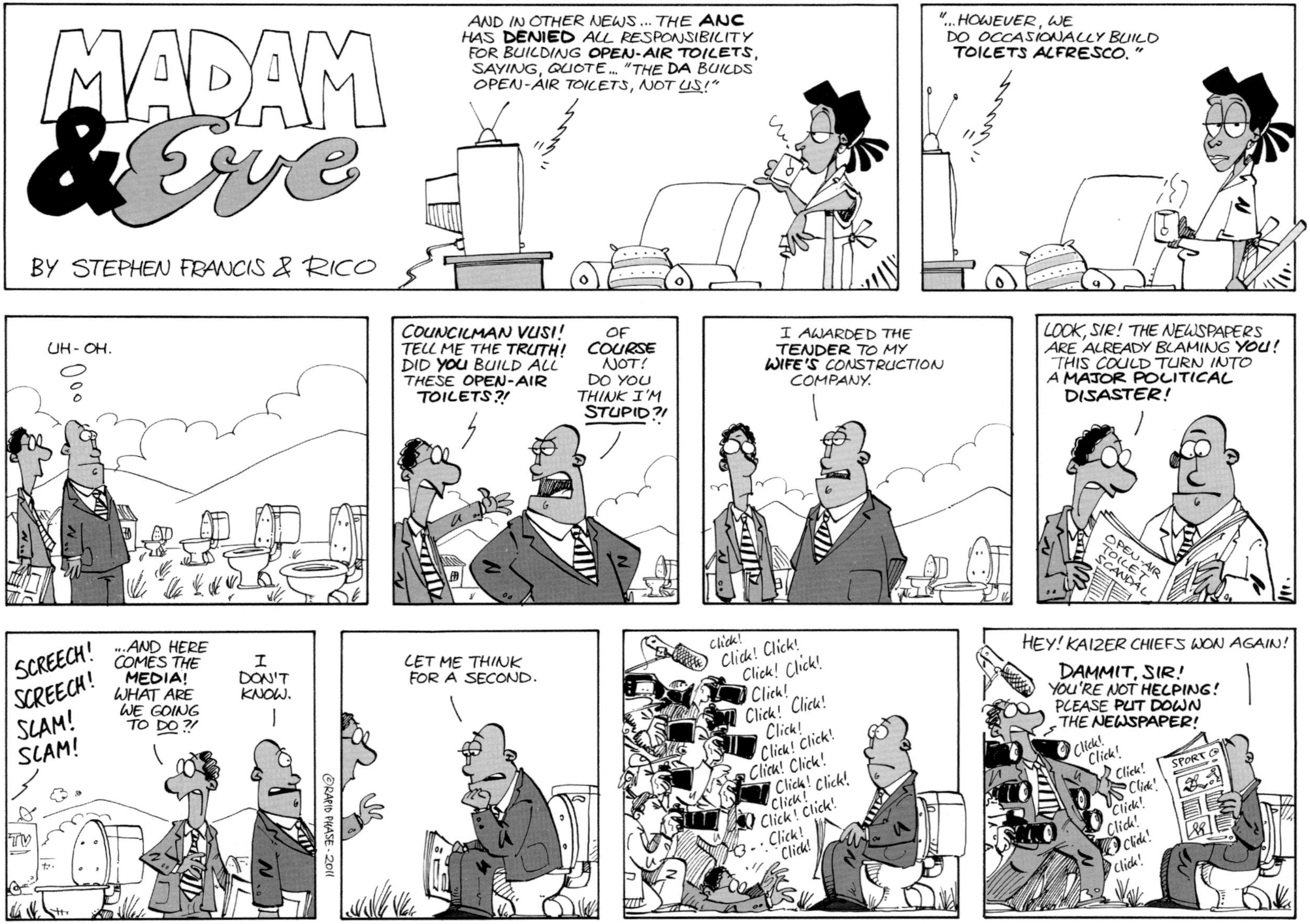
MADAM & Eve
BY STEPHEN FRANCIS & RICO
AND IN OTHER NEWS... THE ANC HAS DENIED ALL RESPONSIBILITY FOR BUILDING OPEN-AIR TOILETS, SAYING, QUOTE... "THE DA BUILDS OPEN-AIR TOILETS, NOT US!"
"...HOWEVER, WE DO OCCASIONALLY BUILD TOILETS ALFRESCO."
UH-OH.
COUNCILMAN VUSI! TELL ME THE TRUTH! DID YOU BUILD ALL THESE OPEN-AIR TOILETS?!
OF COURSE NOT! DO YOU THINK I'M STUPID?!
I AWARDED THE TENDER TO MY WIFE'S CONSTRUCTION COMPANY.
LOOK, SIR! THE NEWSPAPERS ARE ALREADY BLAMING YOU! THIS COULD TURN INTO A MAJOR POLITICAL DISASTER!
OPEN-AIR TOILET SCANDAL
SCREECH! SCREECH! SLAM! SLAM!
...AND HERE COMES THE MEDIA! WHAT ARE WE GOING TO DO?!
I DON'T KNOW.
TV
©RAPID PHASE 2011
LET ME THINK FOR A SECOND.
Click! Click!
HEY! KAIZER CHIEFS WON AGAIN!
DAMMIT, SIR! YOU'RE NOT HELPING! PLEASE PUT DOWN THE NEWSPAPER!
Click! Click! Click! Click! Click! Click! Click! Click!
SPORT

COUNCILMAN VUSI--WOULD YOU CARE TO COMMENT ON THE **OPEN-AIR TOILETS** DISCOVERED IN YOUR DISTRICT?
IT'S A **LIE**!
ACCORDING TO OFFICIAL **ANC** POLICY... "**WE DON'T BUILD** OPEN-AIR TOILETS! ONLY THE **DA** BUILDS **OPEN AIR TOILETS**!"
©RAPID PHASE · 2011
THEN WHAT DO YOU CALL **THESE**?
"TOILETS ALFRESCO."
... AND WHEN I GET MY HANDS ON THIS **AL FRESCO**, HE'S GOING TO HAVE SOME **EXPLAINING** TO DO!

CONGRATULATIONS, COUNCILMAN VUSI. NOW THAT YOU'VE BEEN **RE-ELECTED**, WHAT CAN THE VOTERS **EXPECT** DURING THE NEXT FOUR YEARS?
MORE OF THE **SAME**.
... HE MEANS MORE OF THE SAME **GOOD GOVERNANCE** AND SPEEDY **SERVICE DELIVERY**.
THANK YOU.
©RAPID PHASE · 2011 www.madamandeve.co.za
SHE DOUBLES AS MY P.R. PERSON.

EVE! YOU DIDN'T FINISH THE IRONING!
IT DOESN'T MATTER. THE **END** OF THE **WORLD** IS COMING.
YOU GOT THE **DATE** WRONG! THE END OF THE WORLD WAS SUPPOSED TO BE **LAST SATURDAY**!
YOU MEAN I **MISSED** IT?
TELL YOU WHAT. WHEN THE END OF THE WORLD REALLY **DOES** COME... YOU CAN HAVE THE DAY OFF.
WITH PAY!
©RAPID PHASE · 2011 www.madamandeve.co.za
AND PEOPLE SAY WE'RE STINGY.
WHEN THE END OF THE WORLD DOES COME -- MAYBE I'LL FINALLY **DO** THE **WINDOWS**!

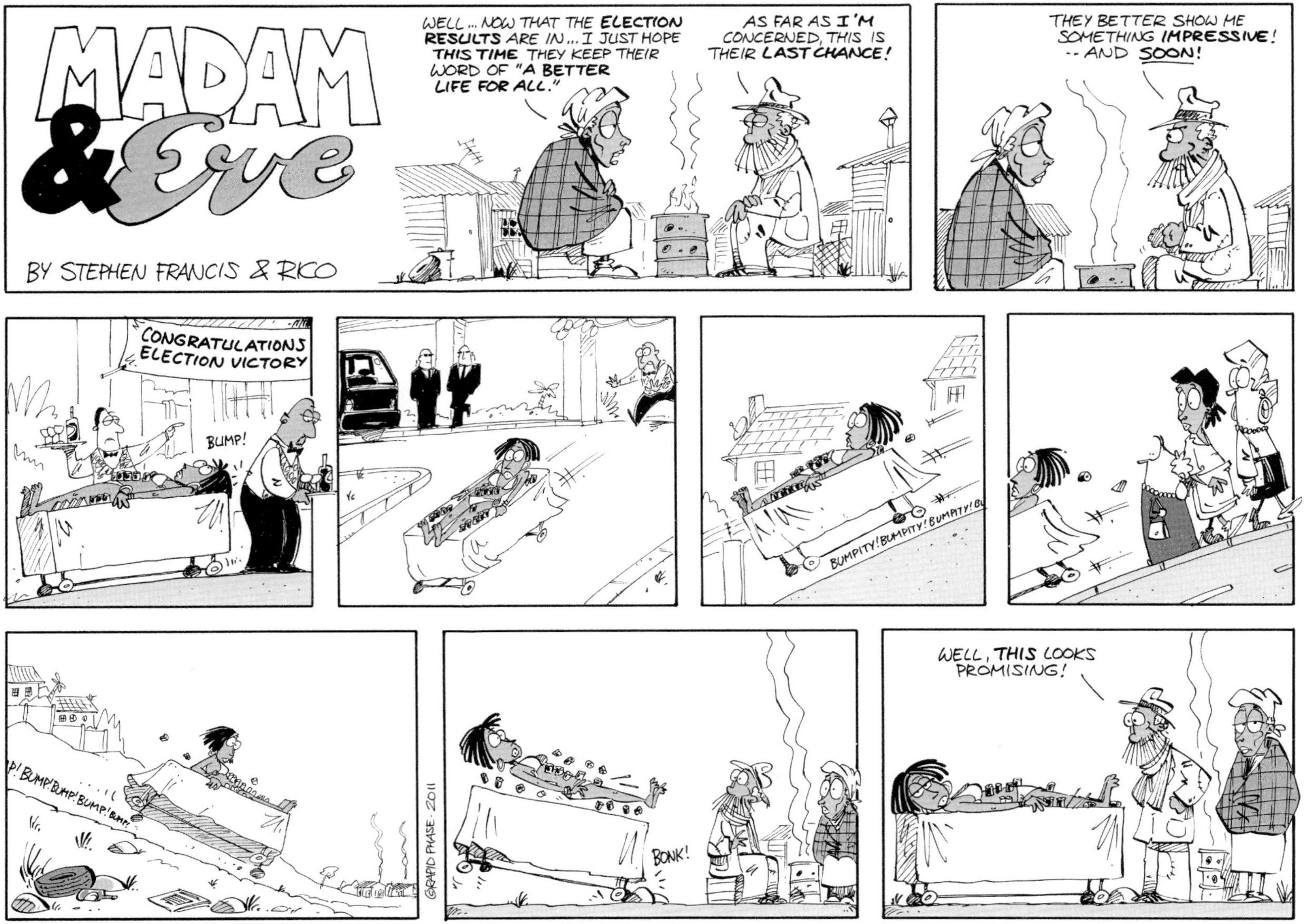
MADAM & Eve
BY STEPHEN FRANCIS & RICO
WELL... NOW THAT THE ELECTION RESULTS ARE IN... I JUST HOPE THIS TIME THEY KEEP THEIR WORD OF "A BETTER LIFE FOR ALL."
AS FAR AS I'M CONCERNED, THIS IS THEIR LAST CHANCE!
THEY BETTER SHOW ME SOMETHING IMPRESSIVE! -- AND SOON!
CONGRATULATIONS ELECTION VICTORY
BUMP!
BUMPITY! BUMPITY! BUMPITY! BU
P! BUMP! BUMP! BUMP! BUMP!
©RAPID PHASE · 2011
BONK!
WELL, THIS LOOKS PROMISING!

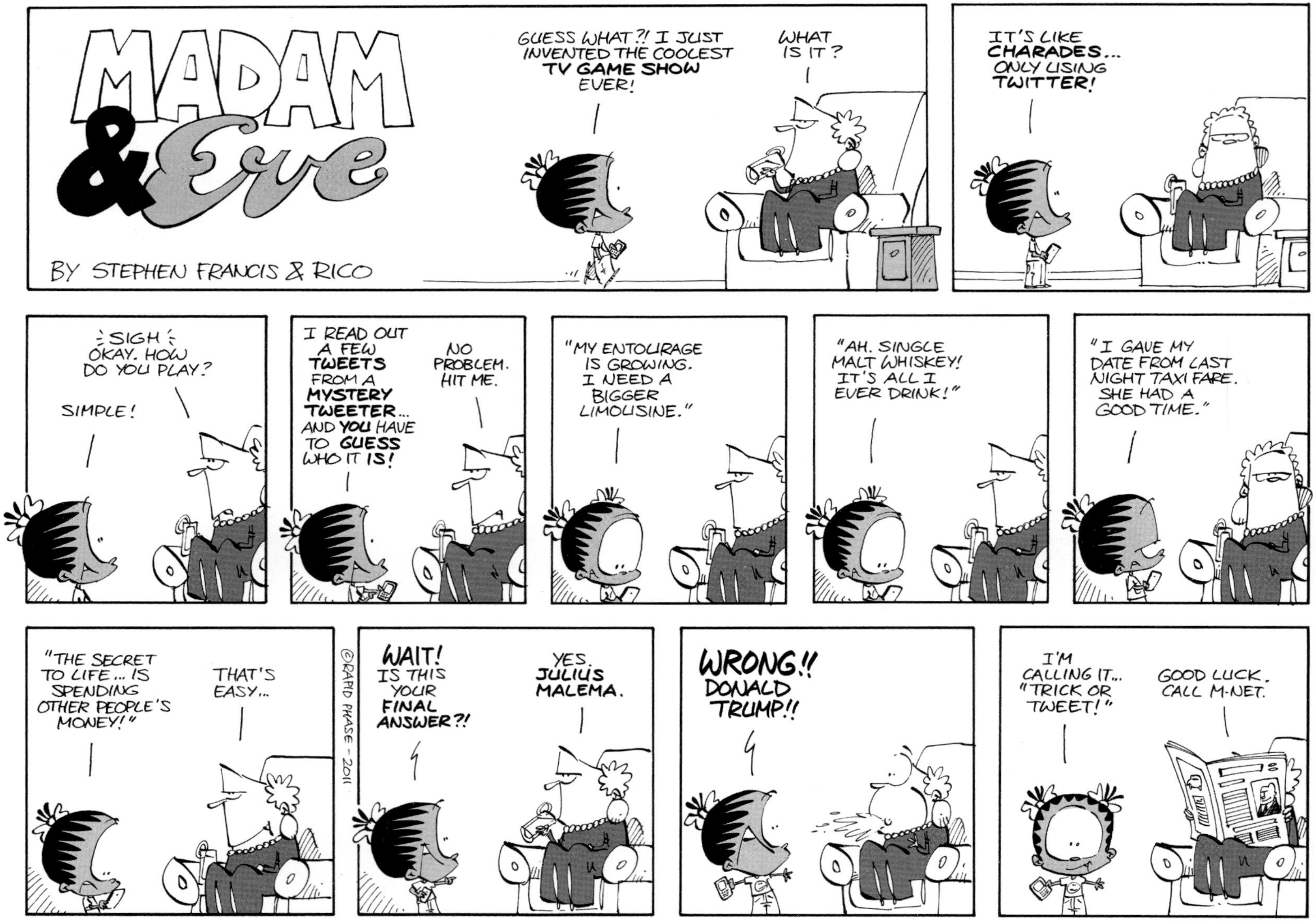
MADAM & Eve
BY STEPHEN FRANCIS & RICO
GUESS WHAT?! I JUST INVENTED THE COOLEST TV GAME SHOW EVER!
WHAT IS IT?
IT'S LIKE CHARADES... ONLY USING TWITTER!
:SIGH: OKAY. HOW DO YOU PLAY?
SIMPLE!
I READ OUT A FEW TWEETS FROM A MYSTERY TWEETER... AND YOU HAVE TO GUESS WHO IT IS!
NO PROBLEM. HIT ME.
"MY ENTOURAGE IS GROWING. I NEED A BIGGER LIMOUSINE."
"AH. SINGLE MALT WHISKEY! IT'S ALL I EVER DRINK!"
"I GAVE MY DATE FROM LAST NIGHT TAXI FARE. SHE HAD A GOOD TIME."
"THE SECRET TO LIFE... IS SPENDING OTHER PEOPLE'S MONEY!"
THAT'S EASY...
©RAPID PHASE - 2011
WAIT! IS THIS YOUR FINAL ANSWER?!
YES. JULIUS MALEMA.
WRONG!! DONALD TRUMP!!
I'M CALLING IT... "TRICK OR TWEET!"
GOOD LUCK. CALL M-NET.

COUNCILMAN VUSI... DO YOU THINK THE PEOPLE HAVE LOST FAITH IN LOCAL GOVERNMENT?
WELL...
...THAT TODAY'S CANDIDATES ENTER POLITICS NOT TO SERVE THEIR COMMUNITY, BUT TO "GET RICH QUICK?"
WELL...
IN FACT, THEY'VE EVEN COINED A NEW BUZZ PHRASE... ANC VULTURES.
THAT'S RIDICULOUS! TYPICAL HOSTILE LIBERAL MEDIA!
©RAPID PHASE - 2011
...RIGHT, BOB?
YOU GOING TO EAT THAT DRUMSTICK?

COUNCILMAN VUSI-- I CAN'T BELIEVE THE MEDIA COINED THE PHRASE ANC VULTURES!
SQUAWK!
©RAPID PHASE - 2011
MAYBE WE CAN GET HIM REDE-PLOYED.
HOW DO YOU REDEPLOY A VULTURE?
SQUAWK
IT'S BEEN DONE BEFORE, SIR.
SQUAWK!
AAAAH!!
www.madamandeve.co.za
AND FOR GOODNESS SAKE... KEEP HIM AWAY FROM OUR SUSHI PARTIES!
MUNCH! MUNCH! MUNCH!

LOOK AT THIS--ALWAYS TALKING ABOUT SERVICE DELIVERY PROBLEMS. WELL, WE HAVE SERVICE DELIVERY PROBLEMS OF OUR OWN...
EVE!! IT'S AFTER FIVE! WHERE'S MY GIN & TONIC?!
SEE? NO SERVICE AND NO DELIVERY.
©RAPID PHASE - 2011
AND WAIT TILL SHE FINDS OUT THERE'S NO GIN.

HI. GWEN ANDERSON HERE WITH A GREAT NEW INFOMERCIAL FOR A GREAT NEW PRODUCT! DO YOU SUFFER FROM MALEMAPHOBIA?!
JULIUS MALEMA! DON'T EVEN MENTION THAT NAME! I--
PSSSSSH.
SO... WHAT DO YOU THINK OF JULIUS NOW?
JULIUS? WHO IS JULIUS?
©RAPID PHASE - 2011 www.madamandeve.co.za
Now available at your local chemist!
MALEMA-AWAY
MALEMA-AWAY
GET YOURS NOW!

HI, EVERYONE! WE'RE BACK... WITH ANOTHER EXCITING INFOMERCIAL!
"MALEMA-AWAY" SOLD OUT IN SECONDS!
©RAPID PHASE - 2011 www.madamandeve.co.za
NOW... INTRODUCING "CORRUPTION AWAY!"
(SHAIK WELL BEFORE USING.)
YES, JUST ONE SPRAY OF "CORRUPTION-AWAY" AND --
PSHHHHH!!
HEY! WHAT HAPPENED?
I GRABBED THE WRONG PRODUCT. THIS IS POWER-AWAY BY ESKOM!!

WHAT'S THAT?
THE "MALEMA EARLY WARNING ALARM SYSTEM."
MALEMA ALARMS
Only 50 RAND
IT'S CONNECTED TO ALL MEDIA. EVERY TIME HE SAYS OR DOES SOMETHING IDIOTIC, IT...
BUZZZ!!
SEE? HERE IT GOES.
BUZZZ!!
THEY'RE VERY POPULAR.
BUZZZ!!
OOPS... THERE IT GOES AGAIN.
BUZZZ!!
©RAPID PHASE - 2011
LOOKS LIKE IT'S OVER-HEATING. WHERE IS HE... AT A PRESS CONFERENCE?
ACTUALLY, HE'S ASLEEP.
BUZZ! BUZZ! BUZZ! BUZZ! BUZZ! BUZZ!

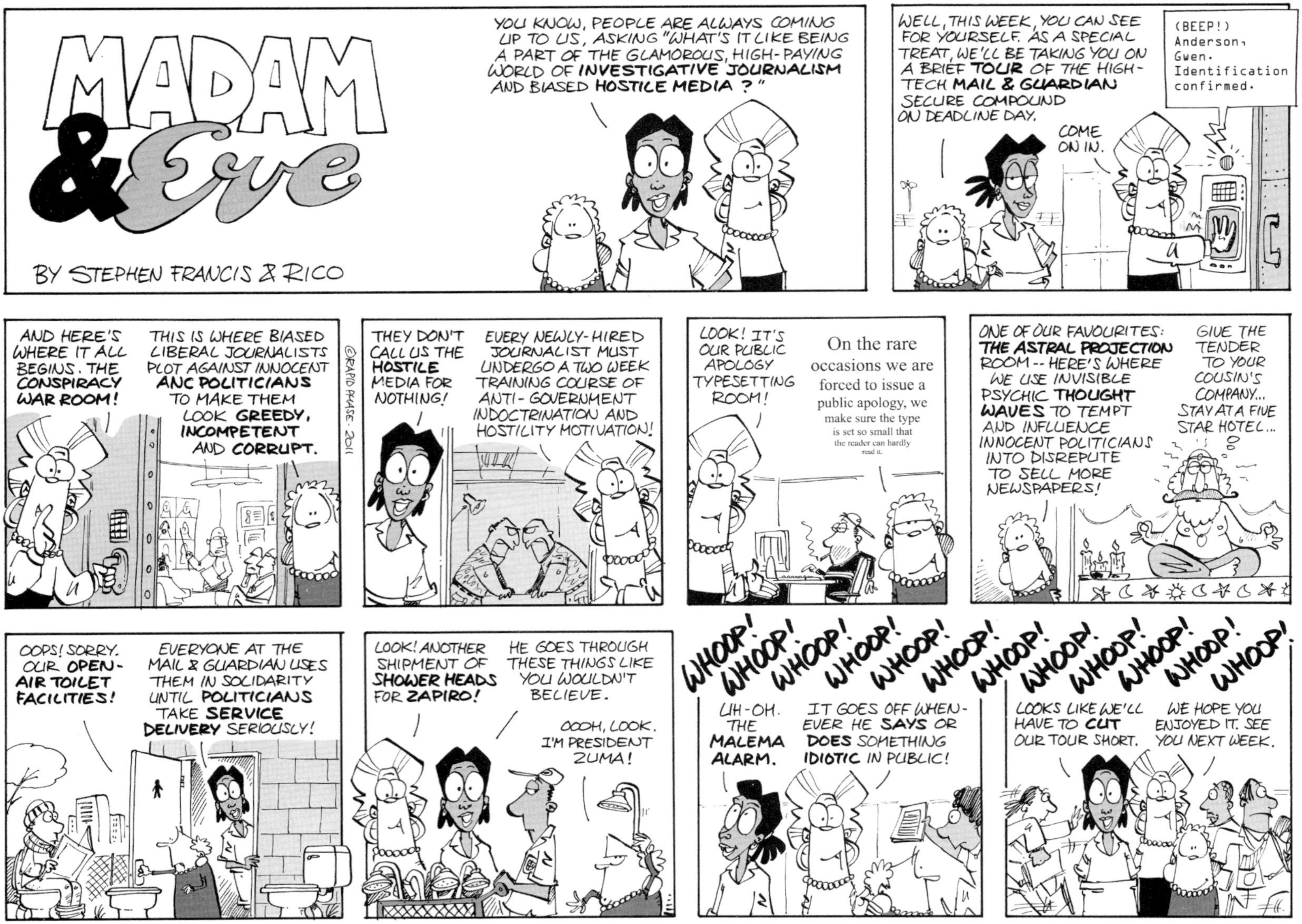
MADAM & Eve
BY STEPHEN FRANCIS & RICO
YOU KNOW, PEOPLE ARE ALWAYS COMING UP TO US, ASKING "WHAT'S IT LIKE BEING A PART OF THE GLAMOROUS, HIGH-PAYING WORLD OF INVESTIGATIVE JOURNALISM AND BIASED HOSTILE MEDIA ?"
WELL, THIS WEEK, YOU CAN SEE FOR YOURSELF. AS A SPECIAL TREAT, WE'LL BE TAKING YOU ON A BRIEF TOUR OF THE HIGH-TECH MAIL & GUARDIAN SECURE COMPOUND ON DEADLINE DAY.
COME ON IN.
(BEEP!) Anderson, Gwen. Identification confirmed.
AND HERE'S WHERE IT ALL BEGINS. THE CONSPIRACY WAR ROOM!
THIS IS WHERE BIASED LIBERAL JOURNALISTS PLOT AGAINST INNOCENT ANC POLITICIANS TO MAKE THEM LOOK GREEDY, INCOMPETENT AND CORRUPT.
©RAPID PHASE · 2011
THEY DON'T CALL US THE HOSTILE MEDIA FOR NOTHING!
EVERY NEWLY-HIRED JOURNALIST MUST UNDERGO A TWO WEEK TRAINING COURSE OF ANTI-GOVERNMENT INDOCTRINATION AND HOSTILITY MOTIVATION!
LOOK! IT'S OUR PUBLIC APOLOGY TYPESETTING ROOM!
On the rare occasions we are forced to issue a public apology, we make sure the type is set so small that the reader can hardly read it.
ONE OF OUR FAVOURITES: THE ASTRAL PROJECTION ROOM -- HERE'S WHERE WE USE INVISIBLE PSYCHIC THOUGHT WAVES TO TEMPT AND INFLUENCE INNOCENT POLITICIANS INTO DISREPUTE TO SELL MORE NEWSPAPERS!
GIVE THE TENDER TO YOUR COUSIN'S COMPANY... STAY AT A FIVE STAR HOTEL...
OOPS! SORRY. OUR OPEN-AIR TOILET FACILITIES!
EVERYONE AT THE MAIL & GUARDIAN USES THEM IN SOLIDARITY UNTIL POLITICIANS TAKE SERVICE DELIVERY SERIOUSLY!
LOOK! ANOTHER SHIPMENT OF SHOWER HEADS FOR ZAPIRO!
HE GOES THROUGH THESE THINGS LIKE YOU WOULDN'T BELIEVE.
OOOH, LOOK. I'M PRESIDENT ZUMA!
WHOOP! WHOOP! WHOOP! WHOOP! WHOOP! WHOOP! WHOOP! WHOOP! WHOOP! WHOOP! WHOOP! WHOOP!
UH-OH. THE MALEMA ALARM.
IT GOES OFF WHENEVER HE SAYS OR DOES SOMETHING IDIOTIC IN PUBLIC!
LOOKS LIKE WE'LL HAVE TO CUT OUR TOUR SHORT.
WE HOPE YOU ENJOYED IT. SEE YOU NEXT WEEK.

EVE! YOU'RE STILL ON YOUR TEA BREAK?! WHEN DO YOU PLAN TO FINISH THE VACUUMING?!
Recalculating... Recalculating...
...avoid disgruntled and stingy Madam and exit out kitchen door into back yard.
I TOLD YOU NOT TO BUY HER THAT DOMESTIC GPS UNIT!
Proceed to clothesline. Neighbourhood maids available for afternoon gossip.
www.madamandeve.co.za
©RAPID PHASE · 2011

CHECK OUT MY OIL PAINTING! I GOT AN A+ FOR IT!
AN A+?! THIS IS THE WORST PAINTING I'VE EVER SEEN! HOW DID YOU GET AN A+?
HOW DO YOU THINK? I BRIBED THE TEACHER.
www.madamandeve.co.za
YOU BRIBED THE TEACHER TO GET A GOOD MARK FOR YOUR OIL PAINTING?! WHAT KIND OF CLASS IS THIS?!
©RAPID PHASE · 2011
"ARTS AND GRAFT."

YOUR CLOTHES. TAKE THEM OFF AND GIVE THEM TO ME. NOW!!
OOOOH. KINKY.
I'LL BE BACK.
SLAM!!
JUST LIKE LAST TIME! I WON'T HOLD MY BREATH!
www.madamandeve.co.za
HASTA LA VISTA, BABY.
@#*@#OFF!!
©RAPID PHASE · 2011
ARNOLD SCHWARZENEGGER
SLEAZENATOR
COMING SOON TO A THEATRE NEAR YOU.

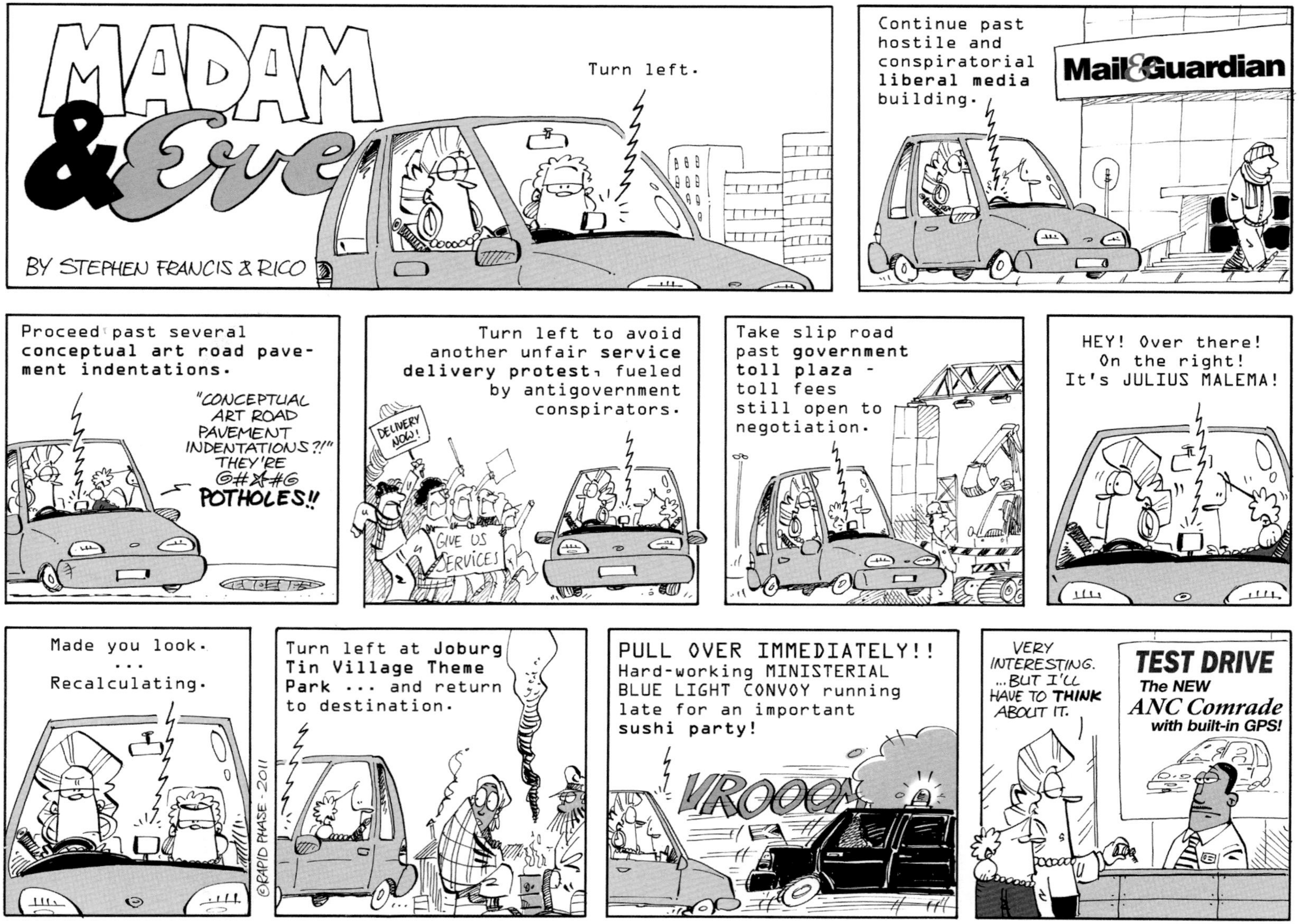
MADAM & Eve
BY STEPHEN FRANCIS & RICO
Turn left.
Continue past hostile and conspiratorial liberal media building.
Mail&Guardian
Proceed past several conceptual art road pavement indentations.
"CONCEPTUAL ART ROAD PAVEMENT INDENTATIONS?!" THEY'RE @#*#@ POTHOLES!!
Turn left to avoid another unfair service delivery protest, fueled by antigovernment conspirators.
DELIVERY NOW!
GIVE US SERVICES
Take slip road past government toll plaza - toll fees still open to negotiation.
HEY! Over there! On the right! It's JULIUS MALEMA!
Made you look. ... Recalculating.
©RAPID PHASE - 2011
Turn left at Joburg Tin Village Theme Park ... and return to destination.
PULL OVER IMMEDIATELY!! Hard-working MINISTERIAL BLUE LIGHT CONVOY running late for an important sushi party!
VROOOM
VERY INTERESTING. ...BUT I'LL HAVE TO THINK ABOUT IT.
TEST DRIVE The NEW ANC Comrade with built-in GPS!

TODAY'S TOP STORY... KIDNEYGATE! MEDICAL COMMUNITY IS STUNNED BY HUNDREDS OF KIDNEYS HARVESTED BY UNSCRUPULOUS DOCTORS!
WHAT'S FOR LUNCH?
©RAPID PHASE - 2011 www.madamandeve.co.za
STEAK AND KIDNEY PIE.
DON'T LOOK AT ME. YOU'RE THE ONE WHO MADE HER WORK ON A HOLIDAY!

EMERGENCY POT-HOLDERS
Only R50
YOU TRY AND SELL THE CRAZIEST THINGS! WHAT ON EARTH WOULD I NEED AN EMERGENCY POTHOLDER FOR?!
©RAPID PHASE - 2011 www.madamandeve.co.za
AAAAH!!
CLUNK!!

OKAY, THANDI! WHERE'S YOUR HOME-WORK?
IT'S POSSIBLE HER DOG ATE IT. WE'RE LAUNCHING A FULL INVESTIGATION.
I WASN'T TALKING TO YOU -- I WAS TALKING TO THANDI!
I'M THANDI'S SPOKESPERSON.
©RAPID PHASE - 2011
...THANDI'S SPOKES-PERSON?
THAT'S RIGHT. ANYTHING YOU WANT TO TELL HER, TELL ME FIRST.
NEXT TIME, JUST SAY WE'RE "UNAVAILABLE FOR COMMENT." ...UNAVAILABLE FOR COMMENT!!
PRINCIPAL

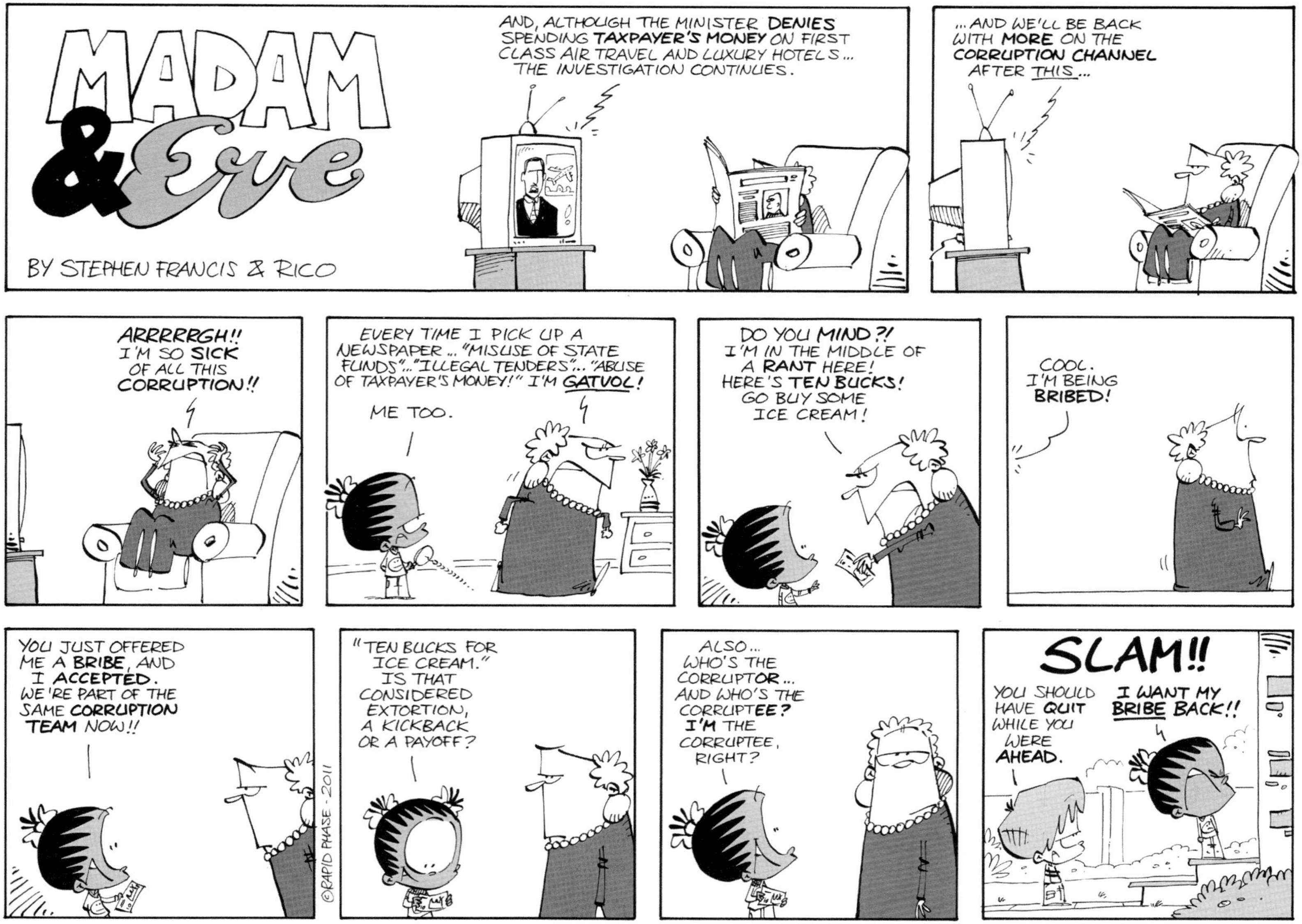
MADAM & Eve
BY STEPHEN FRANCIS & RICO
AND, ALTHOUGH THE MINISTER DENIES SPENDING TAXPAYER'S MONEY ON FIRST CLASS AIR TRAVEL AND LUXURY HOTELS ... THE INVESTIGATION CONTINUES.
... AND WE'LL BE BACK WITH MORE ON THE CORRUPTION CHANNEL AFTER THIS ...
ARRRRRGH!! I'M SO SICK OF ALL THIS CORRUPTION!!
EVERY TIME I PICK UP A NEWSPAPER ... "MISUSE OF STATE FUNDS"... "ILLEGAL TENDERS"... "ABUSE OF TAXPAYER'S MONEY!" I'M GATVOL!
ME TOO.
DO YOU MIND?! I'M IN THE MIDDLE OF A RANT HERE! HERE'S TEN BUCKS! GO BUY SOME ICE CREAM!
COOL. I'M BEING BRIBED!
YOU JUST OFFERED ME A BRIBE, AND I ACCEPTED. WE'RE PART OF THE SAME CORRUPTION TEAM NOW!!
©RAPID PHASE · 2011
"TEN BUCKS FOR ICE CREAM." IS THAT CONSIDERED EXTORTION, A KICKBACK OR A PAYOFF?
ALSO... WHO'S THE CORRUPTOR... AND WHO'S THE CORRUPTEE? I'M THE CORRUPTEE, RIGHT?
SLAM!!
YOU SHOULD HAVE QUIT WHILE YOU WERE AHEAD.
I WANT MY BRIBE BACK!!

IT'S THE WHOLE "FACEBOOK" THING, DOCTOR. EVERYWHERE I TURN, IT'S FACEBOOK, FACEBOOK, FACEBOOK!
THAT SOUNDS A LITTLE PARANOID.
I GET MESSAGES FROM FACEBOOK GIVING ME WEEKLY UPDATES! MESSAGES TELLING ME I FORGOT SOMEONE'S BIRTHDAY... OR THAT I OWE SOMEONE A "POKE!"
THAT REMINDS ME. LAST WEEK I REQUESTED YOU TO BE MY FACEBOOK FRIEND... AND YOU DIDN'T RESPOND.
YOU'RE MY PSYCHIATRIST! YOU'RE NOT MY FRIEND!!
©RAPID PHASE · 2011
SOB! FINE! FORGET I EVEN ASKED!
I HATE SOCIAL MEDIA.

TODAY'S TOP STORY... YET ANOTHER PERSON CAUGHT TAKING PERFORMANCE-ENHANCING SUBSTANCES.
WHAT'S GOING ON? IS EVERYONE TAKING PERFORMANCE-ENHANCING SUBSTANCES?!
©RAPID PHASE · 2011
...NOT EVERYONE.
www.madamandeve.co.za
IS THERE SUCH A THING AS NON-PERFORMANCE-ENHANCING SUBSTANCES?
FUNNY. ...NOT.

WHAT'S WRONG, MOM?
OTHER CARTOONISTS ARE GETTING SUED! BUT NOT US.
DO YOU REALLY WANT TO BE INVOLVED IN A LAWSUIT?
DUH. YOU CAN'T BUY PUBLICITY LIKE THAT!
©RAPID PHASE · 2011
WHAT ARE YOU GOING TO DO? MAKE RUDE GESTURES AND INSULT THE PRESIDENT?
GOOD IDEA! HEY ZUMA! WATCH THIS!!
LET ME OUT OF THE BOX-- I WAS ONLY THINKING OUT LOUD!

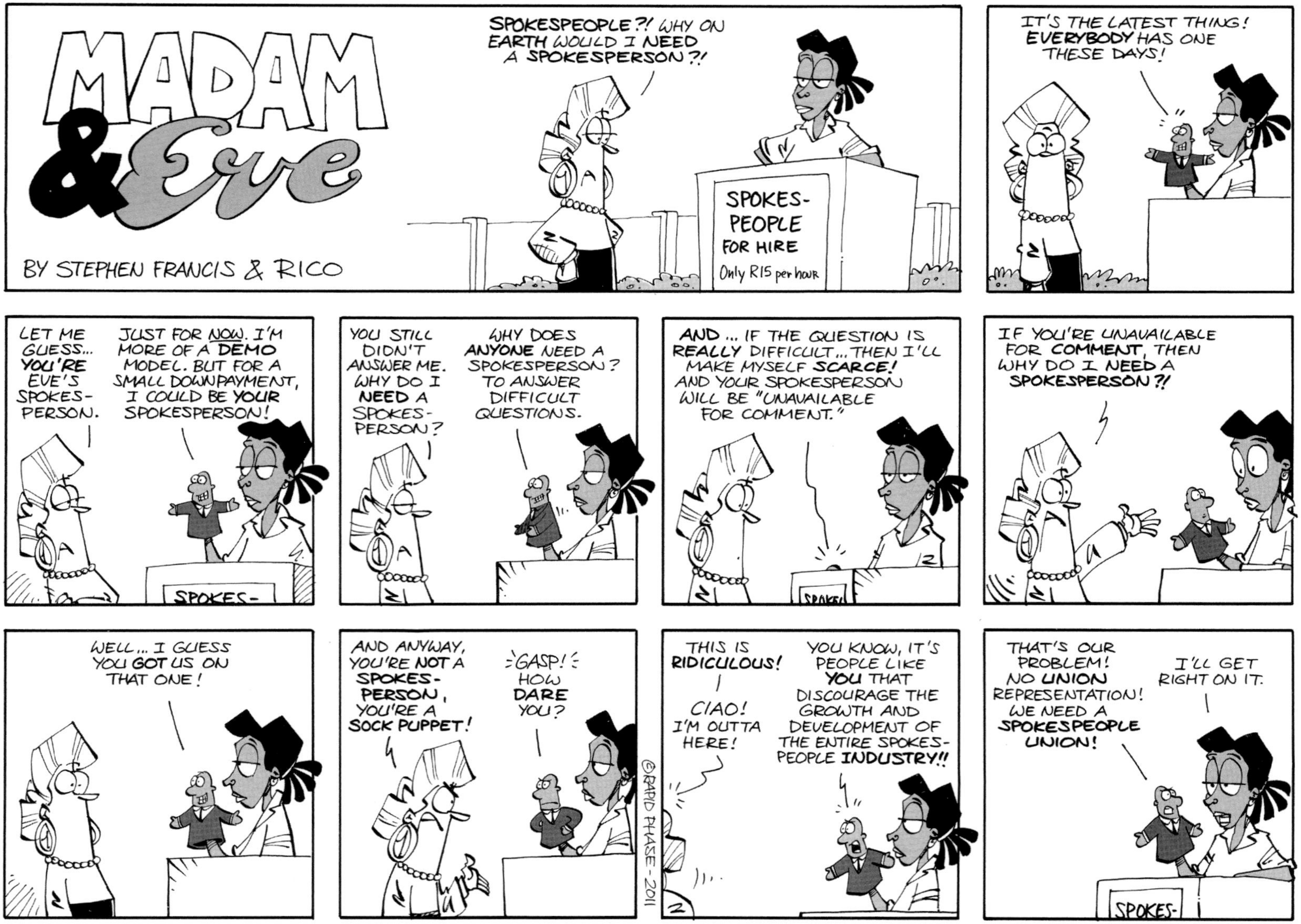
MADAM & Eve
BY STEPHEN FRANCIS & RICO
SPOKESPEOPLE?! WHY ON EARTH WOULD I NEED A SPOKESPERSON?!
SPOKES-PEOPLE FOR HIRE
Only R15 per hour
IT'S THE LATEST THING! EVERYBODY HAS ONE THESE DAYS!
LET ME GUESS... YOU'RE EVE'S SPOKES-PERSON.
JUST FOR NOW. I'M MORE OF A DEMO MODEL. BUT FOR A SMALL DOWNPAYMENT, I COULD BE YOUR SPOKESPERSON!
SPOKES-
YOU STILL DIDN'T ANSWER ME. WHY DO I NEED A SPOKES-PERSON?
WHY DOES ANYONE NEED A SPOKESPERSON? TO ANSWER DIFFICULT QUESTIONS.
AND... IF THE QUESTION IS REALLY DIFFICULT... THEN I'LL MAKE MYSELF SCARCE! AND YOUR SPOKESPERSON WILL BE "UNAVAILABLE FOR COMMENT."
IF YOU'RE UNAVAILABLE FOR COMMENT, THEN WHY DO I NEED A SPOKESPERSON?!
WELL... I GUESS YOU GOT US ON THAT ONE!
AND ANYWAY, YOU'RE NOT A SPOKES-PERSON, YOU'RE A SOCK PUPPET!
GASP! HOW DARE YOU?
©RAPID PHASE-2011
THIS IS RIDICULOUS!
CIAO! I'M OUTTA HERE!
YOU KNOW, IT'S PEOPLE LIKE YOU THAT DISCOURAGE THE GROWTH AND DEVELOPMENT OF THE ENTIRE SPOKES-PEOPLE INDUSTRY!!
THAT'S OUR PROBLEM! NO UNION REPRESENTATION! WE NEED A SPOKESPEOPLE UNION!
I'LL GET RIGHT ON IT.
SPOKES-

AND IN OTHER NEWS... THE VOLCANIC ASH CLOUD FROM CHILE'S VOLCANO IS HEADING TOWARDS SOUTH AFRICA!
I DON'T BELIEVE IT! IT'S HERE ALREADY!
©RAPID PHASE · 2011
THAT'S ODD. IT SMELLS LIKE... IT SMELLS LIKE...
www.madamandeve.co.za
EVE!! ARE YOU WATCHING THE APPLE PIE IN THE OVEN?!
UH-OH.

AND IN OTHER NEWS... THE CHILEAN VOLCANIC ASH CLOUD IS DRIFTING THIS WAY.
IT'S COVERING ALL OF JOHANNESBURG!
©RAPID PHASE · 2011
UNBELIEVABLE! IT'S FILLING UP EVERY SINGLE POTHOLE!!
LET'S HEAR IT FOR NATURE!!
SHOULD I WAKE UP YOUR MOTHER?

HAVE YOU SEEN EVE?
LAST TIME I SAW HER, SHE WAS HANGING UP THE LAUNDRY.
ODD. MARGE FROM NEXT DOOR CAN'T FIND HER MAID, EITHER.
©RAPID PHASE · 2011
www.madamandeve.co.za
WELL, THEY'VE GOT TO BE AROUND HERE SOMEWHERE...
BISCUIT?

THE A TEAM
©RAPID PHASE · 2010
www.madamandeve.co.za
THE BEE TEAM

GIVE ME YOUR LUNCH MONEY!!
OK, HERE.
WHY DIDN'T YOU STAND UP TO HIM? THAT BULLY WAS HALF YOUR SIZE!
I KNOW... I KNOW...
www.madamandeve.co.za
WHAT A ZUMA YOU TURNED OUT TO BE.
©RAPID PHASE · 2010
TOWNSHIP SLANG... CATCHES ON FAST THESE DAYS.

AND THE WINNER IS...
... GAUTENG!
©RAPID PHASE · 2010
YAY!! THAT'S GREAT! WHAT DID WE WIN?!
www.madamandeve.co.za
SOUTH AFRICAN CRIME STATISTICS: "MOST DANGEROUS CITY."

NO WORK.
No Food.
No Money.
NO MONEY
©RAPID PHASE - 2011
HI MICHELLE! WELCOME TO SOUTH AFRICA!
www.madamandeve.co.za
THESE AMERICAN SECRET SERVICE GUYS ARE GOOD.
HI MICHELLE! WELCOME TO SOUTH AFRICA!

UNITED STATES FIRST LADY MICHELLE OBAMA VISITS SOUTH AFRICA. JOHANNESBURG METRO POLICE SPRING INTO ACTION!
WE CAN FORGET THE SPEEDING FINE IF YOU BUY US A "COOL DRINK."
HEY! YOU LOOK LIKE THE WIFE OF THE AMERICAN PRESIDENT!
www.madamandeve.co.za ©RAPID PHASE - 2011

BY A STRANGE QUIRK OF FATE, JULIUS MALEMA'S MOTORCADE ACCIDENTALLY RUNS INTO MICHELLE OBAMA'S MOTORCADE.
DO YOU KNOW WHO I AM?!
UH... NO, ACTUALLY.
www.madamandeve.co.za ©RAPID PHASE - 2011

THE BIG SEVEN: LION, LEOPARD, RHINO, BUFFALO, ELEPHANT, MICHELLE, OPRAH.
Click! Click! Click!
Click! Click! Click! Click!
Click! Click! Click!
Click! Click! Click!
Click! Click! Click!
©RAPID PHASE·2011

NO WORK NO FOOD JUDGE MOTATA ALMOST HIT ME!
www.madamandeve.co.za
©RAPID PHASE·2011

Madam & Eve's South African Best-Sellers
ROBERT LUDLUM
THE BOURNE APOLOGY
A Julius Malema Mystery
www.madamandeve.co.za
Harry Squatter and the Goblet of Fire
©RAPID PHASE·2011
RICH MINISTER,
EVEN RICHER MINISTER

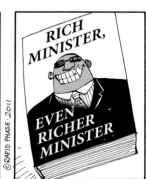

HAHAHAHA! HEEHEEHEE!! HOHO HOHO! HEE HEE!
HA HA!
HAHAHAHA!! HOHOHOHO!! HEE HEE!!
©RAPID PHASE·2011
AND WE'LL BE RIGHT BACK WITH TODAY'S TOP STORY... THE TAXI INDUSTRY PLAN TO LAUNCH THEIR OWN AIRLINE.
www.madamandeve.co.za
BWA-HAHA HAHA!!
HEE! HEE!
AND PEOPLE WONDER WHERE WE GET OUR IDEAS.

©RAPID PHASE·2011 www.madamandeve.co.za
IT SAYS WE FORGOT TO RICA EVE AND NOW SHE HAS SHUT DOWN AND STOPPED WORKING.
DOES THAT MEAN I HAVE TO MAKE MY OWN GIN & TONICS?

©RAPID PHASE·2011
www.madamandeve.co.za
ALRIGHT! WHO SUPERGLUED MY GIN & TONIC TO THE END TABLE?!!
WOW. YOU ARE GOOD.
GET READY TO RUN.

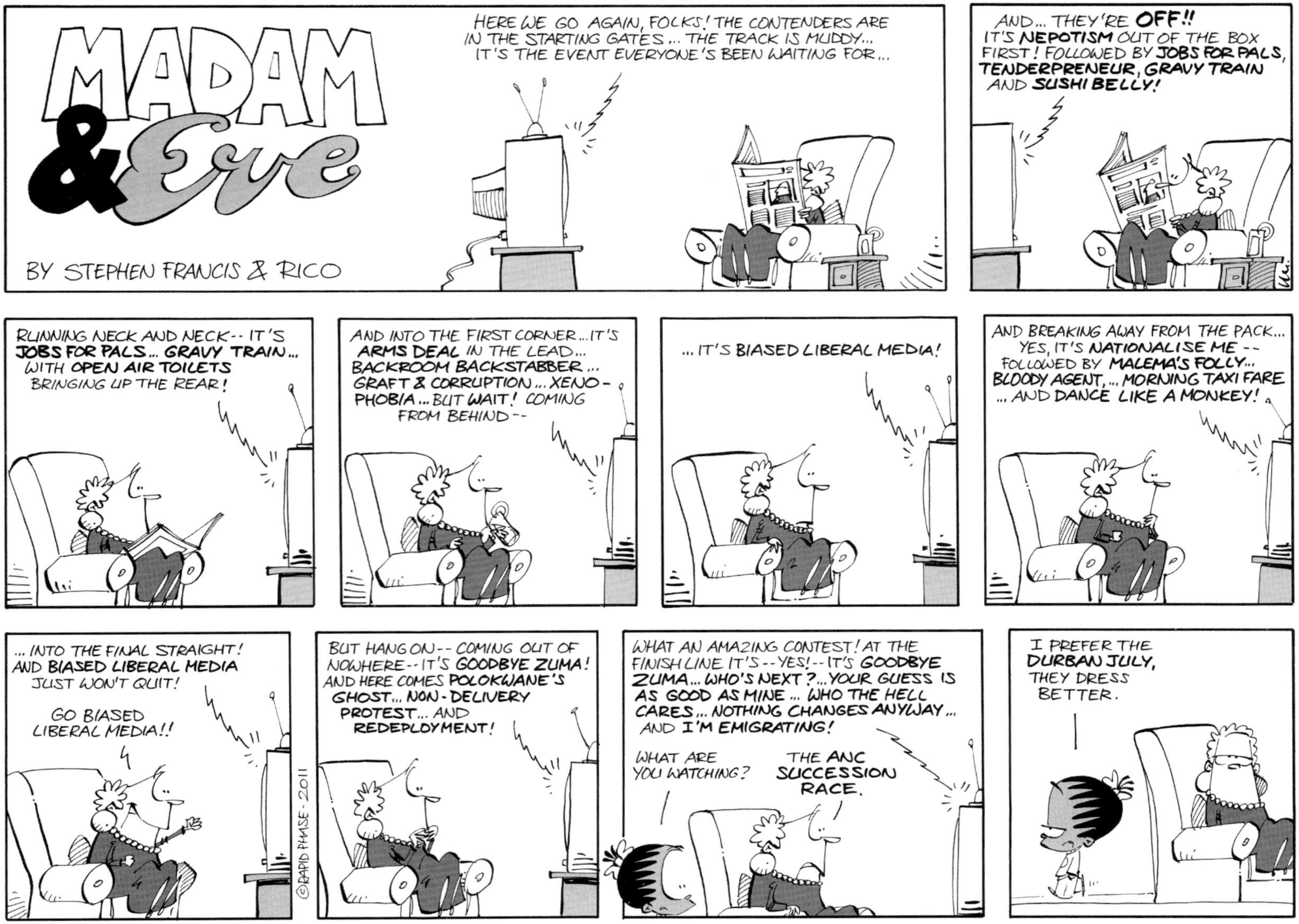
MADAM & Eve
BY STEPHEN FRANCIS & RICO
HERE WE GO AGAIN, FOLKS! THE CONTENDERS ARE IN THE STARTING GATES... THE TRACK IS MUDDY... IT'S THE EVENT EVERYONE'S BEEN WAITING FOR...
AND... THEY'RE OFF!! IT'S NEPOTISM OUT OF THE BOX FIRST! FOLLOWED BY JOBS FOR PALS, TENDERPRENEUR, GRAVY TRAIN AND SUSHI BELLY!
RUNNING NECK AND NECK-- IT'S JOBS FOR PALS... GRAVY TRAIN... WITH OPEN AIR TOILETS BRINGING UP THE REAR!
AND INTO THE FIRST CORNER... IT'S ARMS DEAL IN THE LEAD... BACKROOM BACKSTABBER... GRAFT & CORRUPTION... XENO-PHOBIA... BUT WAIT! COMING FROM BEHIND--
... IT'S BIASED LIBERAL MEDIA!
AND BREAKING AWAY FROM THE PACK... YES, IT'S NATIONALISE ME -- FOLLOWED BY MALEMA'S FOLLY... BLOODY AGENT,... MORNING TAXI FARE ... AND DANCE LIKE A MONKEY!
... INTO THE FINAL STRAIGHT! AND BIASED LIBERAL MEDIA JUST WON'T QUIT!
GO BIASED LIBERAL MEDIA!!
©RAPID PHASE · 2011
BUT HANG ON-- COMING OUT OF NOWHERE-- IT'S GOODBYE ZUMA! AND HERE COMES POLOKWANE'S GHOST... NON-DELIVERY PROTEST... AND REDEPLOYMENT!
WHAT AN AMAZING CONTEST! AT THE FINISH LINE IT'S --YES!-- IT'S GOODBYE ZUMA... WHO'S NEXT?... YOUR GUESS IS AS GOOD AS MINE... WHO THE HELL CARES... NOTHING CHANGES ANYWAY... AND I'M EMIGRATING!
WHAT ARE YOU WATCHING?
THE ANC SUCCESSION RACE.
I PREFER THE DURBAN JULY, THEY DRESS BETTER.

"MY DOG ATE MY HOMEWORK" - A SCIENCE PROJECT BY THANDI SISULU. I HAVE OBSERVED THAT MANY OF YOU DO NOT BELIEVE THAT THE DOG ATE MY HOMEWORK! MY HYPOTHESIS IS THAT YOU ARE WRONG.
I HAVE HERE A DOG AND AN ACTUAL HOMEWORK PAGE!
www.madamandeve.co.za
NOW WATCH... GO ON BOY. EAT THE HOMEWORK! GOOD DOG! EAT THE HOMEWORK! YUM! LOOK AT THE NICE HOMEWORK! GO AHEAD-- EAT IT!!
©RAPID PHASE · 2011
MAYBE HE'S FULL.
SNORT!
SO MUCH FOR GROUND-BREAKING SCIENTIFIC RESEARCH.
PRINCIPAL
WHINE.

HERE BOY... GO ON... THAT'S IT!
SNIFF! SNIFF!
www.madamandeve.co.za
YOU'RE MY WITNESS. THE DOG JUST ATE MY MATHS HOMEWORK... DIPPED IN BEEF MINCE.
MUNCH. MUNCH. MUNCH.
©RAPID PHASE · 2011
DIPPED IN BEEF MINCE? WHY GO THROUGH ALL THE TROUBLE? JUST TELL THE TEACHER HE ATE IT!
YOU MEAN LIE?!
BECAUSE I HAVE INTEGRITY!!
ER... HE JUST ATE YOUR PENCIL BOX.
CHOMP! CHOMP! CHOMP!

THANDI--WHERE'S YOUR HOMEWORK?!
THE GOGO NEXT DOOR ATE IT.
©RAPID PHASE · 2011
DON'T YOU MEAN... "YOUR DOG ATE YOUR HOMEWORK?"
NOPE. THE GOGO NEXT DOOR.
HOW CAN THE GOGO NEXT DOOR EAT YOUR HOMEWORK ASSIGNMENT?!
YOU SURE YOU WANT TO DO THIS?
DESPERATE TIMES... DESPERATE MEASURES...
ZZZZZZZ

EVERYTHING MUST GO!
Only 10 Rand
© RAPID PHASE · 2011
OKAY-- HERE'S **TEN BUCKS.** NOW WHAT?
EVERYTHING MUST GO!
EVERYTHING MUST **GO!**
EVERYTHING MUST GO!
Only 10 Rand
www.madamandeve.co.za
DID YOU JUST TELL **EVE** TO TAKE THE ENTIRE DAY **OFF** WITH **PAY?!**

"QUESTION ONE: GIVE AN EXAMPLE OF **TRANSFORMATION** IN SOUTH AFRICA AND PROVIDE ILLUSTRATION."
© RAPID PHASE · 2011
www.madamandeve.co.za
TRANSFORMATION
1 Dark of the Moon

RECYCLED CARTOONS
Only 10 Rand
© RAPID PHASE · 2011
OKAY... HERE'S TEN BUCKS. **NOW** WHAT?
RECYCLED CARTOONS
Only 10 Rand
RECYCLED CARTOONS
Only 10 Rand
OKAY... HERE'S TEN BUCKS. **NOW** WHAT?
RECYCLED CARTOONS
Only 10 Rand

WEATHER REPORTS AND OPPORTUNISTIC MARKETING
Only 10 Rand
OKAY. HERE'S MY **TEN BUCKS.** WHAT'S THE...?
RAIN.
RUMBLE!
©RAPID PHASE · 2011 www.madamandeve.co.za
CHEAP UMBRELLAS
Only 20 Rand

MIELLLIES!!
TROMP! TROMP! TROMP! TROMP! TROMP!
©RAPID PHASE · 2011 www.madamandeve.co.za
THE RUNNING OF THE MIELIE LADIES, PARKTOWN NORTH

MADAM... CAN YOU SETTLE AN ARGUMENT? WHICH IS BETTER-- A **KINDLE**... AN **IPAD**... OR GOOD OLD FASHIONED **NEWSPRINT?**
WELL... I'M NO EXPERT, BUT THERE ARE QUALITIES THAT **ELECTRONIC** PUBLISHING JUST CAN'T MATCH ... LIKE **TOUCH**... THE **TEXTURE** OF PAPER, THE SMELL OF **INK**...
THANKS MADAM.
NO PROBLEM. I CALL IT LIKE I SEE IT.
©RAPID PHASE · 2011 www.madamandeve.co.za

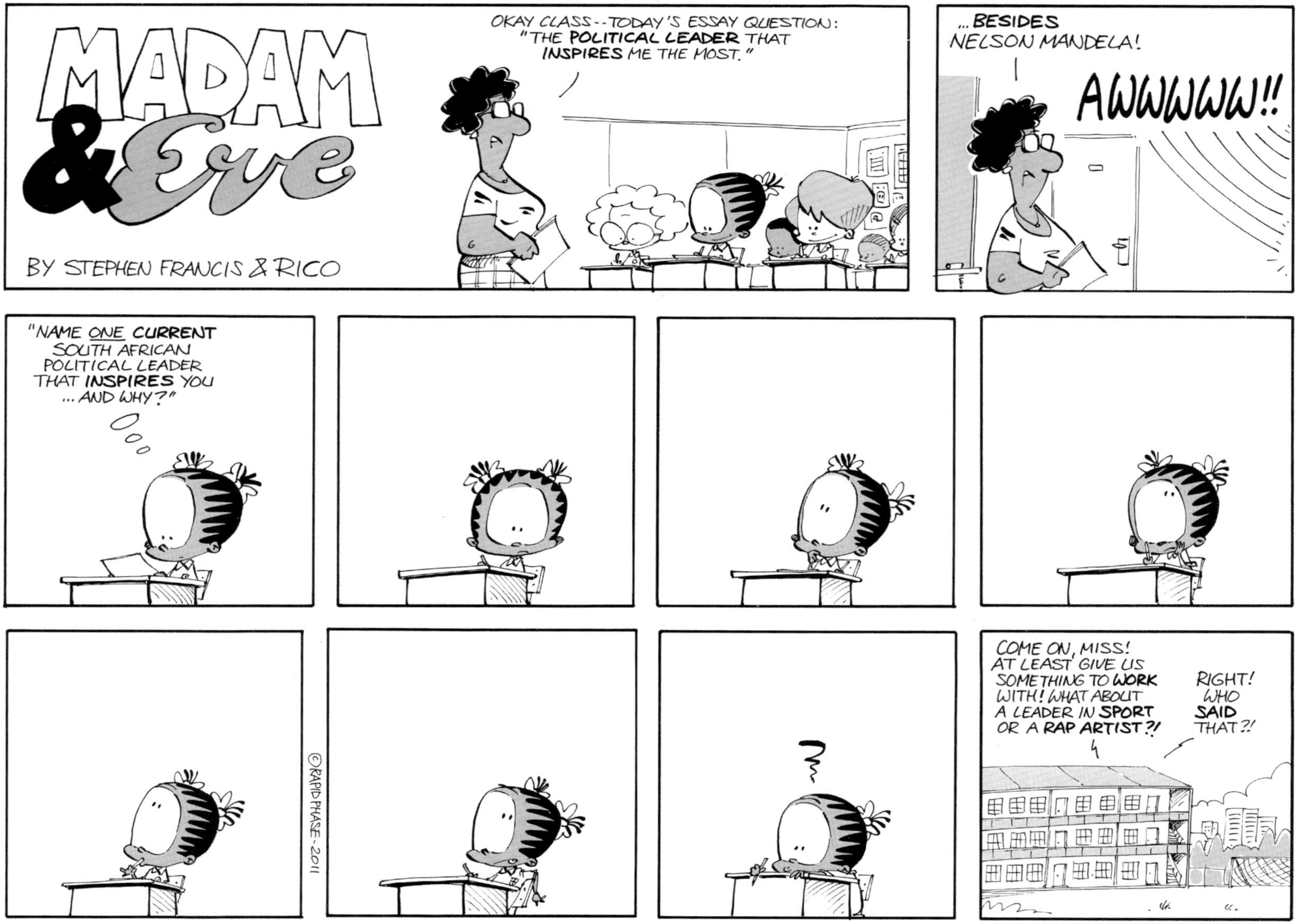
MADAM & Eve
BY STEPHEN FRANCIS & RICO
OKAY CLASS--TODAY'S ESSAY QUESTION: "THE POLITICAL LEADER THAT INSPIRES ME THE MOST."
...BESIDES NELSON MANDELA!
AWWWWW!!
"NAME ONE CURRENT SOUTH AFRICAN POLITICAL LEADER THAT INSPIRES YOU ...AND WHY?"
©RAPID PHASE-2011
COME ON, MISS! AT LEAST GIVE US SOMETHING TO WORK WITH! WHAT ABOUT A LEADER IN SPORT OR A RAP ARTIST?!
RIGHT! WHO SAID THAT?!

WHEN A JOURNALIST CALLED ANC YOUTH LEAGUE SPOKESMAN **FLOYD SHIVAMBU** TO ASK ABOUT A LAVISH THREE-DAY SAFARI LEAGUE PRESIDENT JULIUS MALEMA TOOK RECENTLY...

...THE CONVERSATION GOT **UGLY** AND SHIVAMBU REPORTEDLY SAID "G#✳@ YOU" TO THE JOURNALIST.

THE ANC **DISTANCED** ITSELF FROM SHIVAMBU'S COMMENTS -- IF HE INDEED SAID "G#✳@ YOU."

THE **NATIONAL PRESS CLUB** CONDEMNED SHIVAMBU'S COMMENTS, SAYING HIS BEHAVIOUR WAS "TOTALLY UNACCEPTABLE AND COMPLETELY OUT OF G✳#$@✳ LINE."

YOUNG FLOYD SHIVAMBU, FUTURE ANCYL SPOKESMAN

I will not use the f-word in class. I will not use the f-word in class.
I will not use the f-word in class. I will not use the f-word in class.
I will not use the f-word in class. I will not use the f-word in class.
I will not use the f-word in class. I will not use the f-word in class.
I will not use the f-word in class. I will not use the f-word in class.
I will not use the f-word in class.
I

JULIUS, WHERE'S YOUR HOMEWORK?

HIS **DOG** ATE IT, MISS.

I'M **NOT TALKING** TO YOU, **FLOYD**. I'M ADDRESSING **JULIUS!**

BUT I'M HIS **SPOKES-PERSON.**

SPOKESPERSON?! RIGHT! DETENTION FOR **BOTH** OF YOU!

G#✳#G.

BLOODY AGENT.

The Adventures of the

ANCRYYL

(The ANC Really Young Youth League)

Coming soon to SABC 2.

128

EMPOWER-MINCE
Only 10 Rand
OKAY... HERE'S TEN BUCKS.
AND HERE'S YOUR **EMPOWER-MINCE BURGER**.
www.madamandeve.co.za
CHOMP CHOMP
IT'S SPICY AND DELICIOUS! BUT WHEN WILL I **FEEL EMPOWERED?**
©RAPID PHASE-2011
...USUALLY WHEN THE **CHILI** HITS YOUR **LOWER INTESTINE**.

THEY'RE **DELICIOUS.** I'VE ALREADY HAD **TWO.**
EMPOWER MINCE BURGERS
Only 10 Rand
HMPH. THE "KITCHEN" DOESN'T LOOK VERY **CLEAN.**
NOT **CLEAN?!** WHY, I **PERSONALLY** MAKE SURE THAT... THAT...
EMPOWER MINCE
www.madamandeve.co.za
©RAPID PHASE-2011
SMACK!
SORRY... **FLY.** ...WHAT WERE YOU SAYING?
...ISN'T THAT A **SPATULA?**

I am an 80 year-old white woman looking to meet a black man between 80 and 85...
GASP!
TIC TIC TIC TIC TIC
PLOP!!
...who drives a 2009 silver BMW and reversed into my tail light in the Sandton City parking lot last Tuesday.
©RAPID PHASE-2011
JUST GOES TO SHOW -- PEOPLE SHOULDN'T JUMP TO CONCLUSIONS.

EMPOWERMENT
BEE DEAL
SUPEREMPOWERMENT
MISS EMPOWERMENT
DISEMPOWERMENT
@#$@# ESKOM.
www.madamandeve.co.za ©RAPID PHASE-2011

Madam & Eve's
CARTOON PANEL INSTANT FEEDBACK SYMBOLS
514 000 people like this cartoon panel.
238 people dislike this cartoon panel.
1402 people want to PUNCH this cartoon panel.
1413 people are picking their nose while reading this cartoon panel.
132 people got a paper cut from this cartoon panel.
146 people want to make shadow puppets on this cartoon panel.
www.madamandeve.co.za
©RAPID PHASE-2011

Madam & Eve's
EVERYDAY INSTANT FEEDBACK SYMBOLS
620 786 people like the job President Jacob Zuma is doing.
878 901 people dislike the job President Jacob Zuma is doing.
16 800 people are telling their bartender to "Make it a double!"
8 456 309 people are taking a minibus taxi to get to work in the morning.
206 594 madams believe their domestic worker needs to do more dusting.
21 484 people want a tip to watch your car while you are shopping.
www.madamandeve.co.za
©RAPID PHASE-2011

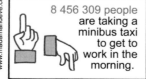

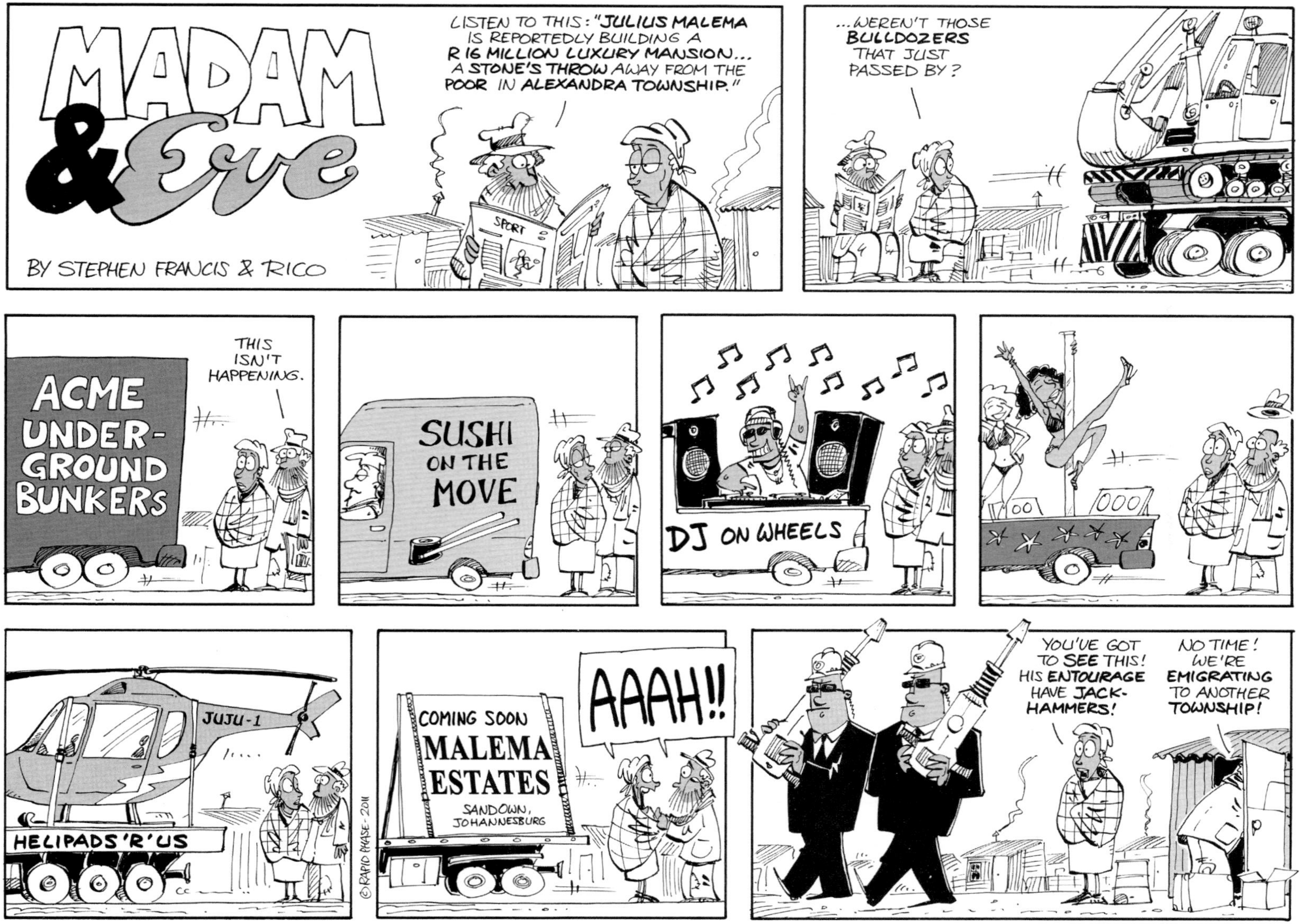
MADAM & Eve
BY STEPHEN FRANCIS & RICO
LISTEN TO THIS: "JULIUS MALEMA IS REPORTEDLY BUILDING A R16 MILLION LUXURY MANSION... A STONE'S THROW AWAY FROM THE POOR IN ALEXANDRA TOWNSHIP."
SPORT
...WEREN'T THOSE BULLDOZERS THAT JUST PASSED BY?
ACME UNDER-GROUND BUNKERS
THIS ISN'T HAPPENING.
SUSHI ON THE MOVE
DJ ON WHEELS
JUJU-1
HELIPADS'R'US
!....
COMING SOON
MALEMA ESTATES
SANDOWN, JOHANNESBURG
AAAH!!
©RAPID PHASE-2011
YOU'VE GOT TO SEE THIS! HIS ENTOURAGE HAVE JACK-HAMMERS!
NO TIME! WE'RE EMIGRATING TO ANOTHER TOWNSHIP!

THANK YOU FOR BEING PATIENT. THE **MALEMA** AND **ANC YOUTH LEAGUE** PRESS CONFERENCE WILL BEGIN IN FIVE MINUTES.
EXCUSE ME.
COMING SOON.
RACE CARD
©RAPID PHASE · 2011
SORRY.
PARDON ME.
RACE CAR
www.madamandeve.co.za
JUST PUT IT ON THE EASEL.
SIGH I'VE GOT A BAD FEELING ABOUT THIS.
ME TOO.

MISTER PRESIDENT-- FORGIVE ME FOR SAYING THIS-- BUT YOU'VE GOT TO GET YOUR **HEAD** OUT OF THE **SAND**!
HUH? WHAT ARE YOU **TALKING** ABOUT?!
www.madamandeve.co.za
THE PUBLIC PROTECTOR'S DAMNING REPORT ON **BHEKI CELE**! RAMPANT STATE **CORRUPTION**! **SERVICE DELIVERY** PROBLEMS! DECLINING SUPPORT BY THE **ANCYL**! STRIKES **CRIPPLING** THE ECONOMY! THINGS ARE **CRUMBLING** AROUND YOU AS WE SPEAK!
©RAPID PHASE · 2011
AND YET... YOU SEEM TO BE IN SOME SORT OF **DENIAL**... JUST LIKE **MBEKI** USED TO BE!
WHAT?! ARE YOU COMPARING **ME** TO **PRESIDENT MBEKI**?
WELL, SIR... NOW THAT YOU **MENTION** IT.
IS IT JUST **ME** ... OR IS IT GETTING **DARK** EARLIER THESE DAYS?
SAND

MISTER PRESIDENT. DUE RESPECT, SIR. BUT YOU'VE GOT TO GET YOUR **HEAD** OUT OF THE **SAND**!
WHAT ARE YOU TALKING ABOUT? I'M ON TOP OF **EVERY-THING**!
I THINK HE'S STILL IN **DENIAL**.
SAND
©RAPID PHASE · 2011 www.madamandeve.co.za
SIR-- YOU'VE GOT TO SHOW SOME **LEADERSHIP**! ...TAKE **ACTION**... OR YOUR ENEMIES **WILL**!
HA! ENEMIES! **WHAT** ENEMIES?!
OW! SOMETHING JUST **BIT** ME!
I'LL GRAB THE BUCKET, YOU GRAB HIS LEGS.
SAND

NATIONALISE THE MINES!
©RAPID PHASE - 2011 www.madamandeve.co.za
NATIONALISE THE MINES!
NATIONALISE THE MINES!
NATIONALISE JULIUS MALEMA'S TRUST FUND!

LIFE-STYLE AUDITS
Only 10 Rand
©RAPID PHASE - 2011 www.madamandeve.co.za
OKAY. HERE'S TEN BUCKS. WHAT ADVICE CAN YOU GIVE ME ABOUT MY LIFESTYLE?
WELL, FOR STARTERS, YOU SPEND WAY TOO MUCH MONEY ON FRIVOLOUS AUDITS.
NOBODY ENJOYS BEING AUDITED.
LIFE-STYLE AUDITS
Only 10 Rand

WHAT'S GOING ON?
EVE'S PERFORMING A LIFESTYLE AUDIT ON ME.
TO FULLY UNDERSTAND YOUR LIFESTYLE ... I MUST THINK LIKE GWEN ANDERSON ... I MUST ACT LIKE GWEN ANDERSON... I MUST BE GWEN ANDERSON.
www.madamandeve.co.za
HEY! AREN'T THOSE YOUR GOOD SHOES?!
I MUST WEAR SHOES LIKE GWEN ANDERSON!
©RAPID PHASE - 2011
I HAVE NOW ATTAINED... A COMPLETE STATE OF GWEN ANDERSON.
TELL ME YOU'RE NOT PAYING FOR THIS...

DO YOU THINK MAYBE ONE DAY I'LL HAVE A SECRET TRUST FUN LIKE JULIUS MALEMA?
FUND! NOT "FUN." HE HAS A SECRET TRUST FUND!
A 16 MILLION RAND LUXURY MANSION WITH UNDER-GROUND GARAGE AND BUNKER... PARTY DECK... SWIMMING POOL...
www.madamandeve.co.za ©RAPID PHASE · 2011
... SURE SOUNDS LIKE HE'S HAVING FUN TO ME.

I DON'T GET IT. EVERYBODY WANTS TO INVESTIGATE JULIUS MALEMA'S BANK ACCOUNT.
NOBODY BELIEVES HIM WHY IT WAS SET UP. NOBODY BELIEVES HIM WHERE THE MONEY CAME FROM.
©RAPID PHASE · 2011
NOBODY BELIEVES HOW THE MONEY IS BEING SPENT.
SO?
www.madamandeve.co.za
SO WHY DO THEY CALL IT A TRUST FUND?

SIGH EVERYBODY'S SUING EVERYBODY ELSE!
EDITORS SUING COLUMNISTS... COLUMNISTS SUING EDITORS... PRESIDENTS SUING CARTOONISTS...
www.madamandeve.co.za
SO? WHAT LESSON DO YOU TAKE AWAY FROM ALL OF THIS?
...WHEN I GROW UP, I'M GOING TO BE A LAWYER!
© RAPID PHASE · 2011
SLAM!!
SOMEHOW, I DON'T THINK THAT WAS THE ANSWER SHE WAS LOOKING FOR.

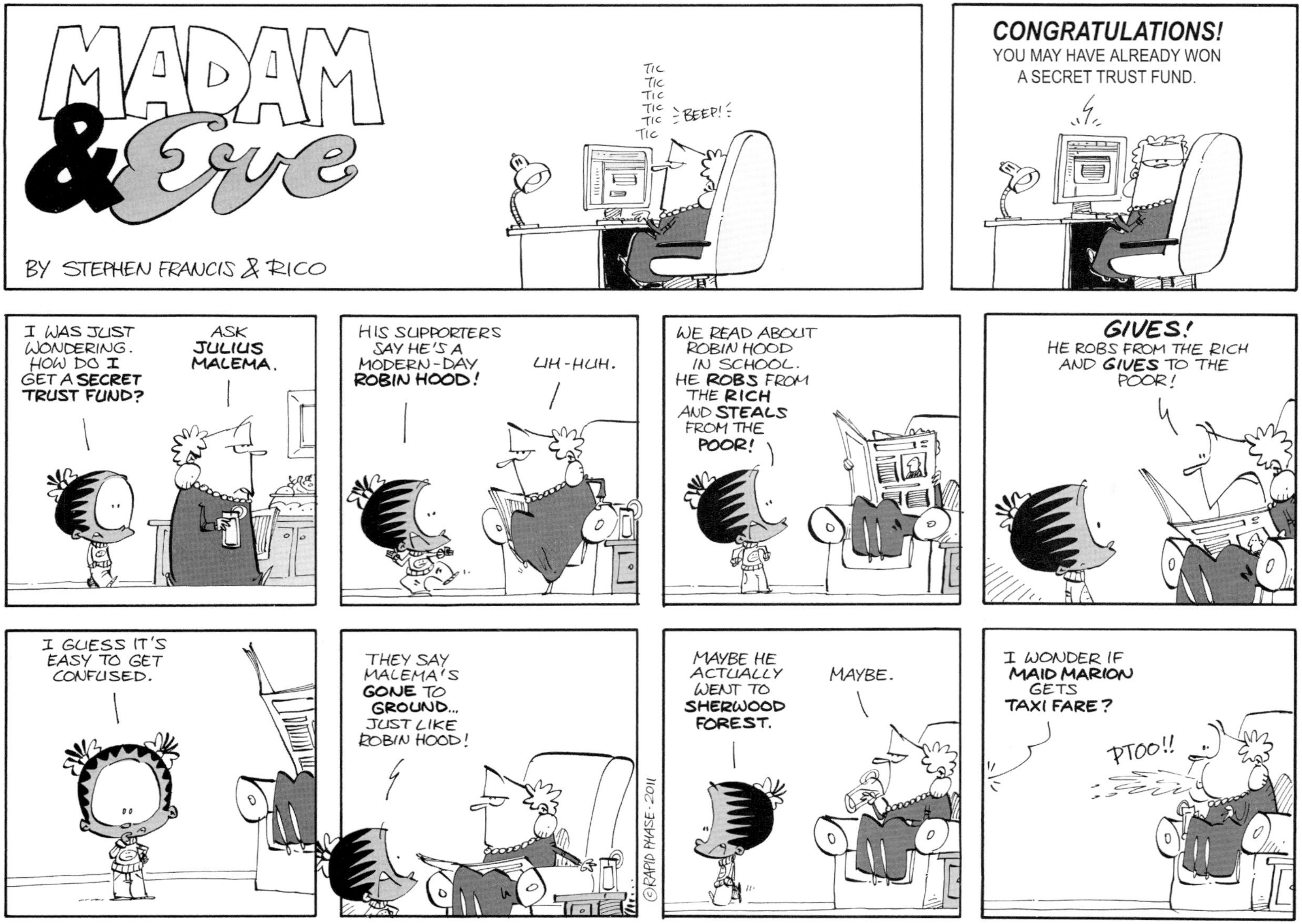
MADAM & Eve
BY STEPHEN FRANCIS & RICO
TIC TIC TIC TIC TIC TIC
BEEP!
CONGRATULATIONS!
YOU MAY HAVE ALREADY WON A SECRET TRUST FUND.
I WAS JUST WONDERING. HOW DO I GET A SECRET TRUST FUND?
ASK JULIUS MALEMA.
HIS SUPPORTERS SAY HE'S A MODERN-DAY ROBIN HOOD!
UH-HUH.
WE READ ABOUT ROBIN HOOD IN SCHOOL. HE ROBS FROM THE RICH AND STEALS FROM THE POOR!
GIVES! HE ROBS FROM THE RICH AND GIVES TO THE POOR!
I GUESS IT'S EASY TO GET CONFUSED.
THEY SAY MALEMA'S GONE TO GROUND... JUST LIKE ROBIN HOOD!
©RAPID PHASE · 2011
MAYBE HE ACTUALLY WENT TO SHERWOOD FOREST.
MAYBE.
I WONDER IF MAID MARION GETS TAXI FARE?
PTOO!!

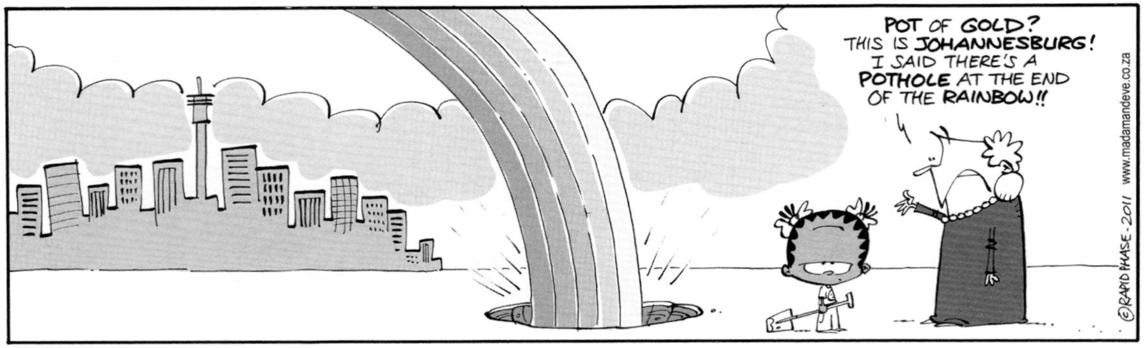
POT OF GOLD? THIS IS JOHANNESBURG! I SAID THERE'S A POTHOLE AT THE END OF THE RAINBOW!!
©RAPID PHASE-2011 www.madamandeve.co.za